Speaking & Listening

for preschool
through third grade

New Standards

Speaking and Listening Committee

Illustrated by Garin Baker

NEW STANDARDS®

Copyright © 2001 National Center on Education and the Economy and the University of Pittsburgh. All rights reserved.

Illustrations © 2001 Garin Baker.

In this book is the poem "A Lazy Thought" from JAMBOREE *Rhymes for All Times* by Eve Merriam. Copyright © 1962, 1964, MATERIAL REQUESTED AND ACKNOWLEDGMENT: 1966, 1973, 1984 by Eve Merriam. All rights renewed. Used by permission of Marian Reiner.

New Standards® is a registered trademark of the National Center on Education and the Economy and the University of Pittsburgh.

No part of this publication may be reproduced or transmitted in any form or by any means, electronic or mechanical, including photocopy, recording, or any information storage and retrieval system without permission from the National Center on Education and the Economy permissions department.

Editorial and design by KSA-Plus Communications, Inc.

Printed in the United States of America by Peake Printers.

ISBN 1-889630-41-1

e-mail: info@ncee.org

Preface

Speaking and listening are to reading and writing what walking is to running. Babies have to learn to walk before they can run — but once they do, nothing can stop them. So too with language. Children understand spoken language many years before we expect them to read on their own. And they can make their thoughts understood in speech well before they can write.

Speaking and listening are the indispensable foundations of reading and writing. A child who does not have a large and fluent vocabulary will have difficulty with every aspect of reading, from recognizing and sounding out words to making sense of a story or a set of written directions. A child who can't tell a story orally surely will have trouble writing one. Parents and educators know this instinctively. But until now they have had little detailed guidance in what speaking and listening abilities they should expect from children at different ages.

Here is help. Prepared as a companion to the popular *Reading & Writing grade by grade*, this book offers a detailed map of children's oral language development from preschool through third grade. It outlines when, where and what kinds of talk we should expect from children at each major stage of development. By description and example, it shows how children should be growing in their ability to converse with others, use oral language to talk themselves through plans and actions, and simply play with words and sentences. It describes several specific kinds of oral language skills children need: narrative, explaining and seeking information, oral "performances," and giving and understanding directions. It outlines a sequence of expectations for the conventions of speech, from turn-taking to word choice and grammatical awareness. Performances of children at different ages participating in "book talks" illustrate what the children should sound like and help make the link to reading and writing explicit.

A CD-ROM for each standard provides "live" video examples from preschool and primary-grade classrooms, along with a summary of the expectations themselves and commentaries explaining why each example was selected.

The idea for *Speaking & Listening for preschool through third grade* came from the committee that guided the development of *Reading & Writing grade by grade*. Members of the Primary Literacy Committee stated over and over again how important it was to develop a clear set of expectations for speaking and listening. But as work progressed, everyone

> This book outlines when, where and what kinds of talk we should expect from children at each major stage of development.

New Standards

realized that to do justice to the importance of oral language and to benefit from the enormous and growing scholarship in the field, we would need a separate committee and a separate book. To head the new committee, we turned to Catherine Snow of Harvard University. Snow is a world-renowned expert in children's language development who also had headed the team that produced the National Research Council's influential book *Preventing Reading Difficulties in Young Children*. With Snow's help we recruited a distinguished group of researchers and educators to guide the crafting of the standards laid out here. Their biographies appear on pages 1–6.

The process was an adventure for us all, for while researchers and expert teachers know a great deal about children's language development, no one had translated that knowledge into a clear set of statements that could guide everyday practice in classrooms across our vast and varied country. We are pleased to bring *Speaking & Listening* to you. We hope it will help you make a difference in your children's progress toward powerful literacy.

Lauren B. Resnick
Co-director
New Standards

Marc S. Tucker
Co-director
New Standards

Funders

Support for the development of these speaking and listening performance standards was provided by the **U.S. Department of Education's Office of Educational Research and Improvement.** These standards build on the New Standards® primary literacy standards in reading and writing, supported by **The Pew Charitable Trusts,** the **John D. and Catherine T. MacArthur Foundation,** and the **Noyce Foundation.**

This generous funding also is supporting a companion resource to help Spanish-speaking English language learners meet the New Standards primary literacy standards. This new book, to be released in 2001, will describe the advantages that Spanish-speaking students bring to learning to read and write in a second language, the specific obstacles that impede their progress, and effective instructional strategies that teachers can use to help these children learn.

Coming Soon:

Strategies for Teaching Spanish-Speaking Students

The New Standards primary literacy standards in reading, writing, speaking and listening are rigorous, fair and reasonable for students who are proficient in English. As teachers well know, however, increasing numbers of students in the United States do not speak English well because English is not their native language.

While there are hundreds of languages spoken in our nation's schools, Spanish is by far the most prevalent. Moreover, Spanish-speaking students are the fastest growing segment of the U.S. student population. For these students — and for all students — the goal is to increase their proficiency in English, which remains the language of opportunity in this country.

Soon, teachers will have a new resource available to help Spanish-speaking English language learners meet the New Standards primary literacy standards. This new book will describe the advantages that Spanish-speaking students bring to learning to read and write in a second language, the specific obstacles that impede their progress, and effective instructional strategies that teachers can use to help these children learn.

Table of Contents

New Standards Speaking & Listening
Committee Members . . . . *page* 1

Learning to Speak & Listen . . . . *page* 7
        Habits / *page 11*
        Kinds of Talk and Resulting Genres / *page 23*
        Language Use and Conventions / *page 29*

About the New Standards
Speaking & Listening Standards . . . . *page* 35

Preschool . . . . *page* 39
        Standard 1: Habits / *page 46*
            Introduction
            Talking a Lot
            Talking to One's Self
            Conversing at Length on a Topic
            Discussing Books
        Standard 2: Kinds of Talk and Resulting Genres / *page 72*
            Introduction
            Narrative
            Explaining and Seeking Information
            Getting Things Done
            Producing and Responding to Performances
        Standard 3: Language Use and Conventions / *page 98*
            Introduction
            Rules of Interaction
            Word Play, Phonological Awareness and Language Awareness
            Vocabulary and Word Choice

Kindergarten & First Grade . . . . *page* **121**

Standard 1: Habits / *page 128*
- Introduction
- Talking a Lot
- Talking to One's Self
- Conversing at Length on a Topic
- Discussing Books

Standard 2: Kinds of Talk and Resulting Genres / *page 151*
- Introduction
- Narrative
- Explaining and Seeking Information
- Getting Things Done
- Producing and Responding to Performances

Standard 3: Language Use and Conventions / *page 180*
- Introduction
- Rules of Interaction
- Word Play, Phonemic Awareness and Grammatical Awareness
- Vocabulary and Word Choice

Second & Third Grades . . . . *page* **193**

Standard 1: Habits / *page 200*
- Introduction
- Talking a Lot
- Talking to One's Self
- Conversing at Length on a Topic
- Discussing Books

Standard 2: Kinds of Talk and Resulting Genres / *page 228*
- Introduction
- Narrative
- Explaining and Seeking Information
- Getting Things Done
- Producing and Responding to Performances

Standard 3: Language Use and Conventions / *page 252*
- Introduction
- Rules of Interaction
- Word Play and Grammatical Awareness
- Vocabulary and Word Choice

Appendix . . . . *page* **264**

Glossary / *page 265*
Committee's Selected Bibliography / *page 266*
Acknowledgments / *page 270*

About New Standards . . . . *page* **272**

Index . . . . *page* **273**

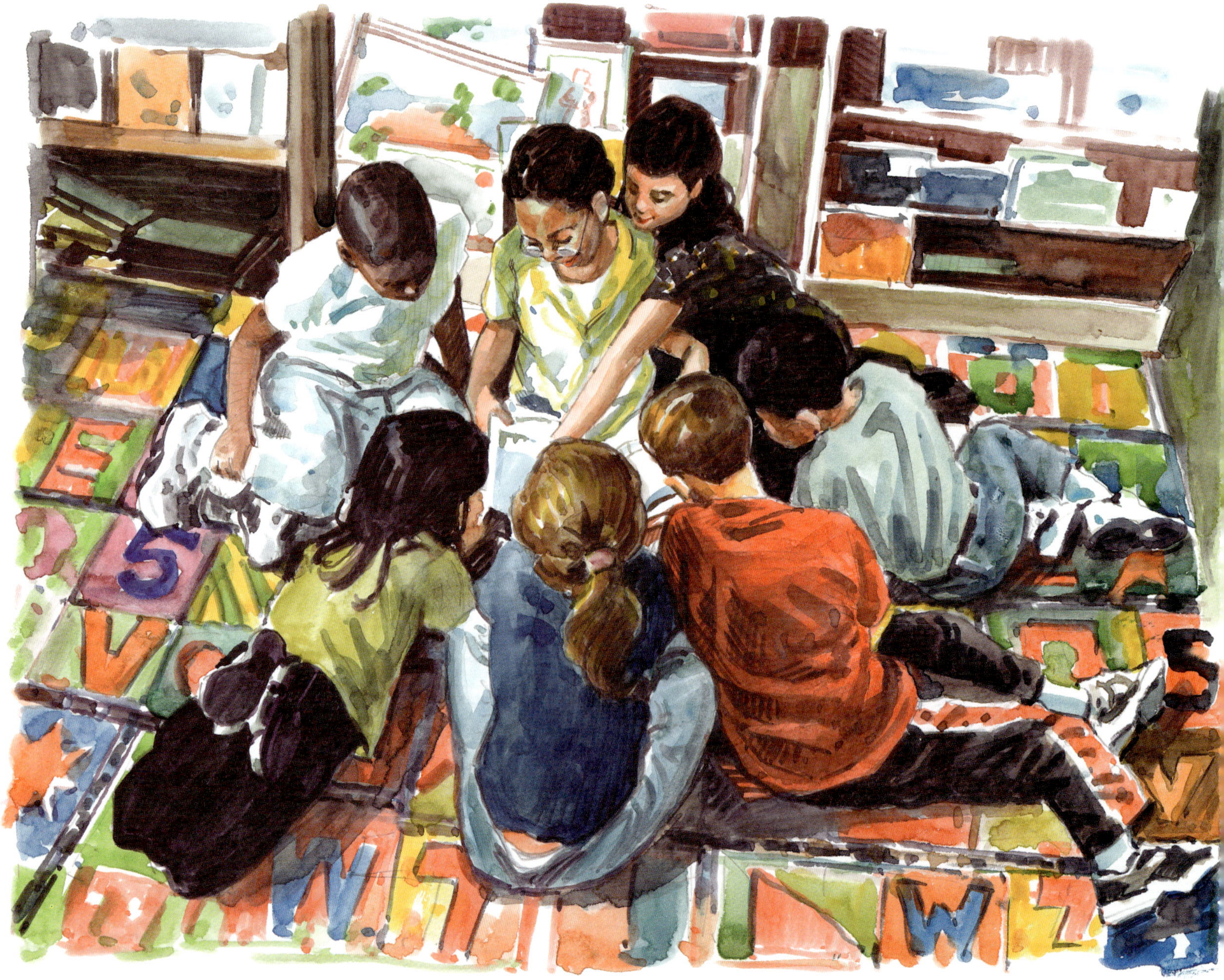

Committee Members

Diane E. Beals, Ed.D., is an assistant professor of education at the University of Tulsa. She has been a member of the Home-School Study research team since 1989. Her research on the project has focused largely on the use of narrative and explanation in family mealtime conversations, beginning with her dissertation, *'I know who makes ice cream': Explanations in Mealtime Conversations of Low-Income Families of Preschoolers,* which was completed in 1991. From 1991 to 1999, she was an assistant professor at Washington University in St. Louis. She went on to the University of Tulsa in 1999, where she has continued her research on the development of children's abilities to use different genres of discourse. In collaboration with Patton Tabors, she has expanded this work to examine whether using rare vocabulary (words preschoolers would not be expected to know) within these discourse genres and situations is informative.

Courtney B. Cazden is the Charles William Eliot Professor of Education Emerita at Harvard University. A former primary-grade teacher, her research and teaching have focused for more than 30 years on the oral language and literacy of young children, especially children from language and cultural minorities. Her most recent book is *Whole Language Plus: Essays on Literacy in the United States and New Zealand.*

Phil Daro is director of teacher education and professional development for the University of California Office of the President. He served as executive director of New Standards and the director of research and development for the National Center on Education and the Economy. His career has included tenures as the director of the Office of Project Development with the California Department of Education, the executive director of the American Mathematics Project and the executive director of the California Mathematics Project. He received his bachelor of arts in English from the University of California, Berkeley, with a minor in mathematics.

The illustrations of committee members are the work of Alison and Robyn Gillum.

New Standards Speaking & Listening Committee Members

Roberta K. Deal has been an elementary school teacher for the Pittsburgh Public Schools for eight years. She also taught for three years in Prince George's County, Md. She earned a bachelor's degree in early childhood education from Kent State University in 1988 and a master's degree in child care and child development from the University of Pittsburgh in 1998. She is a fellow of The Writing Project, served on the Pittsburgh Public Schools' African Centered Task Force, conducts in-services for teachers on technology and writing, and sponsors her school's Writer's Club and newspaper.

David Dickinson is a senior research scientist at the Education Development Center (EDC) and recognized researcher in the area of emergent literacy and early childhood education. He directs the New England Research Center on Head Start Quality, which is examining the impact of Head Start on children's language and literacy development and on families. Also, in 1994, he and colleagues at EDC began to develop an approach to helping preschool teachers adopt more effective practices to support children's language and literacy. This effort resulted in the Literacy Environment Enrichment Project, an intervention designed for teachers and their supervisors. He and others at EDC are developing and researching a version of this program that can be delivered using the Internet in combination with interactive television.

Dorothy Fowler is a primary language arts specialist for the National Center on Education and the Economy. Previously, she taught in public schools from Virginia to Louisiana and in elementary schools on military bases in Europe.

She also taught courses at George Mason University in Fairfax, Va., on beginning reading strategies for teachers in that county.

She has written curriculum and resource guides for teachers in Fairfax. She also has been published in education journals on how to teach reading and has presented at conferences on the topic.

She earned her bachelor's degree in education at the University of Toledo and her master's degree from the University of New Mexico. She also is certified by the National Board and is a Reading Recovery teacher.

New Standards Speaking & Listening Committee Members

Jean Berko Gleason is a professor in the psychology department at Boston University (BU). She is a faculty member and former director of BU's graduate program in applied linguistics and a research fellow in the department of cognitive and neural systems. She has been a visiting scholar at Stanford University, Harvard University and the Linguistics Institute of the Hungarian Academy of Sciences in Budapest.

She was president of the International Association for the Study of Child Language. She is the author and editor of a leading textbook, *The Development of Language*. She co-edited the textbook *Psycholinguistics* with Nan Bernstein Ratner.

She has conducted research and published in the areas of language development in children, aphasia, language attrition, lexical development and developmental sociolinguistics.

Sally Hampton is senior scholar at the Carnegie Foundation for the Advancement of Teaching. She served as director of research on curriculum and instruction and English language arts for the National Center on Education and the Economy. Since 1991, she has been involved with New Standards, developing both performance standards and a reference exam in English language arts. She worked as a classroom teacher for nearly 16 years and then joined the Fort Worth Independent School District to develop a research-based writing program. She has spoken and published widely on the subject of student writing.

Gail Jordan is an associate professor of education at Bethel College in St. Paul, Minn., where she teaches undergraduate and graduate classes in literacy and educational psychology. Her interests include early literacy development, parent education and text comprehension. Her recent work has been as a reading specialist for the White Bear Lake Schools in White Bear Lake, Minn. There she has taught and developed literacy programs for kindergarten through eighth grades. She initiated a parent education program for literacy development called Project EASE (Early Access to Success in Education). Her graduate work is from the University of Wisconsin and the University of Minnesota.

New Standards

Brian James MacWhinney, Ph.D., is a professor of psychology at Carnegie Mellon University. He received his doctorate in psycholinguistics from the University of California, Berkeley. He also has been a Ford Fellow at the Hungarian Academy of Sciences and taught elementary school in the Oakland, Calif., public schools. With Catherine Snow, MacWhinney was instrumental in developing the Child Language Data Exchange System (CHILDES), a database and software program for the study of child language. He published *The CHILDES Database* and has edited a book on language development, *The Emergence of Language.* He has published numerous articles on aspects of children's language and reading development in refereed journals, focusing recently on those processes in children with various types of brain injury.

Allyssa McCabe, Ph.D., is an associate professor of developmental psychology at the University of Massachusetts, Lowell. With Carole Peterson, she has written on the development of narrative structure and co-edited *Developing Narrative Structure* on narrative development at home and in school settings. She has written a book on cultural differences in narrative structure for teachers, *Chameleon Readers: Teaching Children to Appreciate All Kinds of Good Narrative.* She founded and co-edits the journal *Narrative Inquiry* and also published a book for parents on how to facilitate oral language acquisition.

McCabe was instrumental in preparing initial drafts of these performance standards and related information regarding language development. Her assistance in preparing project staff to collect, select and write commentary on the student performances, which illustrate the standards, was invaluable.

Sharon Nelson-Barber, a sociolinguist, is director of the Language and Cultural Diversity Program, a cross-program effort responding to the need for schools and communities to improve services to students from diverse linguistic, cultural and racial backgrounds. Because sociocultural factors often contribute to students' lack of success in school, she is committed to exploring ways teachers can teach more effectively the full spectrum of students in today's classrooms. Her work spans the lower 48 states, Alaska and the northern Pacific islands of Micronesia. She has published extensively, is active in major organizations and meetings in anthropology and education, and serves on a number of national advisory boards and steering committees on teaching and learning in culturally diverse settings.

New Standards Speaking & Listening Committee Members

Lauren B. Resnick is co-founder and co-director of New Standards, and she also founded and directs the Institute for Learning, which focuses on professional development based on cognitive learning principles and the development of effort-oriented educational programs. A professor of psychology at the University of Pittsburgh, she directs the university's Learning Research and Development Center. Her research has focused on standards and assessment, effort-based education, the nature and development of thinking abilities, and socializing intelligence, with special attention to literacy and mathematics. She has written or edited 10 books and more than 125 articles and book chapters. She has served as president of the American Educational Research Association and as a member of the Harvard Board of Overseers and the Smithsonian Council, along with several boards and committees of the National Research Council.

Catherine Snow is the Henry Lee Shattuck Professor of Education at the Harvard Graduate School of Education. Her research interests in children's language development, including the role of the family and cultural differences in family roles, have expanded to include literacy development, social and familial influences on literacy development, acquisition of English and bilingualism in language-minority children, and literacy acquisition in a second language. She has co-authored books on language development (*Pragmatic Development* with Anat Ninio) and literacy development (*Unfulfilled Expectations: Home and School Influences on Literacy*, with W. Barnes, J. Chandler, I. Goodman and L. Hemphill) and has published many articles in refereed journals and chapters in edited volumes.

She chaired the National Research Council Committee on Preventing Reading Difficulties in Young Children, which produced a report that has been widely adopted as a basis for reform of reading instruction and professional development.

Grover J. (Russ) Whitehurst is leading professor of psychology, professor of pediatrics and chairperson of the psychology department at the State University of New York at Stony Brook. He also has been senior lecturer at the University of New South Wales and academic vice president of the Merrill-Palmer Institute. He is editor of *Developmental Review*, the principal journal for theoretical and review papers in the field of developmental psychology. His research focuses on the prevention of reading problems in children from low-income backgrounds and the nature and consequences of early language delay.

He is a member of the National Research Council's Committee on Early Childhood Pedagogy, the U.S. Department of Education's Family Literacy Synthesis Panel, the National Academic Council of Intelecom, and the U.S. Department of Health and Human Services' Committee on Head Start Research and Evaluation. He is a recipient of the Microsoft Innovators in Higher Education Award.

Sally Mentor Hay directed the development and production of this publication, including the CD-ROMs. She also produced the award-winning *Reading and Writing grade by grade,* the accompanying parents' guide, a book on helping English language learners meet the standards, and videos on literacy program practices. She currently leads a team producing standards-based instructional materials in English language arts for grades K–10. She also is engaged in the design of a four-year professional development program that will prepare school-based literacy coaches to provide in-classroom assistance for teachers and will train them in the effective use of standards-based materials for teaching reading and writing.

Mentor Hay was executive director of New Standards and deputy superintendent of the California State Education Department. She is recognized as the founder of the California School Leadership Academy and has worked as a teacher, reading specialist, principal, curriculum director and associate superintendent for elementary and secondary schools.

Jerlean Daniel is associate professor of education at the University of Pittsburgh and an associate at the Learning Research and Development Center. In this role, she led staff efforts in support of the Speaking and Listening Committee. Along with Allyssa McCabe, she produced the initial drafts of the standards and supporting material about language development. She also was instrumental in the selection and production of the videos and written commentaries of student performances. Her work included support and guidance for a book on helping English language learners meet reading and writing standards and videos on literacy program practices.

Daniel is one of the on-air faculty for Heads Up! Reading, a joint project of the National Head Start Association, the Council for Early Childhood Professional Recognition and Rise Learning Solutions. She also is a past president of the National Association for the Education of Young Children and was director of a child care center for 18 years. She has written articles on transitions for infants, toddlers and difficult children in child care.

Learning to Speak & Listen

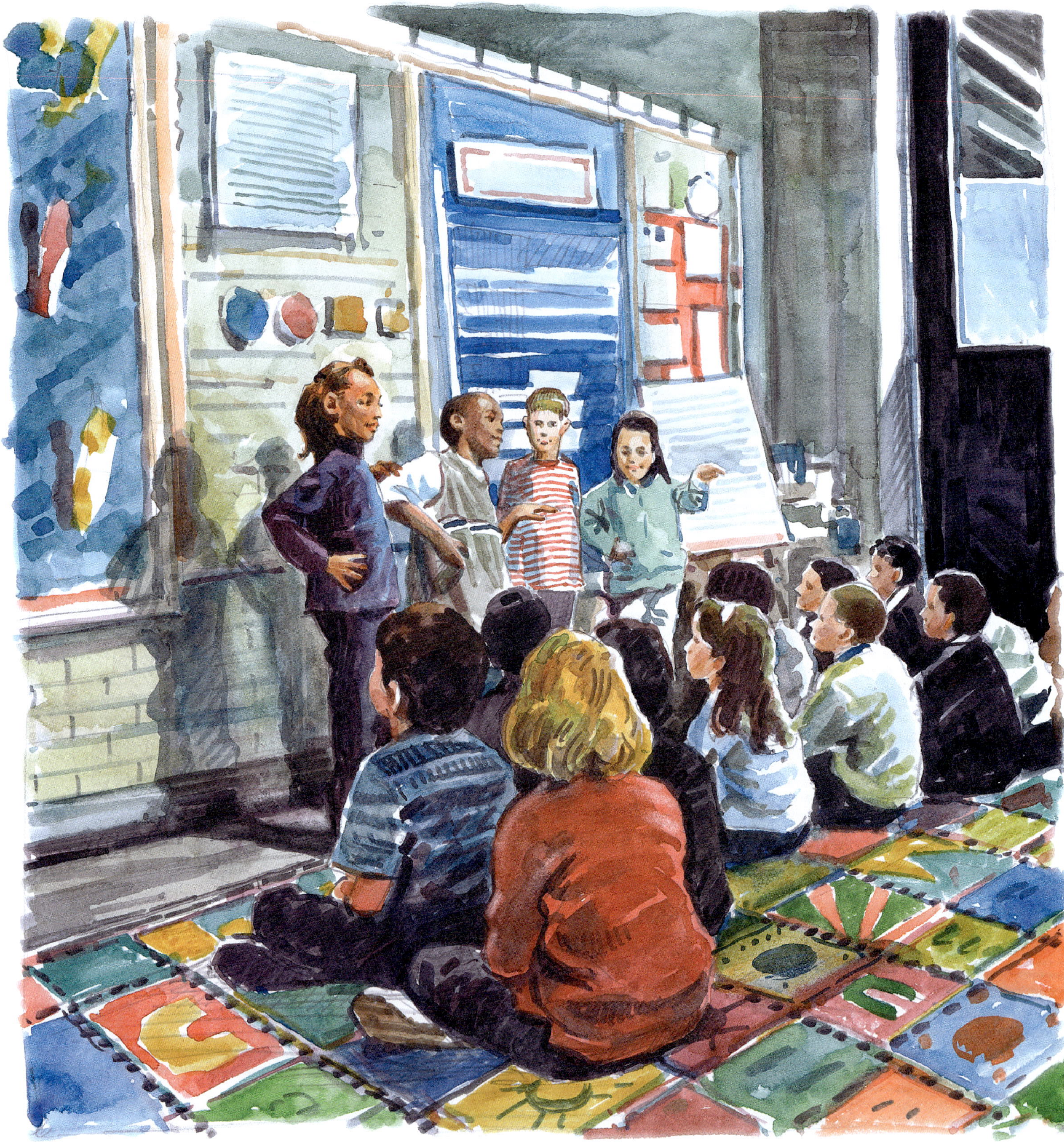

Learning to Speak & Listen

In a room full of children chattering about their work, it may be hard to imagine the great accomplishment reflected in a child's urgent request: "I need the green crayon, please, to color my Triceratops!"

Learning a native language is an amazing — and complex — process. While young children seem to learn to talk quickly and easily, they actually work very hard at it, making many charming errors along the way. People continue to learn new language skills well into adulthood, but the most dramatic language development happens when they are much younger.

Today, we know that it is critical for young children to practice and master their native language for three important reasons:

Speaking and listening are the foundation skills for reading and writing. To read and write well by the end of third grade — a goal that most parents and teachers agree is a key to success in school and life — children must have a solid foundation in oral language. By talking, children encounter sounds, words and language uses that, together, make a natural bridge to sounding out words, understanding stories and writing to communicate.

Speaking and listening make children smarter. By "thinking out loud," asking questions, listening to others, discussing topics, and collaborating and solving problems with others, for example, children learn about the objects, facts, people and ideas that make up their world. Talking makes children familiar with words and knowledge that they need to enjoy and understand fiction and nonfiction books, including math, science, history, art and other academic subjects that they will encounter later on in school.

Speaking and listening are academic, social and life skills that are valued in school and the world. Children who can talk about what they know, hold a polite conversation, take turns in a discussion and perform in front of a group, for example, hold a distinct advantage in school and social situations. Academically, children are judged, in part, by what they say and how they say it.

This book is a companion volume to *Reading & Writing grade by grade* — primary literacy standards for kindergarten through third grade that spell out exactly what students should know and be able to do to read and write well by the end of third grade. *Speaking & Listening for preschool through third grade* spells out exactly what children in preschool through third grade should know and be able to do in the foundation skills of speaking and listening to become good readers and writers — and smart people who are comfortable talking with others.

These speaking and listening standards are organized for three distinct age groups:

◆ preschoolers (three- and four-year-olds), who are just beginning to acquire formal literacy skills;

◆ kindergarten and first graders (five- and six-year-olds), who are making the transition into formal literacy; and

◆ second and third graders (seven- and eight-year-olds), who are solidifying formal literacy skills.

Children learn language at considerably different paces, so these two-year age spans are intentionally broad. To subdivide further by age or grade would be artificial and misleading.

What Should Children Talk About?

To talk a lot, children need topics to talk *about*. Preschoolers tend to talk about whatever is at hand — literally. They need toys, flexible figures, blocks, building sets, books, art supplies, puppets, make-believe and dress-up clothes, and child-size kitchen items, for example, to hold, touch, play with and manipulate. Their talk focuses on the here and now of what they're doing with their hands or about relatively recent events. In fact, preschoolers cannot talk much about ordinary events that happened yesterday or even this morning; *now* is all that counts. However, they can remember significant events from the past, even though their understanding of time is fuzzy. And most preschoolers cannot chat or make small talk about the weather or abstract concepts; they need tangible — and interesting — "props" to talk *about*.

Props also enable children to engage in fantasy play, which is very important for language development. When children play house or cops and robbers or knights and dragons, they use more interesting and challenging language. To say, "You be the mommy, and I'll be the daddy" requires a child to use language to change perspective. Or to whine in a baby's voice, "I'm hungry, Mommy!" requires a child to take on the talk of another character. This is known as *transformational* use of language — and it's actually a very sophisticated form of talk.

Teachers and child care providers can encourage talk with a wide variety of materials in their classrooms. They need to refresh or add to these materials frequently, so children have something new to explore — and talk about — all the time. Surprises spark conversations. Children are most likely to have long talks about topics that they are familiar with and that are interesting to them — *not* about topics that are still very new to them or about topics that bore them.

Likewise, to carry on lengthy conversations, children need meaty topics. The question, "What did you eat for breakfast?" is not likely to lead to a lengthy conversation. On the other hand, conversations about why we classify plants as living creatures, why characters in books act the way they do or — for elementary students — about the results of the Civil War can go on and on. These topics spring from content-rich learning units, beginning in preschool, and from a rigorous core curriculum in elementary school.

As children grow older, they talk longer and in more detail about events they experienced in the past and about their own future plans — as well as those of others. They use their imaginations to talk about fantasies and about "what if?" situations. They have full discussions on topics, negotiating several different and complex perspectives. The seeds for these conversations — in the form of knowledge and language — are nurtured in the minds of three- to eight-year-olds.

Learning to Speak & Listen

For K–3 students, the speaking and listening standards go hand-in-hand with the reading and writing standards; in many cases, students can meet both sets of standards with carefully planned teaching and learning activities.

The following sections give child care providers and preschool and K–3 teachers a preview of the three standards:

◆ Habits;

◆ Kinds of Talk and Resulting Genres; and

◆ Language Use and Conventions.

These standards focus on research that tells us what *students* need to know and be able to do to succeed academically — and on the skills and knowledge that *teachers* actually can teach in their classrooms, beginning in preschools and child care centers.

Habits

From the time they are infants until they are about eight years old, children learn most of what they know by hearing other people talk: Talking is the main way children get to know the world, understand complex events and encounter different perspectives.

Furthermore, engaging in stimulating talk is the only way young children can expand their *own* language skills — learning words, putting sentences together and practicing the "rules" of talk, such as taking turns in a conversation. In playful word games, discussions, collaborations and problem solving with others, children learn more and more about the world and about language.

"I don't know anything about trains. What can you tell me about trains?"

"Um, there are hopper cars, even box cars, even tank cars, even automobile cars."

"Does it get its name by what it carries, like you said, automobile cars? Does that mean it carries cars? It carries automobiles, rather?"

"Yeah."

Only when they reach third or fourth grade — as fluent readers — can children routinely find out about the world and language in another important way, by reading. Once they can read at a fourth-grade level, they regularly can learn new, more complex words and ideas by reading and writing. *To achieve this level of literacy, however, young children must hear and practice words orally.* They need to hear books read aloud; listen to others speaking; and talk, talk, talk.

Talk is a cultural value of great importance in the United States — but talking a lot may seem strange to students and parents in some communities and cultures. Still, to do well in U.S. schools and, later, in workplaces, young people must speak comfortably and proficiently. In American classrooms, after all, oral participation often counts as part of students' grades. Success on the job usually requires face-to-face job interviews and then competence and confidence in interacting with other people. These standards, then, build in these expectations. (For more, see "Different Cultures, Different Rules," page 24.)

Children learn from the back and forth of speaking and listening — even when they are on the receiving, or listening, end. They learn by observing how other people react to what they say. A puzzled glance shows a child that a comment isn't clear; a hearty chuckle indicates that a friend enjoys a joke.

Listening, in fact, is embedded in all the standards. The best talk comes when children listen attentively to what other people say and then connect their responses to what they have heard. Good conversations build when children extend the remarks other people make — and they can do this only, of course, if they are paying attention.

Children learn by listening to other people's knowledge, insights and different points of view. Purposeful talk about a topic, known as *accountable talk*^{SM}, can occur on

> The shy, quiet and reserved child may seem like a model of good behavior — but that child may be a cause for concern, not celebration. *All* children need opportunities to talk *a lot* to develop word knowledge and language skills.

Learning to Speak & Listen

says, "Which one is yours? The blue cup or the green cup?" the child learns to be more specific to make the meaning clear.

Children also learn from regular, repeated and engaging practice. Suppose a child hears a new word — for example, *insect* — when his teacher reads aloud a book in class. If the child hears *insect* just once, for that fleeting moment, he may well forget it. But if the word *insect* pops up over and over in carefully planned classroom talks, the word becomes familiar. The teacher can draw attention to the word, explaining that *insect* is another word for *bug*. She can set up opportunities for children to use the word *insect* in their daily talk — by hunting for insects outdoors; creating habitats for ants, crickets or butterflies in the classroom; drawing insects and labeling their parts; adding *insect* to a word wall; making ladybugs for an art project; and so on. When children hear *insect* again and again — and have the chance to use the word themselves — they are more likely to remember it. The word *insect,* then, becomes part of their working vocabulary.

And so it goes for many, many words — in settings that support language development. (For more, see "Settings That Get Children Talking," page 17.)

Knowing all of this, teachers and child care providers no longer can take stock in the old

Talk: A Very Important Topic

Talk about talk — the rules for speaking and listening and the meaning of words and language — is especially important in the classroom. With the teacher's guidance, children should pay attention to words and talk about language. By doing so, they learn a great deal about language. For example, words such as *dressing, light* and *bug* can have distinct, but related, meanings, depending on how they are used:

- salad *dressing,* window *dressing, dressing* up, *dressing* down, *dressing* someone down;
- *light* a fire, turn on the *light, light* up the night, a butterfly *lights* on a flower, *light*weight fabric, *light* color, *light* meal; and
- the fly is a *bug,* computer *bug,* don't *bug* me, *bug* off.

Children may never notice these multiple meanings unless a teacher — or another student — points them out. English language learners, in fact, often use words, ask questions and construct sentences that make children notice different ways to use language. For this reason, non-native English speakers are an important resource in classrooms.

Noticing the different uses of words prepares children for words they will learn later in school. In fifth grade, for example, they may encounter words such as *dissolution* and *suspension*. These words have different, but related, meanings, depending on whether they come up in a discussion about science or government.

Word relationships should be a topic of conversation, beginning in preschool. How else is a child later supposed to make sense of the difference between dissolving sugar in water and dissolving parliament or between suspension bridges and suspension of *habeas corpus*? By the same token, if children know the meaning of words in one context, they can make leaps of understandings to other contexts — if they know that words can have multiple meanings.

New Standards

"Can you remember what it was like when you didn't know how to read and what it felt like to you?"

"I got jealous of some people because I know somebody in this classroom that was a pretty fast reader to me and I was like, oh, why am I not reading that fast and like, um, like, um, why am I not learning and why am I not just getting the hang of it?"

"And what did you do to change that?"

"I practiced every day."

saying, "Children should be seen and not heard." The shy, quiet and reserved child may seem like a model of good behavior — but that child may be a cause for concern, not celebration. *All* children need opportunities to talk *a lot* to develop word knowledge and language skills. That said, teachers must understand that children have different temperaments. Some children are chatty, while others are better listeners. Some children enjoy an audience; others balk at the attention. These differences are natural. Children also come to school with different cultural and social expectations about speaking and listening. (For more, see "Different Cultures, Different Rules," page 24.)

Teachers and child care providers have to recognize reluctant speakers — and provide extra attention or opportunities for them to use language. Children who fear a classroom presentation, for example, likely will do better if they practice in advance with their teacher, parents or another adult "coach."

The standards, then, lay out several different and important ways for children to develop the habits of speaking and listening:

◆ talking a lot;
◆ talking to one's self;
◆ conversing at length on a topic; and
◆ discussing books.

New Standards

Talk, Talk and Talk Still More

Children need to talk *a lot* to develop oral language fully — and playfulness may be the key element in this process. In a playful, purposeful environment of talk, talk, talk, children learn more than in classrooms where only the teacher's voice is heard. Put another way, oral language development cannot be a spectator sport. A lively hum of focused conversations in a classroom is a sign that talk is valued. This is true not only in preschool, but also throughout the elementary school years. By the same token, rambunctious shouting or arguing are signs of a less purposeful learning environment.

Teachers should be mindful, however, that a lively hum may conceal the silence of some children in the classroom. Teachers need to pay attention to who's talking — and nudge the quiet students to join the dance of conversations.

'Air Time' and 'Ear Time'

Children need both "air time" — opportunities to talk a lot — and "ear time" — the attention of fluent, responsive adults — to develop oral language skills. Even the best schools do not give students enough opportunities and attention to engage in interactive conversations. In classrooms where the student-teacher ratio is 30-to-1, children simply cannot get enough practice talking with adults.

Teachers, then, need to arrange other opportunities for children to have these conversations. One option is a new kind of homework, oral language homework, which builds on topics discussed in class or prepares students for the next day's activities. For example, after the teacher reads aloud a story in the classroom, she may give students the assignment of retelling the story to their parents or caregivers at home. After older students read the first few chapters of a book, they may be asked to discuss the plot and characters with their parents and talk together about the language of the author. After they conduct a science experiment in class, students may be asked to explain the results at home. Or parents may serve as the audience when students rehearse the alphabet, nursery rhymes, poems, book reports or science project presentations.

This kind of homework requires clear and consistent communication between teachers and parents, which does not have to be elaborate. A simple note works: "Today we are studying the food groups in class. At dinner tonight, your child may have a lot to tell you about what you are eating."

Many parents are willing and able to provide their children with ample "air time" and "ear time." Other parents cannot serve as fluent speakers and responsive listeners. For their children, schools and teachers may recruit older students; parent volunteers; and other volunteers from the neighborhood, businesses or community organizations.

Finally, teachers need to give parents and volunteers clear guidelines about these conversations. Children make the most progress with kind adults who recognize their best contributions with interest and praise — *not* with adults who scold them when they make a mistake. Adults should teach by speaking well themselves rather than by pointing out children's inadequacies. Children will correct their mistakes spontaneously when they have the chance to talk with people they like about topics that interest them.

Talking a lot boosts academic success

Willingness and ability to talk a lot, under a variety of circumstances, is a standard in its own right.

Talking a lot helps children do well in school. Certain kinds of talk — discussing, collaborating and problem solving with peers — help children learn academic subjects, research shows. These kinds of talk put children in situations where they can:

- observe how other people react to what they say;
- hear and respond to other people who ask them to clarify what they say;
- hear their own ideas reflected in other people's comments;
- hear children and adults repeat, revise or improve on what they say; and
- learn the rules of speaking and listening, such as taking turns.

These interactive skills contribute to academic success. Children who participate in sharing time, small-group learning activities or whole-class discussions meet academic expectations. In part, teachers judge children's academic potential on their ability to listen to others and express themselves in these situations. Children who *don't* talk much often are deprived of the circumstances that promote language growth.

Talking a lot is not easy for all children. Some children can talk one on one but find it hard to talk in small groups and even harder to talk in large groups. Most children need to feel comfortable talking in small groups before they tackle large ones. Beginning in preschool, these standards expect children to expand their conversations from one-on-one exchanges to small groups. Preschoolers are not necessarily expected to speak *in front of* a group, but they should speak *with* other children in small gatherings — circle time, block play, snack time and dramatic play, for example — to share personal stories, express their preferences or talk about topics that interest them.

By kindergarten and first grade, children also should be able to talk about their own writings and drawings, present an event or object to the class, play and learn with others, teach and learn new techniques from others, read aloud, and listen and respond to questions and comments about books they have read or books that have been read aloud to them.

By second and third grades, children should be able to speak in front of larger groups, such as the whole class or a parent audience. They can recite poems; perform, with others, parts they have memorized in plays; give a book talk; and present a science project.

In addition to anxiety or shyness, talking a lot may require children to overcome other obstacles to participating. Different social groups and cultures have varying expectations about talking in school. Some children are reluctant to speak, while others tell their tales in styles that are different from the European American norm. Teachers should recognize this diversity — and support all children in meeting the standards in ways that are right and rigorous for them. To do this, teachers need to

> This is a six-year span of great importance that sets the stage for children's future education.

Settings That Get Children Talking

When, where and how do children talk? Talk, of course, happens in many *settings* — the places and social situations of talk. *And setting changes the possibilities for the conversations.* People talk face to face, one on one, on the telephone, in small groups, in crowds. Every setting is different, depending on:

◆ *Who gets to talk?* Talk among children is different from talk between an adult and a child. Talk with an expert is different from talk among people who don't know very much about a topic.

◆ *What are the rules?* In some settings, one person is in control, talks as long as she wants, and decides if and when others get to talk. Most classrooms operate like this at times. In other settings, such as two-person conversations, people take turns talking in response to one another, and both have responsibilities to do some of the talking. They participate as equals, speaking and listening in response to one another. In other settings, say family dinner table conversations, several people share the floor. Everyone has to jump in, coordinating their timing or negotiating an opening in the conversation, when they have something to say.

◆ *What is going on — and where?* Some talk is fine in one setting but not in another. For example, yelling on the playground is acceptable, while softer voices are appropriate indoors. Likewise, a five-year-old playing house with a friend has the right to say, "You have to eat your peas!" Role playing is fine in this setting — but if this command is issued to a classmate during lunch, the child is considered bossy. In science, elementary school students often are expected to describe exactly what they see. But during art class, children are expected to go beyond describing only what they see in a painting, for example, to talking about their interpretation of the image and their reaction to it.

Children need to talk in many social settings. Talking one on one with adults, discussing in small groups, performing in front of a group, collaborating and resolving disputes — each of these settings gives children different opportunities to learn by speaking and listening. The settings should change significantly through the years. Dramatic play, for example, is an excellent setting for preschoolers to meet speaking and listening standards. Formal, curricular settings such as math and science lessons are more appropriate for second and third graders meeting the same standards.

For children to meet the standards, teachers must take settings and classroom discussions seriously, teaching the rules of participation and expecting children to respect everyone's contributions. Teachers must share the responsibility for introducing new topics with everyone in the classroom, so children learn to talk about their own perspectives — and listen attentively to those of others. And teachers must model the give and take, back and forth of polite conversation, offering evidence or justification to support what they say, so children learn to share ideas, negotiate and even disagree without being disagreeable.

For Talk at Its Best, Try Familiar, Informal and Comfortable Settings

As parents and teachers know — and as research shows again and again — children, especially young children, do not talk comfortably or well in all situations. Children produce longer and more complex language when conversing with familiar, trusted peers and adults. They perform best in familiar, informal and comfortable surroundings. Familiarity is the most important factor for long, interesting conversations. Children talk most — and with the most complex words and sentences — when they are talking about subjects they are familiar with, but not so familiar that they are bored with the subject.

The teacher's challenge, then, is to create a classroom that invites high levels of purposeful talk from children. A classroom that is familiar, comfortable and stimulating is the best setting for fostering and evaluating children's language skills.

understand the storytelling styles of the different cultures represented in their classrooms. (For more, see "Different Cultures, Different Rules," page 24, and "Cultural Differences in Narrative Form," page 231.)

Talking to one's self guides thinking, language skills

Researchers in child development made an important discovery in the early 20th century: Children learn a lot when they talk out loud to themselves. Preschoolers delight in their newfound ability to put thoughts into words, an ability they first display by talking out loud to themselves. During free play at preschool, about 40 percent of children's talk is directed at themselves, not at other preschoolers or adults. This "private speech" is a key way for children to practice language and guide themselves through their actions.

For example, a preschooler painting at an easel may say, "I'm making a flower. I'm making a red flower . . . and green grass . . ." and so on, in a running monologue to no one in particular. Talking helps organize thinking and behavior — and it helps control impulses as well. For example, a preschooler approaching a hot stove will say, in her mother's voice, "No!" The child will voice her thoughts to control her own impulses, a critical aspect of socialization.

Talking to themselves or others, children begin to notice when familiar words don't sound right — and they attempt to correct themselves. Beginning in preschool, the standards expect children to focus on language this way and, in doing so, try to get the words right. So, for instance, a child may say, "I'm hoppy — I mean *happy!*" The correction does not have to be perfect. What matters is that the child notices a mistake and tries to correct it.

By kindergarten and first grade, children talk or mutter out loud to plan ahead or figure something out, such as a math problem. Talking out loud indicates that they are working hard on a task; indeed, it helps them stay focused on a challenge. By second and third grades, children also use self-monitoring strategies — thinking silently or muttering quietly to themselves — to:

Learning to Speak & Listen

- check their understanding of words and meaning as they read;
- rehearse steps to solve a problem; and
- recite information they have learned or memorized.

Conversing at length on a topic

Between the ages of three and eight, children develop the capacity to stay on and extend the *topic*, or shared focus, of a conversation. Children younger than three respond to questions, but they usually do not develop the topic by asking questions or expanding on responses to their own questions.

When they are three or four years old, though, children start to ask questions to seek information *about topics they are interested in*. Parents, child care providers and teachers will recognize this curiosity in familiar, insistent questions, such as, "Why is the sky blue?" At this age, children can stay on a topic — and extend the topic — with their own questions and responses.

This is a six-year span of great importance that sets the stage for children's future education. In classrooms, the curriculum drives topics of talk: *Children talk about what they are learning.* It is critical, then, for the curriculum to include good topics that foster engaging talk

The Joy of Collecting Words

Every day, preschoolers and elementary school students should expand their vocabularies by learning a handful of new words. This puts them on track to learn hundreds or thousands of new words every year — a reasonable expectation as they progress through school. The *worst* way for children to learn new words is with vocabulary drills — giving students lists of words to memorize or look up in a dictionary.

Instead, teachers should encourage children to become *word collectors*, people who notice new words and scoop them up for their personal collections when they hear, see or read them. Teachers can model this behavior by:

- calling attention to new or interesting words and expressions in books and conversations;
- giving students new words to describe what they are doing or learning;
- rephrasing students' remarks with more sophisticated vocabulary and sentence structure;
- praising students when they try out new words in speaking or writing;
- playing word games with students;
- encouraging children to keep and use personal dictionaries for new words they learn; and
- adding new words to well-organized, thoughtful word walls displayed in the classroom.

In preschool, word walls may include action or descriptive words with pictures. In first grade, they may include words with similar phonemes or graphemes, which are written representations of words. By third grade, word walls may be organized with labels for the parts of speech, such as nouns, verbs, adverbs and adjectives.

Children who collect words can "unlock their word-hoards," to borrow from *Beowulf*, when they speak and write.

Meaningful Differences and Implications for Schools and Teachers

Some differences in children's speaking and listening skills stem from their everyday circumstances at home. A landmark study of toddlers and preschoolers in professional, working-class and welfare families found huge differences in children's language development over time. The study, described in the book *Meaningful Differences* (Hart and Risley, 1995), makes clear the significant advantages for children whose parents talk, talk and talk still more to them. These parents talk regularly about the stuff of daily life, listen carefully to what their children say, try to be nice and positive, and ask for their children's opinions. These kinds of interactions require no special training, just an active conviction that their children are interested — and interesting — people.

The study documented that children in families with the highest income and education levels have bigger and more expressive vocabularies and use more sophisticated sentence structures than children from the poorest families. Their parents seem to be preparing them to participate in a culture where words are important. Just by being around people who talk to them all the time, *three-year-olds* in professional families talk more and use more complex language than *adults* in welfare families do. In fact, the study estimates that by the age of three, children in professional families have heard 30 million words, children in working-class families 20 million and children in welfare families 10 million.

This study underscores the vital role teachers and school communities play in helping to support the language development of children who come to school with very little language experience. These children have a special need for intensive talk time and focused attention on their language learning. Teachers have a responsibility to help children catch up on speaking and listening in school.

---

with new words and ideas. Children may have deep, abiding interests in certain topics. Dinosaurs, trucks, dolls, pets or some more idiosyncratic passions may dominate their conversations. Attentive teachers can turn these personal topics into curriculum topics — and turn the floor over to the resident child expert, who can guide the talk and the discoveries.

Focusing on children's interests to promote learning is particularly important in the preschool years. A curriculum that capitalizes on children's curiosity and helps them expand what they know about the world gives them new ideas and the words to go with them. (For more, see "Talk, Talk and Talk Still More," page 15.)

The challenge in preschool and early primary grades, then, is for teachers to refresh the curriculum, activities, materials — *and conversations* — regularly. This variety ensures that children always have new topics at hand to talk and hear about. This doesn't mean flitting rapidly from topic to topic, television style. Nor does it mean moving at the pace of the teacher, who may get bored with a topic before children do. Children need time to linger on topics and

Learning to Speak & Listen

explore them deeply at their own pace. Engaging topics, explored in depth, introduce new ideas and new words — which expand children's knowledge and vocabularies.

For example, preschoolers are not likely to hear words such as *hose, pump, ladder, engine* and *oxygen* unless they are learning — and talking — about firefighting (in the context, say, of a field trip to the neighborhood fire station). Nor are first graders likely to hear words such as *mollusk, bivalve* and *crustacean* unless they are studying shellfish (in the context of a hands-on science unit). Nor will most third graders hear words such as *solid, density* and *porous* unless they are learning — and talking — about the physics of matter (in the context, say, of floating and sinking objects at a water table).

Different topics also introduce different kinds of talk, such as facts and opinions, explanations, and stories. Only when children have many different, interesting topics to discuss in their classrooms can teachers be sure that there are enough opportunities to learn, practice and display a wide range of language skills.

The standards expect children to keep up a conversation on a topic. In preschool, children are expected to talk for four or more exchanges, or turns, with a teacher or another student. By kindergarten and first grade, the conversations should extend to six or seven exchanges. By second and third grade, the conversation should extend to eight or more exchanges.

Discussing books leads to meaningful topics

Talking about books challenges and stimulates children's learning — and gives them interesting topics of conversation. Books are more than the sum and substance of the words. They are filled with opportunities for making meaning — and talking about books helps children reach a deeper understanding of their meaning. Discussing books also helps children practice the kind of academic talk that is expected in school. For example, children learn to:

◆ state their points to others;

◆ back up their remarks with the words in the text;

◆ politely discuss and defend their remarks;

◆ "read into" the words in the text, or make inferences about what the author is saying;

◆ discover new or multiple meanings for words and new perspectives on themes; and

◆ collaborate with others to build an understanding.

Beginning in preschool, children regularly can and should discuss books that teachers read to them. Teachers can read aloud to the whole class or small groups of children. Book talk can occur in one-on-one conversations with the teacher, small groups and large groups. In these settings, the teacher can lead children in discussions of the pictures, words, literary conventions (capital letters, commas, periods, exclamation points and question marks), literary devices ("Once upon a time"), plot and information in the book.

The quality of book talk builds over time — with regular practice and rereading of good books. When children read books over and over again, they notice more and can talk more about them. The discussions are better when the books give children something to chew on as well — a quirky plot, a character torn by a dilemma, a haunting theme, an ambiguous or

New Standards

unexpected ending, or an imaginative use of language or illustrations.

Typically, very young children talk about books as they relate to their own lives and experiences. Talking about the *Spot* or *Clifford* books, for example, children may tell about their own pets. Teachers, then, should carefully select books with their students in mind, books that reflect students' perspectives, interests, values, cultures and genders.

In book talks, the standards expect children to name and describe characters and objects, repeat information, use the text to predict what will happen next, and talk about why characters act the way they do. And they should begin to notice titles, authors, plots and topics — the literary conventions of books.

Kindergartners and first graders should be reading and talking about longer, more challenging books as they relate to other people's lives and experiences, not just to the children's own. They should compare books by the same author and refer back to the text to make a point, get information or write about their reading. Similarly, they should compare books by different authors in the same genres. Also, children at this age should be more aware of what other students have to say about books. They should respond to other students' remarks by asking questions or relating their own observations to what others already have said.

In second and third grades, the quality of book talk increases dramatically — because by this age, children should be independent readers and writers. The standards expect children to use their reading and writing knowledge to talk about books. By this age, children should discuss the details of books, including word meanings, word choices, literary devices, subplots, character motivation and main ideas. They also should give oral reports about books in front of the class.

"I really like this book because of all the interesting language it had. Let me see if I can find it, like, where is it? 'The older children waved flags and headbands and shouted at the top of their lungs until the mountain echoed the noise like rumbling thunder.'"

"Well, I agree with you. I mean, and I think that some of these interesting words are kind of interesting, like Byrd Baylor's words."

". . . Yeah, they're, like, connected in some way."

New Standards

Kinds of Talk and Resulting Genres

Like adults, children talk for a variety of reasons, or *purposes*. Among the major reasons people talk are to:

- inform, entertain and persuade others;
- present themselves, their topic or their point of view to others;
- negotiate or propose relationships with others;
- evaluate people, information or events; and
- think, teach and learn.

By the time they are three years old, children already talk for many of these purposes. They can discuss a joint focus of attention (for example, a stack of blocks), tell about recent and sometimes more distant past events (a visit to the zoo), and share their feelings and reactions (loneliness when a friend is away) as well as those of others. They can talk about their actions; ask people to explain what they mean; and talk about changing objects, actions and people in pretend play. Typically, then, three-year-olds use language to get what they want or to express their point of view. They do not use language much yet to express high-level social messages to others. They also usually don't make "small talk" just to pass the time. (For more, see "What's the Point? Talking for a Purpose" at left.)

People who listen, speak and use language well are more likely to succeed in their purposes than people who struggle to express themselves. This is true in academic and social situations in school and elsewhere. The standards do not cover all the many and varied styles and intentions of language. Rather, they lay out several different and important academic forms, or *genres*, of speaking and listening in which children can practice and accomplish a variety of purposes:

- narrative;
- explaining and seeking information;
- getting things done; and
- producing and responding to performances.

These are the same genres for which students are expected to meet academic standards in *Reading & Writing grade by grade*. Exploring the genres orally, beginning in preschool, prepares children to meet standards in reading

What's the Point? Talking for a Purpose

For children, speaking appropriately for a purpose is as much a matter of social skills as it is a matter of language and words. Children need to understand classroom expectations for speaking and listening — and often that knowledge comes from social situations and social signals that may not be obvious.

Children first encounter many of the purposes and genres of talk in preschool and elementary school. Teachers need to give children opportunities to discover the rules of communicating for different purposes and genres — through lots of practice and, at times, through clear instruction. Teachers need to talk about different forms of purposeful talk and help children figure out how to use stories, questions, reports and recitations to accomplish their own academic purposes.

Children cannot respond appropriately to adults unless they have a basic understanding of the expectations for the situation.

Different Cultures, Different Rules

The social and grammatical rules of interaction in these standards spring from a distinct point of view: They are widely shared by speakers of mainstream English, the primary language of school and business. But different social groups share different rules for "knowing how to talk" — and teachers should be very aware of this diversity.

Asian American preschoolers, for example, address their teachers respectfully as "Teacher" or "Miss Juanita," while mainstream American preschoolers seem to know that "Juanita" is fine. In some cultures, it is a sign of respect for students to avoid eye contact with teachers, but this deference may be mistaken for inattentiveness or embarrassment in U.S. classrooms.

Often, the ability to use more than one set of language rules is an advantage, allowing children to communicate with different social groups. Sometimes, though, children are handicapped academically when they make social or grammatical errors in mainstream English. They may not participate as much or as effectively in classroom talk. All students should learn the shared rules of standard English — but not in ways that tread on their heritage.

Social Dialects and Code Switching

Some children use nonstandard English dialects, such as "he don't," "I ain't," "birfday" for *birthday* and "aks" for *ask*. Preschoolers and kindergartners may not know standard English when they enter school, so teachers cannot expect them to use it proficiently. Students who have been in school for a few years should be expected to use standard English for academic purposes but not necessarily in social conversations.

Many students know the rules of more than one social dialect or language. When pairs or groups of Hispanic children talk, for example, they may mix the rules and words of both languages, a practice known as code switching. Code switching comes into play when children can't recall the right rules or words in a second language, when they want to respond politely to a friend's code switching or stress their own belonging to the group, or when it's easier to talk about certain topics in one language or the other. In such circumstances, refusing to code switch may be socially inappropriate. On the other hand, people who don't understand Spanish may judge code switching as a conscious rejection — even if the Hispanic students are using the strategy to try to understand English.

and writing. The literacy standards build on and complement the oral language standards.

Often, purposes and genres overlap and blend together. Indeed, genres are not rigid forms in speaking *or* writing; genres are flexible forms that take on different shapes, depending on the purpose. For example, children can tell a narrative story to inform, entertain, persuade or negotiate, and the story changes to adapt to the purpose. To inform, a child may stick to a simple recounting of significant events: "Well, first I went to my grandma's house and then we played bubbles and then it got dark and we came home." To entertain, the child may

Learning to Speak & Listen

embellish the story: "Guess what! We played bubbles at my grandma's house, and I blew a bubble as big as a basketball!" To persuade, the child may add emphasis and pick just the right detail to share: "I *really* like playing bubbles. Grandma bought us some bubbles, and she says I blow the biggest bubbles she ever saw. Can you *please* buy me some bubbles to play with at home?" To negotiate, the child may adapt the story in this way: "If you buy me some bubbles, I'll play with them outside just like I did at Grandma's house, OK? I promise I won't drip them in the house."

✓ In preschool, children are just beginning to produce language with characteristics of different genres. But they generally do not make conscious choices from among the genres. By third grade, children understand some differences among the genres, and they can choose consciously from among them — and adapt them intentionally — to accomplish their purpose. To a large extent, third graders know when to tell a story, explain and argue a point.

Narrative talk: why tell stories

Children begin to tell stories, or *narratives,* every day as soon as they can put sentences together — when they are about two years old. ✓ By the time they get to preschool, their personal oral narratives can be well developed; children have a natural ability to tell tales. Most storytelling occurs at home, but children benefit from frequent exposure to narratives —

through oral storytelling and books read aloud — and from opportunities to tell their own stories at school.

Children from different cultures bring different styles to the stories they tell. The best-known fairy tales of European American storytellers follow a distinct pattern with predictable organizational elements, which together are known as *story grammar.* At its simple

> People who listen
> and use langua
> are more likely to
> in their purpos
> people who st
> to express the

plotted on a line — first this happened, then that happened and then the next thing happened.

Other cultures tell tales in circular, spiral, web or haiku patterns. Hispanic children, for example, often people stories with friends and relatives, whether or not they are central to the theme or main event. These stories are just as well constructed as those of the brothers Grimm or Hans Christian Andersen, but they reflect the Hispanic culture's value of family relationships. African American children often organize their stories by recounting a series of events and descriptions that may seem isolated but that actually build meaning or lead to the point of the story. This circling around the theme is typical of African tribal narratives. Japanese American children, meanwhile, often pare their stories down to short, concise accounts that mirror the artistic precision of haiku poems.

(For an understanding of how the different cultural narratives meet the standards, see the examples in the preschool, kindergarten and first-grade, and second- and third-grade sections of this book.)

In preschool, children should tell many kinds of narratives, including personal memories, imaginary stories, story or television retellings, and stories made up to go with pictures or storybooks without words. Narratives can be true, made up, or a blend of fact and fiction. Often, children recount real events or retell stories they have heard.

Teachers play a critical role in creating opportunities for children to tell stories, and they should create settings that nurture stories. For example, sharing time invites personal narratives; storyboard stations, dolls and animals encourage made-up stories. Children bubble up with stories whenever their teacher stays still and approachable — during morning hellos and afternoon good-byes, over snacks and lunch with students, on the playground. Teachers should plan for these "spontaneous" moments to happen. And when they do, teachers should help children tell longer, more detailed stories. When children are telling about an experience the teacher has shared, she can ask pointed questions to push the conversation. Children tend to tell longer stories, though, about unshared events. Teachers can extend these stories with general, open-ended remarks, such as, "Tell me more" or "Really! I didn't know that!" or "You must have been scared [or happy or surprised] when that happened." Stories about shared and unshared events develop children's ability to talk at length about the past.

Eventually, children are expected to read classic and contemporary fiction stories — and to write their own stories. Telling stories aloud and listening to stories spoken and read aloud prepares children to read and write narratives later on in school. The standards expect children to develop oral narratives that are more and more detailed — and more like *written* stories, with story lines and characters, for example — as they grow older.

> Teachers play a critical role in creating opportunities for children to tell stories, and they should create settings that nurture stories.

Explaining and seeking information gets children ready for reports

In academic and social situations, children are expected to seek information and communicate it to others. In elementary school and beyond, this genre takes the form of information reports, essays, and other written and oral work — and it becomes increasingly important as students grow older.

For preschool children, this genre takes the form of talking to inform and explain. Preschoolers often use narrative stories for this purpose, embedding information in the story so the two genres blend together: "My dad took me to the park, and we caught two frogs. Did you know that frogs eat flies? I wanted to take them home, but my dad made me put them back near the water."

However, by the end of preschool, children should be telling stories and giving information in distinctly different ways. To do this, children need real knowledge and a vocabulary to describe their knowledge — exactly what they should be learning in preschool. With a content-rich curriculum, teachers should guide children through experiences that help them understand — and talk about — the world.

For example, a study of rocks would include collecting local rocks; sorting rocks by color, shape, weight or size; learning the names of specific rocks (*granite, limestone, coal, quartz, slate, amethyst, diamond*) or rock types (*igneous, sedimentary, metamorphic*); and visiting a rock display at a museum. This kind of intense study gives children hands-on, physical knowledge of rocks and a real vocabulary to describe them and explain how some rocks are formed. Their talk, then, should move from a story about rocks ("We looked for rocks today") to vivid questions and explanations about rocks ("How did erosion make this rock smooth?" and "This basalt rock came from the lava in a volcano!").

Thematic studies and a rigorous core curriculum in preschool and elementary school give children opportunities to seek and provide information in formal and informal settings. At times, the teacher provides the information. At other times, the standards expect children to talk about what they know — or want to know. In elementary school, children should be giving oral reports (and writing) about topics they know about, using language that is used in the real world.

Getting things done — with words *and* strategies

In school and life, children need to talk to get things done. They need to be able to ask for and give help, follow directions, and work with others to solve problems. Children should start learning these important communication skills in preschool.

✓ In preschool, children can ask or tell someone how to work a new toy, try to convince a friend to stop coloring a picture and play blocks instead, or persuade a classmate to take turns with the puppets. Preschool children still need help from teachers who can act as role models to give and follow directions, negotiate, and solve problems with others. Most of these activities are simple and self-centered, focused on what children want or need to do for themselves.

In kindergarten and first grade, children can listen to, understand and carry out longer and more detailed directions. They begin to consider other people's perspectives as well, elaborating on directions or explanations for someone else's benefit. They ask for clarifications when they need them — and will push for more information to understand things or

Ordering the World with Superordinates and Subordinates

No word is an island. Words are useful to people only as they relate to and connect to other words to make meaning. As children learn language, therefore, they lump like words together into knowledge domains, or broad spheres of knowledge. So, for example, *transportation* is a knowledge domain, while *boats* is one top-level category, or superordinate, within that knowledge domain. *Rowboat, canoe, ferry* and *tanker* are subordinates within that superordinate.

Children need to develop a vocabulary that encompasses many knowledge domains. Infants and toddlers begin acquiring this knowledge when they learn animal sounds: *meow, bark, moo, oink* and *baa*, for example.

get things done. They use writings or drawings to explain their thinking, drawing a diagram to show their precise meaning, for example. And they engage in longer conversations to work through a problem, speaking and listening in turn.

In second and third grades, children give and receive even more specific and complex directions and explanations. They are much more capable of seeing the world from somebody else's perspective. They do more than listen to what others say; they truly *collaborate* with others to get things done. They disagree with others politely but offer alternative solutions to smooth out arguments. In addition, they are more likely to reason with others with evidence or logic, rather than with an outburst of anger or tears.

Producing and responding to performances

By their nature, speaking and listening activities imply that there is an audience. These standards make that connection explicit by expecting students to give and respond to performances. At many times during their school years, students will be expected to read aloud, give oral reports or speeches, present their reactions, respond to literature, and so on. With practice, children can present themselves and their points of view successfully and comfortably.

In preschool, children can venture into performances in simple ways. They can pay attention to short performances, such as listening to a story read or told aloud. In a voice that can be heard by others, they can join in on the refrain of song or give a brief performance of a song, nursery rhyme or short play that they know. Preschoolers also can respond briefly to a performance. And they can ask questions when they don't understand.

In kindergarten and first grade, students talk more about performances, making more evaluative comments about why they like or don't like what they've seen. These comments are the beginning stages of responses to literature, for which students are expected to discuss books. At this age, students also can memorize, rehearse and deliver a few lines of a poem or play with others in the classroom. They also can read aloud from their own writing, another kind of performance that is linked to writing. And they can respond with targeted comments when other students perform in this way as well.

For second and third graders, performances and responses become more sophisticated. Students can sit through longer performances — and they can absorb and learn from performances with educational, not just entertainment, value. Their own performances will be longer and more elaborate and will take place in front of the whole classroom or larger groups. For example, students may present a play or a report on the solar system with visual aids, costumes, props or sound effects.

> Language is the primary means for making social contact and creating social relationships.

Learning to Speak & Listen

Language Use and Conventions

To thrive academically and throughout their lives, children need to become skilled conversationalists, people who can use language to present themselves — and the topics they talk about.

Language, after all, is not merely a tool for people to get things done or even to get what they want ("May I *please* have another cookie?"). More important, language is the primary means for making social contact and creating social relationships. People do this in subtle and not-so-subtle — but mostly learned — ways: by greeting people, making small talk, being polite and respectful even in brief exchanges, paying compliments, listening to others with interest, and so on.

People use language to communicate who they are, to establish a personal identity. Like clothing, jewelry, hairstyle, makeup and body art, for example, the language that people choose represents them. Almost inevitably, language often reveals glimpses of people's geographic and ethnic origin, social class, and educational background. Language also may indicate membership, or the desire to belong, to various social groups. Language, then, carries a heavy social burden.

There are three main ways for children to develop into skilled, mature conversationalists — by learning the social rules of conversation, the grammatical rules of language, and enough words to keep the conversation lively and interesting. This sounds beguilingly simple, but it is actually incredibly complex work. Moreover, this work is complicated by culture, race, ethnicity, class, family background and a host of other variables. Even so, with good instruction and practice in a language-rich environment, children can master the art of conversation and, for school, accountable talk for academic purposes.

The standards lay out these elements for children to become skilled conversationalists:

- rules of interaction;
- word play and language awareness; and
- vocabulary and word choice.

Take Time to Listen and Model Good Habits

Standards in speaking and listening imply that children have someone to talk *to*. With that in mind, here are a few suggestions for teachers:

- **Stop and listen.** Make time every day to stop and sit with your students to listen. Make sure no chores or distractions come between you and your students. Make yourself available and welcoming for students to come up to you and talk, talk, talk.

- **Read and learn.** Read newspapers, magazines and books about topics that are new to you. Watch educational television shows about current events, history, science and the arts. Refresh *your* mind. Follow *your* curiosity. Challenge *yourself*. Get excited about learning!

- **Model language and literacy habits and skills.** Talk to children in the ways you are trying to help *them* learn to talk. Make sure students see *you* reading and writing for pleasure or to get things done. Model the habits and skills of language and literacy in your daily life.

"There's a word for it, I don't know, you're like older and you don't need to pay as much money."

"Senior, senior citizens."

"Senior is all the way up."

"Yeah, like over 50."

Rules of interaction

Beginning in infancy and continuing through the elementary years and beyond, children learn the rules of the game of conversation. It is crucial for teachers to understand that the conversational rules they themselves know and follow are *social* rules, which for the most part are rooted in the customs of a primarily European American society. In other cultures and societies, even within the United States, the rules of interaction are different — but no less worthy. (For more, see "Different Cultures, Different Rules," page 24.) Nevertheless, the rules stand as an accepted compact among most Americans — and children who fail to understand them suffer academic and social consequences. Therefore, children should learn and practice the most widely shared rules of interaction.

In most of U.S. society, people are expected to take turns when they talk: One person speaks, and the other listens. Interruptions are a breach of etiquette that call for an "excuse me" or an "I'm sorry." Some kinds of utterances, such as questions, demand responses.

People are expected to be polite in their interactions as well, saying "please," "thank you" and "you're welcome." In classrooms, children often are expected to raise their hands before they can talk. Even when they have to deliver news that may not be well received, children must learn to disagree without being disagreeable. For example, if two children are vying for the same metric ruler, one of them may offer a polite solution instead of an argument: "How about if I measure my rectangle first, and then you can be next, okay?"

Children also learn to address people appropriately, depending on whether they are superiors, subordinates or equals. "Miss Linda" may be appropriate for preschool teachers, for example, while "Mrs. Mooney" is expected in elementary school. Even preschoolers will adjust their language to their audience, using baby talk with infant siblings, taboo words with playmates, and, if taught, polite words such as "please" and "thank you" with parents and other adults.

Preschoolers generally understand that they are expected to take turns and be polite — but they often forget their manners in the heat of the moment. In kindergarten and first grade, children should be better adjusted to the rules of interaction. By the second and third grades, children should master the social graces of school interactions — one on one, in small groups and in whole-class settings. There are different rules in different settings; children need to participate effectively in a variety of circumstances.

Word play and language awareness

Just as kicking a ball around helps children develop soccer skills, playing around with words helps them develop language skills. The T-shirt philosophy applies to both: If you want to play, practice. If you want to play better, practice harder.

With language, the emphasis is on *play*. Children should be encouraged to play with words every day — rolling them around in their mouths, stretching them out and turning them all about — to get a keen sense of the sounds that words are made of. This sense, known as phonemic awareness, is an important skill that helps children understand letter-sound relationships. Phonemic awareness helps children crack the print-sound code, sound out words and learn to read.

Moreover, word play builds confidence, empowering children to take risks with language. Children who are comfortable being silly with sounds are more likely to take a chance at sounding out words, guess at the meanings of new words and try to spell words they can say but cannot write yet.

Preschoolers engage in word play naturally and enthusiastically. They enjoy nursery rhymes, silly verses, chants and songs. Cadences, melodies, rhythms, rhymes and alliterations are embedded in these playful forms of language — and children absorb these features of language without any formal instruction. They make up their own silly word uses as well, experimenting with word meanings in the process: "Daddy, doggie meow!"

Just by playing with words, preschoolers develop a sense of grammar as well. They learn how to string words together into sentences that make sense. They make "smart mistakes" about grammatical rules: "I *goed* to the store," while incorrect, is a smart guess based on a learned pattern of using *-ed* to form the past tense of many verbs.

In kindergarten and first grade, children extend their word play, incorporating jokes and tongue twisters into their repertoire of silliness with words and sentences: "She sells seashells by the sea shore." They begin to use words with double or multiple meanings. Their phonemic awareness is more conscious; they produce and recognize rhyming words, and they learn to sound out words. Likewise, their grammatical awareness, though still largely unconscious, is stronger as well; there are fewer mistakes in their word choices and sentence structures.

In the second and third grades, children continue to experiment with words, adding puns, riddles, made-up languages and secret codes to their language tricks. At this age, word play and sentence play are more sophisticated. Children pick up on nuances of meaning in words and on inflection or emphasis in spoken words as well. Their grammatical awareness is stronger at this age — but this may have a sad side effect. Children start conforming to more "expected" grammatical rules, shying away from using original metaphors to describe things, for example. Teachers can encourage children to notice bold language and continue taking risks with words in their own writing.

Basic Linguistics: What Should Children Learn?

Children need to know a certain number of words — and a great deal *about* these words — to participate effectively in school. There are, in fact, five kinds of information that apply to every word. This information is a complex rule system that the human brain uses — often subconsciously — to recognize, decode, sort, understand and use words. Children start learning this rule system in preschool and even earlier, but a full understanding takes years. With good instruction and practice, though, children get better and better at calling upon the rules of language automatically and simultaneously when they speak, listen, read and write.

Consider two words, the noun *cabinet* and the verb *cooperate*, to appreciate the sweeping complexity of language development.

Phonology: What does it sound like? The first impression a word makes is its sound. When the brain hears *cabinet*, it breaks down the word into sequences of sounds, or phonemes. When the brain can't remember *cabinet*, it roots around for matching sounds — and it may come up with *bassinet, castanet* and (oh, yes!) *cabinet*. With practice, the brain memorizes these sounds in the right order and recalls them to recognize and say *cabinet* accurately. When the brain hears *cooperate*, it recognizes the /ate/ at the end of the word and, knowing words such as *create* and *anticipate*, sorts *cooperate* with the verbs.

This abstract, often subconscious, thinking about the sounds of words is called phonological representation. The brain is clever about sound in other ways as well. It recognizes that *cabinet* is an authentic English word, unlike *burrito* or *blitzkrieg*, which don't fit standard English sound patterns. It will modify words to match its own dialect — even if it hears the words from somebody who speaks a different dialect. And it knows that the plural of *cabinet* ends with an /s/ sound, while the plural of *bird* ends with a /z/ sound.

Semantics: What does it mean, and where does it belong? To understand what *cabinet* means, the brain tries to connect it to the meanings of other words already in its familiar vocabulary. So *cabinet* goes with *cupboard, dresser, bookcase, armoire, sideboy* and other pieces of furniture used to contain or store things. But *cabinet* is actually slightly different in size, location and utility from these other items. So the brain tries to further nail the meaning of *cabinet* by organizing it into categories — top-level, or superordinate, categories, such as *furniture;* same-level categories, such as *dresser* and *sofa,* which are subsets of *furniture;* and specific, or subordinate, categories, such as *kitchen cabinet, bathroom cabinet* and *file cabinet*. The brain can even make up its own categories that follow these rules: *CD cabinet, rock cabinet, sticker cabinet*.

This thinking about word meanings and connections is known as semantics. Eventually, the brain can crack the meaning of *cabinet* when it is used as a metaphor, as in *the president's kitchen cabinet*.

Learning to Speak & Listen

Syntax: What kind of word is it? In the process of learning new words, the brain figures out which other words can come before, after or with them: *a* cabinet, *the* cabinet, *this* cabinet and *that* cabinet, for example, are cues that *cabinet* is a noun. *The boys cooperate* and *Estelle cooperated with Sarah* are cues that *cooperate* is a verb and that word order and endings such as *-ed* mark it as such. But *the window cooperates* and *they cooperated the homework* make no sense; the brain learns that *cooperate* needs an animate, or living, subject and a prepositional object.

This kind of understanding about word usage and context is known as syntactic knowledge.

Morphology: What is its form, and how can it change? With a deep understanding of words, the brain knows that *cooperate* has a prefix, *co-*, that means "with" or "together" and that the *-ate* on the end strongly suggests that it is a verb.

The brain also knows that *cooperate* needs changes to its ending, or morphological markers, depending on its use: he cooperate*s*, she's cooperat*ing*, they cooperat*ed*. Moreover, the brain eventually can figure out that *cooperative, cooperation, cooperatively* and *co-op* are related to *cooperate* — and, indeed, that rules known as morphological procedures can transform one word into another. These rules may be somewhat unpredictable, but with practice, the brain masters the rules.

Pragmatics: How is it used? People who have a full command of words have a kind of street-smart savvy, an ability to choose language well for the desired effect. For example, a preschool teacher may tell her students, "You need to *work together* on this project." But she may write in a progress report to parents, "Sally is learning to *cooperate* with others." This is a subtle nuance that, with these relatively common and neutral words, may not seem like a big deal.

Sometimes, though, word choice matters deeply. Some words are loaded with subtle and not-so-subtle meaning. For example, is it appropriate to use *Hispanic* or *Latino*? *Nerd* or *honor roll student*? *Comment* or *complain*? The wrong word choices can insult, disdain or ridicule other people. This ability to make the right word choices depending on the audience, situation and intent is known as pragmatic knowledge.

Clearly, mastering the phonological, semantic, syntactic, morphological and pragmatic knowledge of words takes time. A full command of these five domains of linguistics, then, cannot be expected in preschool or elementary school. Still, children who are immersed in reading, writing, speaking and listening will begin to notice and think about words. ("Is a cabinet a little cabin?" "Does the president let the people out of his cabinet on the weekend?") This conscious thinking about words is called metalinguistic awareness — and it is a crucial step toward mustering word knowledge to analyze words and meanings and to choose words carefully.

Vocabulary and word choice

Vocabulary, along with the rules of interaction and the rules of language, is the third necessary ingredient to good social and academic conversations. Vocabulary development is an ultimate goal of many speaking and listening exchanges in preschool and elementary school. Research shows a direct and positive relationship between vocabulary development and academic success. Simply put, the more words children know, and the more they know about these words, the better they do in school — and the faster they learn more new words. (For more, see "Basic Linguistics: What Should Children Learn?" pages 32–33.)

The size of children's vocabularies varies enormously, depending on the quantity and quality of speaking and listening at home and elsewhere. Talking a lot, and talking about interesting topics that go beyond the here and now, introduces children to words and meanings they aren't likely to encounter frequently in any other way.

There is no particular list or set of words that children should know; the idea is that they should add at least 5 to 10 new words to their working vocabularies every day. Children need to "own" the words; they need to understand and use them in everyday talk. The words need to resonate with meaning gained through personal experiences or encounters. For some words, once or twice is enough. For more complex words, it may take dozens of encounters in a meaningful context, which is why vocabulary drills are the least effective way for preschoolers and K–3 students to learn new words.

Beginning in preschool, children should be exposed to new words — and the ideas and concepts that give them meaning — every day. By hearing books read aloud to them and by talking about interesting topics, children learn new words, including nouns, verbs, adjectives and adverbs. They begin to make word choices to capture their meaning when they talk. They learn how words "fit" with their understanding of the world. For example, a *wolf* is an *animal*, a *mammal* and a *canine* that is related to a *dog*. (For more, see "Ordering the World with Superordinates and Subordinates," page 27.)

In kindergarten and first grade, children think about and use words more deliberately. They build classroom "word maps" that categorize word relationships. They define words they know and recognize multiple meanings of words. They study word families and clusters of words that show different perspectives. They choose words that fit their audience. Most important, they acquire words at a rapid clip; their vocabulary likely will double from the preschool years.

In the second and third grades, children continue cataloging and grouping words, but now the words are more sophisticated. They learn specialized vocabulary about school subjects, such as ancient Egypt and Rome in history, the parts of a plant in science, and addition and subtraction in math. They learn more about word parts and word meanings, such as prefixes, suffixes, synonyms and antonyms. Children continue learning new words at a phenomenal rate, often now by reading on their own and still by hearing books read aloud to them. Their vocabularies may double yet again from the kindergarten and first-grade years to the second- and third-grade years.

About the New Standards Speaking & Listening Standards

The New Standards speaking and listening standards specify the knowledge and skills children should acquire and demonstrate as they progress along the continuum of oral language development, from preschool through third grade.

Students who meet these standards should be on target to meet high oral language and literacy standards in states and local school districts around the country. Educators, child care providers and parents will find these standards a useful companion to their state and local standards. This guide provides examples of real student performances analyzed against the standards and the answers to the question of how good is good enough.

How These Standards Are Organized

These standards are organized by grade span, with sections for preschool, kindergarten and first grade, and second and third grades. Each section begins with a profile of students at that grade span, describing their readiness to learn and activities that will support their progress in speaking and listening.

These profiles are not intended to suggest that all children and all programs are — or should be — alike. Rather, they evoke images of real children in real classrooms learning in rich literacy programs: the ultimate purpose of the standards. The profiles serve as a reminder that, despite the intentionally stark, precise and crisp language of the speaking and listening standards themselves, teaching children to speak and listen is complex work. There are as many nuances to this learning process as there are unique human beings.

Three standards follow the profiles.

Three Sensible Standards

The essential components of learning to speak and listen, like any complex process, can be segmented in many ways. For ease of use, these standards are organized under three broad headings:

1. Habits
2. Kinds of Talk and Resulting Genres
3. Language Use and Conventions

The standards in this book parallel the standards in *Reading & Writing grade by grade*, but speaking and listening are inextricably bound — speakers must have listeners, listeners must be attending to speakers. By their very nature, the performances that demonstrate speaking and listening incorporate both kinds of skills. Therefore, the standards for speaking and listening are presented together. By contrast, reading and writing are related but distinct skills that require very different performances to demonstrate mastery, so the standards for reading and writing are presented separately.

Students meet a standard when their overall performance satisfies the expectations often enough and well enough to indicate mastery. Generally, assessing whether students meet a standard requires evaluating a number of performances rather than an isolated test performance.

Companion CD-ROMs

The New Standards speaking and listening standards are unique and powerful for two reasons. First, they are clear and precise expectations, not fuzzy jargon. Second, student performances accompany standards that define the speaking and listening skills and that exemplify the expectations and the results.

Moreover, the commentary on the student performances explains the qualities of performances that meet the standards and answers the burning question, "How good is good enough?" The student performances, collected from a diverse range of students in a wide variety of settings, show the level of performance expected — and reachable — in these standards.

Video performances also are included on the CD-ROMs that accompany this book. Each CD-ROM shows the performances of children in preschool through third grade, by standard. This format enables teachers to see the progression along the continuum of oral language development. It is important for teachers to understand not only what is expected of the children in their care now, but also what will be expected in the future. With this understanding, presented in powerful video performances of real children in real classrooms, teachers can help their own children develop higher-level oral language skills.

A Healthy Tension Between Theory and Practice

A major challenge in drafting standards is translating abstract theories of learning into concrete language for practice. In these standards, the language is specific enough to be useful, yet general enough to accommodate variability in preschool through third-grade students and literacy programs. At the same time, these standards invite active intellectual engagement from educators who use them in classroom practice.

These standards spell out what students are expected to do, cognitively and behaviorally, rather than what curriculum and instruction should look like. There are, in fact, many effective ideas for organizing strong oral language and literacy programs. All of them offer children supportive, content-rich environments that get children speaking and listening and, in the kindergarten to third-grade years, reading and writing — a lot. To understand what we know about oral language development, turn to **Learning to Speak and Listen,** page 7. This section lays out the assumptions about speaking and listening that are incorporated in the standards.

About the New Standards Speaking & Listening Standards — 37 —

Design Features

◆ Standard name

◆ A site map that shows where you are, where you've been and what comes next. Page numbers refer you to the first page of each standard and subtopic.

◆ Video snapshot from one of the CD-ROMs of students' speaking and listening performances that meet the standard and demonstrate "how good is good enough."

◆ Insightful commentary that explains the student performances.

About the Student Performances

The speaking and listening performances in this book come almost entirely from ordinary preschools and public school classrooms, many of them urban — and not from "gifted and talented" programs. The performances were gathered from schools recognized for their good oral language development programs. Even so, the performances come not from students who are superstars or unusually talented, but from typical, normal children who work hard in good programs.

As a result, the levels of performance represent reasonable, attainable expectations where student effort and the opportunity to learn are in place.

New Standards

Research Perspectives

"What were your first words? Although you probably do not recall uttering those words, your parents or older siblings almost certainly recollect your having spoken them. First words are so important that, in most cultures, they are viewed as a personal landmark, worthy or recording in a baby book or a family Bible. . . . [F]rom the moment of birth, humans seem to be programmed to communicate."

From Christie, J., Enz, B. and Vukelich, C. (1997). *Teaching Language and Literacy, Preschool Through the Elementary Grades.* Addison-Wesley Educational Publishers Inc., 19.

Preschool

Preschool

The language of play has
a strong and direct connection
to reading and writing.
Talking a lot — and
engaging in high-quality,
vocabulary-rich conversations
— builds a solid foundation
for reading and writing.

Preschool: Speaking & Listening

Exploring and Playing with Language

Most preschoolers come to school or child care centers at a turning point in their lives. The intense dependence of the zero-to-three years is ending — and a new age of exploration and understanding is beginning.

At three and four years old, preschoolers have a growing sense of themselves as individuals. They've adjusted to the astonishing awareness, which dawns at about age two, that they are separate from their caregivers. Developmentally, this can be a very peaceful time. Preschoolers are secure in their ability to dress and feed themselves — and they're fairly comfortable with toilet routines. Now, they are gaining confidence, reaching out to other people and making friendships with other children. The preschool years, in fact, are all about stepping out into the world beyond their own families — and figuring out how to get along with people who don't know them as well as their families do. Children's growing facility with language is a critical factor in these new interactions with others.

For preschoolers, all of this exploring and understanding, reaching out and making friends, and stepping out and getting along is encompassed in a main activity: play. Life is play, in the minds of preschoolers. Playing together rather than in the side-by-side, parallel style of toddlers' play, preschoolers explore, organize and make sense of the world. Make no mistake, though: The silliness of dressing up, playing house, acting out stories, pretending and playing games amounts to much of the significant — and crucial — learning that occurs while children play. *And much of the learning comes from the words that bubble up in the giggling and gamboling of play.*

The language of play, in fact, has a strong and direct connection to reading and writing. Talking a lot — and engaging in vocabulary-rich conversations with caring adults — builds a solid foundation for reading and writing. Teachers and caregivers, then, should view play as time filled with teachable moments and opportunities to develop speaking and listening skills. By talking purposefully and focusing on topics of direct interest and connection to children and their lives, teachers can increase children's language proficiency.

Speaking and Listening: What to Expect

Preschool is the time when children learn to "use their words" to get what they want. Words give them the option of communicating their wants, needs and feelings in a more specific, controlled manner than crying, hitting, biting or snatching another child's toy. Still, preschoolers resort to these physical expressions when the words don't come to them — or when others ignore their words.

Typically, three-year-olds are just trying to figure out how to express themselves and understand their place in the world. Four-year-olds are better at it — they can say what they want, when and why. Just a year's practice makes them more skilled at talking things through for the sake of friendships and social relationships. That said, *all* preschoolers still need plenty of language support from caring, capable adults.

When most three-year-olds talk, teachers can understand what they say. Some words come out a bit garbled, especially long or difficult words such as *Thanksgiving*, which may come out "Sanksgiving." Many three-year-olds stutter or stammer, which is normal at this age and not a cause for concern. The words that three-year-olds know depend a lot on the individual child. Children talk about topics that interest them and events of the here and now, or the very recent past. They make "smart mistakes" when they talk, as in "I hi-ed the big boy" for "I said hello to the big boy." This is actually an accomplishment; they are learning that language has rules, even if they don't have the rules down pat yet.

Preschool: Speaking & Listening

Three-year-olds also can connect two events together as cause and effect. Asked, "Why was he crying?" they will say, "He fell down." They can tell a simple, two-event story, as in, "Da puppy taste my knee, and he chase me."

Three-year-olds are "geniuses in terms of metaphor," according to one early childhood language specialist. They dazzle by putting words together as creatively as poets do. For example, a three-year-old who sees a jet's white plume says, "There's a scar in the sky." When they don't have the words to describe something, they cobble together the ones they know — without anyone teaching them how. Three-year-olds play with language — with sounds, words and sentences — just like they make play out of everything.

Three-year-olds also begin to try out reading and writing. Some three-year-olds can recognize the shape of a stop sign and "read" *stop,* for example. Some can page through a book and start "reading" a familiar story, especially a repeated refrain. Some very advanced three-year-olds actually know how to read. In writing, three-year-olds may know some letters. Their "writing" may mix letters and pictures, with a result that looks like hieroglyphics.

Four-year-olds speak in longer sentences, with four or five words to a sentence. When they tell stories, they can put together more than two events. But these longer stories may end up sounding very mysterious; children sometimes omit things and leave people wondering exactly what happened. This is normal, though, and shows that children are taking risks with language to say more.

Sometimes, four-year-olds experiment with language through name-calling, lying, bathroom talk, swearing and other inappropriate expressions. This appalls parents, of course, who want their children to be polite and honest. In reality, this kind of talk signals that preschoolers are beginning to understand the power of language. Both parents and teachers can encourage this interest in words and their effect on others while helping children find more appropriate ways to communicate.

Four-year-olds continue to play with language, making real or nonsense rhymes, such as "ollie, lollie, lollie." They tell silly jokes and laugh at them uproariously, seemingly all out of proportion to the actual humor of the punch line. They continue to make "smart mistakes" about the rules of language, as in, "I have much morer than you" or "Here's hers and mine's."

Four-year-olds, in general, are easier to understand when they talk than three-year-olds are. Many normal children have difficulty pronouncing some words until they are seven or eight years old. There's no reason to worry about them. However, a four-year-old whose pronunciation of words is not comprehensible at all should be a cause for concern. This child may have a hearing loss or other issues that may require attention.

> Three-year-olds are "geniuses in terms of metaphor." They dazzle by putting words together as creatively as poets do.

Developing Oral Language

Preschoolers tend to talk about the here and now of the games they are playing, the food they are eating, the books they are reading — the activities of the moment, in other words, or memorable events in the recent past. They love to dress up and act out the lives of firefighters, astronauts, princesses, doctors, or mom and dad. The rituals of play are important to them; they spend lots of time setting up and planning as part of their playing. Language is becoming a tool for explaining their world, getting things done, sharing stories and talking about books.

Preschool caregivers and teachers, then, should use their words carefully, with the constant awareness that they have a crucial responsibility to help develop oral language. Adults should be ever welcoming and available to talk to children. They should prepare their classrooms or facilities before children arrive and put aside busy work and conversations with other adults until children leave. Interacting with children is the business of the day — all day, every day.

Teachers and caregivers should watch for opportunities to develop preschoolers' talking skills. When squabbles or frustrations arise, adults can help by literally talking children through the situation: "Why don't you tell Nicole how you feel about her playing with your doll?" "I can see that you're both enjoying that spaceship. Juan and Emil, how can each of you have a turn at the control panel?"

Adults should be watchful, positioning themselves in the room so that they can see and hear every child. If there are two or more adults, each should watch from a different spot. If they're spread out, they can be available to all of the children in the room, watching and interacting with the whole group and with smaller groups of children. When tempers rise or words escalate, a teacher should be there to defuse the situation with kind, guiding words. And while an adult's first impulse may be to step in and solve a problem quickly, children will learn more about language and about life if the adult talks through the situation: "I see you're puzzled by how to balance those two blocks on your tower. What else can you try?"

Teachers can help preschoolers by simply giving them the words to express their feelings. Children often know simple words such as *mad, sad* and *happy*. But they can be *frustrated, disappointed, nervous, surprised, excited* and *thrilled* as well — a whole range of emotions that they may not have the words to express. By using these more specific words, teachers

> Adults should prepare their classrooms or facilities before children arrive and put aside busy work and conversations with other adults until children leave. Interacting with children is the business of the day — all day, every day.

New Standards

Preschool: Speaking & Listening

act as translators of students' emotions — and they help children learn to communicate more precisely. Teachers also can encourage children to listen to one another and respect other children's feelings.

Teachers should take advantage of preschoolers' natural tendency to play with sounds and words. Silly nursery rhymes, chants, word games and songs should find a place in everyday activities and conversations.

Teachers can show children that their words are important by writing them down. When children draw, teachers can collaborate with them to write labels or titles on the pictures, using the children's words. Children can tell stories or dictate letters, notes or lists for teachers to write down, post on the walls, or send home to parents or caregivers. Children should be encouraged to "write" down their own ideas to help them make the connection between oral and written language. Teachers can write notes or reminders for themselves as well, showing children that writing is a way to communicate and get things done.

Teachers also can help preschoolers pay attention to the details of the world around them. They can point out colors, shapes, objects and patterns in everyday life. They can look more closely at the "ordinary" — much of which may be new and fresh to children. A walk around the block, for example, can be an opportunity to learn when teachers try to expand conversations with open-ended questions and remarks: "What do you see?" "What do you smell?" "What do you hear?" "How would you describe the maple tree today? Let's look closely."

Teachers should use real words, not baby talk, to label and describe things. It's just as easy for preschoolers to learn *wound* or *bruise* as it is to learn *boo-boo*. A new word is a new word. Preschoolers can and will use complex, grownup words — such as *pyramid, abacus, algae, tarantula, CD-ROM drive, photograph* and *character* — if they hear adults around them using these words.

Indeed, research shows that children who hear these kinds of accurate words in extended talk all day long, starting when they are babies, are better prepared. The gap between the language abilities of young children who have had this rich early language stimulation and those who have not had it is enormous. The implication is clear: All adults, parents, teachers and other caregivers must create opportunities to engage young children in meaningful talk throughout each day.

Standard 1: Habits
Introduction

To sharpen their speaking and listening skills, children must develop certain habits that become a natural part of their social and academic experience. We have identified four habits that can be encouraged as early as preschool: talking a lot, talking to one's self, conversing at length on a topic and discussing books. Children need daily interactions with peers and adults to engage in quality talk and attentive listening and to give and receive useful feedback. These interactions should be in whole-class, small-group and one-on-one settings. Such purposeful talk supports the development of emergent reading and writing skills.

Learning to initiate and sustain lengthier conversations is important at this age. It is important to remember, however, that much of preschool conversation is limited to the "here and now" or to relatively recent events. Personal and cultural variations and home experiences affect children's behavior. Caregivers will notice individual differences in styles of talk and interaction — some children are boisterous and verbose, others like to

Preschool Standards

Standard 1: *Habits*
- Talking a Lot — pg. 48
- Talking to One's Self — pg. 58
- Conversing at Length on a Topic — pg. 60
- Discussing Books — pg. 64

Standard 2: *Kinds of Talk and Resulting Genres*
- Narrative — pg. 74
- Explaining and Seeking Information — pg. 82
- Getting Things Done — pg. 90
- Producing and Responding to Performances — pg. 94

Standard 3: *Language Use and Conventions*
- Rules of Interaction — pg. 100
- Word Play, Phonological Awareness and Language Awareness — pg. 104
- Vocabulary and Word Choice — pg. 112

> Quality preschool programs are rich in literacy. Through read-alouds, drawing pictures to tell stories, captions and print, children see the connection between spoken language and printed words.

joke, and still others may be shy and reticent. Cultural differences also come into play — some children consider brevity important, while others may expect to hold the floor at length. Adults can encourage talk by maintaining a stationary position and focusing their attention on the child. Both "air time" and "ear time" are important — air time refers to the daily opportunities children must have to talk and express themselves; ear time includes the undivided attention of an audience and thoughtful feedback.

Preschoolers who possess the newfound ability to put their own thoughts into words often talk to themselves. This "private speech" is a critical step in socialization and is one of the habits we value. Research shows that during free-play settings, about 40 percent of children's talk is not directed to socializing with other children but to guiding their own behavior or thinking. This "talking to one's self," or thinking aloud, helps to guide cognitive processes and is used extensively as children begin to read.

Quality preschool programs are rich in literacy. Through read-alouds, drawing pictures to tell stories, captions and print, children see the connection between spoken language and printed words. Daily read-alouds should be followed by "book talk" whenever possible. These early opportunities prepare children for more in-depth discussions as they begin to read.

Talking a Lot

Activities involving high-quality, purposeful talk and attentive feedback are critical for the development of language skills. Such talk can occur simultaneously with learning activities, playtime and mealtime. Talking a lot every day provides practice with various genres of talk for specific purposes. But children should experiment and *play* with language daily.

Preschool Standards

Standard 1: *Habits*
- Talking a Lot   pg. 48
- Talking to One's Self   pg. 58
- Conversing at Length on a Topic   pg. 60
- Discussing Books   pg. 64

Standard 2: *Kinds of Talk and Resulting Genres*
- Narrative   pg. 74
- Explaining and Seeking Information   pg. 82
- Getting Things Done   pg. 90
- Producing and Responding to Performances   pg. 94

Standard 3: *Language Use and Conventions*
- Rules of Interaction   pg. 100
- Word Play, Phonological Awareness and Language Awareness   pg. 104
- Vocabulary and Word Choice   pg. 112

Specifically, we expect preschool children to:
- talk daily for various purposes;
- engage in play using talk to enact or extend a story line (for example, taking on roles, using different voices, solving problems);
- playfully manipulate language (including nonsense words, rhymes, silly songs, repetitious phrases);
- express ideas, feelings and needs;
- listen and respond to direct questions;
- ask questions;
- talk and listen in small groups (during playtime or mealtime or more formally at workshop areas or craft tables); and
- share and talk daily about their own experiences, products or writing (for example, explaining their pictures or "reading" their writing attempts).

Personal and Cultural Differences

Informal situations may be most inviting for children who are eager to share their thoughts and experiences. Many shy children, however, prefer the reassurance of structured situations and clear expectations for talk. Cultural differences also are important to consider. For example, research shows that some African American children tell narratives that are organized to present a series of events, each of which may seem minor but that together make the point of the story, rather than focusing (as European American children's stories are more likely to) on the beginning, middle and end of a single event. For more information and examples of cultural differences, especially in narrative, see page 231.

Preschool: Standard 1/Commentary on Student Performances

Alex Expresses a Need

Standard 1: Habits
Talking a Lot

◆ Express ideas, feelings and needs

Small, informal groups provide opportunities for children to meet the standard for talking a lot. In this conversation, Alex expresses his feelings, letting his teacher, Kathy, know what he needs. His twin brother has had numerous opportunities to be with their friend Noah: "Every time when we have small groups, Max goes with Noah, and I don't." He continues, expressing his need, "I want to get a chance to go with Noah."

Kathy reinforces how important it is for Alex to express his feelings when she says, "You do? I'm glad to know that. It's good to tell me those things."

The images and commentary in this section refer to performances available on the accompanying CD-ROMs.

Playful Manipulation of Language

Common forms of language manipulation include rhyming songs; chants; and the silly, repetitious and often alliterative phrases that children tend to repeat. Children are often natural poets. A three-year-old may refer to a jet's trail as "a scar in the sky." Children also will make up words, combining two or more words to create a silly label, "picklepie," "feather head" or "sillyface." Some preschoolers utter profanities or hurtful words that they have learned, often without fully understanding their meaning. Parents may be shocked to be called a "chicken" or "poopie-head," forgetting that they also are called "sweety-pie" or "babycakes." Children might even call their parents by first names — using a number of different words for the same thing shows that a child is tuning in to language. Adults can help children produce gentler names for bantering, while still encouraging fun manipulation of language.

Preschool Standards

Standard 1: *Habits*

- Talking a Lot — pg. 48
- Talking to One's Self — pg. 58
- Conversing at Length on a Topic — pg. 60
- Discussing Books — pg. 64

Standard 2: *Kinds of Talk and Resulting Genres*

- Narrative — pg. 74
- Explaining and Seeking Information — pg. 82
- Getting Things Done — pg. 90
- Producing and Responding to Performances — pg. 94

Standard 3: *Language Use and Conventions*

- Rules of Interaction — pg. 100
- Word Play, Phonological Awareness and Language Awareness — pg. 104
- Vocabulary and Word Choice — pg. 112

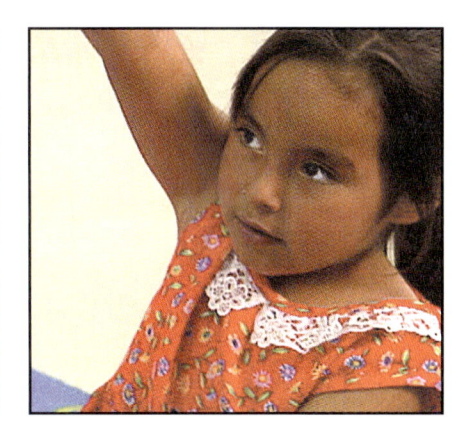

Preschool: Standard 1/Commentary on Student Performances

April's Story

Standard 1: Habits
Talking a Lot

- Talk daily for various purposes
- Listen and respond to direct questions
- Ask questions
- Talk and listen in small groups
- Share and talk daily about their own experiences, products or writing

As a part of this preschool's daily program, one or two children are invited to share the stories they are working on in an informal group setting. Note that the teacher reminds the children that the Author's Chair will come next. This preschool class has implemented a full Writers Workshop, complete with mini-lessons, independent writing time, response groups and an Author's Chair in which one student takes the floor to present a published "book." Even though these children are prereaders and prewriters, they are quite comfortable with the rituals and routines of the workshop setting as they proudly work on their scribblelike writing and phonetic spellings, sometimes even producing two- to three-line stories. They already have internalized the belief that they are readers and writers.

Talking, and talking often, especially about what they have written or read, is critical for students. Having many preschool opportunities to converse provides an important foundation as students entering the lower grades work toward the reading and writing standards.

The teacher says, "Let's listen to April tell her story, and let's be a good listener so we can ask her questions."

Then April begins, "Once upon a time, um, I was at the park. Then, then my cat went to the swings that. . . . I was on the swings with other kids. And then the sun comed up, then the stars and the moons."

The use of "once upon a time" shows that April already is appropriating language that she has heard before by adopting the familiar phrase in her own work. When children are invited to ask questions, one asks, "Where are the kids?"

Notice that the teacher reframes this question in the context of setting, asking April, "Where is your story? Where does it take place? Where are you?"

April answers, "The park."

Another child asks, "Where is the cat?"

April holds up her story, which is part words and part pictures, and points out the cat.

Again, note that the teacher comments in terms of story and characters: "The story is about her cat, isn't it?"

This group is given opportunities to talk daily. They listen attentively, ask questions and signal comprehension by staying on the topic. April is comfortable writing and talking about a personal experience.

New Standards

Informal Snack Table Conversation

Standard 1: Habits
Talking a Lot

- Respond to direct questions
- Talk and listen in small groups
- Share and talk daily about their own experiences, products or writing

Standard 2: Kinds of Talk and Resulting Genres
Narrative

- Give a simple narrative (with adult prompting if necessary), recounting two or more events that are not necessarily in chronological order

Standard 3: Language Use and Conventions
Vocabulary and Word Choice

- Show a general interest in words and word meanings

Snack time is a daily opportunity for conversation in most preschool classrooms. Note that these preschoolers talk over one another and have not yet mastered the art of polite conversation, with each person taking a turn speaking. In this sequence, Kathy, the teacher, prompts informal conversation by saying, "Tell me what you did at T-ball practice. Tell everybody!"

In a typical four-year-old response, everyone speaks at once. When you listen closely, you hear these preschoolers talking for various purposes, including clarifying their own words, sharing experiences, telling narratives, talking about an unshared experience and providing explanations.

Alex can be heard responding to Kathy's question when he says, "We were throwing. We were throwing."

Kathy, talking to Alex's twin brother, Max, tries to restate what she thought she heard him say. "You threw the ball?" she asks.

Max clarifies his words and corrects her, saying, "No, I caught the ball."

Another boy named Alex gains the floor and begins a narrative by directly soliciting the listeners' attention. "You know what?" he says. He orients his listeners to his story by saying, "It was too rainy. We were, we were playing, and then it started to rain hard." He continues, "And then we left and then went out, the three of us, um, the three of us went out to eat."

Evie begins her story before Alex finishes his. She picks up the topic of rain with a personal narrative about getting her pants wet. She says, "And, I, um . . . Alex, do you know what? I slided down the slide. And do you know what? It was really fast. And I got my pants wet. And I had to take them off at home."

Both of these narratives include a story told in chronological sequence, more than one event and a resolution.

The teacher asks Evie, "Where were you that you went down the slide?"

Evie responds to this direct question, saying, "At Blue Park."

This generates a lot of excitement, and several children report playing at the "blue slide park."

When Blue Park first was mentioned, Alex identified it as his park. He repeats, "That's my park, you know."

The teacher asks, "Why is it your park, Alex?"

He explains his thinking and provides a definition by saying, "Because it's close to my house. Whichever park is close to your house is your park."

Alex, the twin, accepts the other Alex's definition and says, "I have my park at my house."

The teacher asks, "What is your park like, Alex?"

Alex uses his hands to indicate the shape of the slide as he says, "It has a slide that turns this way, and you come down this way."

Noah uses a simile to describe his park when he says, "I have a park. I have a park. It's Mellon Park. It's Mellon Park, and there's a wiggly slide, like a snake."

Kathy offers another direct invitation to speak, saying, "Tell us about your park, Evie."

Evie responds with a narrative, using descriptive words and spiral gestures. She says, "It has a slide that turns round and round like this and round and round. And do you know what? One time, I sat down, and someone was holding onto my legs. And do you know what? We fell and down the slide, and it was really fun. And I got socked on my bum. That's what happened."

In this segment, we have evidence that these preschoolers can talk for various purposes; talk and listen in this informal, small-group setting; and talk about their various past experiences at parks. We also see them respond to direct questions, ask questions of each other and tell narratives that meet the standard for preschool.

Water Talk

Standard 1: Habits
Talking a Lot

- Talk daily for various purposes
- Express ideas, feelings and needs
- Respond to direct questions

Claire, the teacher, has gathered the whole class together so that they can help her plan their study of water. She reminds the children of their recent classroom experiences with water. Then she asks, "What do you know about water?"

Individual children share what they know. This collection of facts about water is written on large newsprint and categorized for later use.

The children know the group-time rules of interaction. They raise their hands and wait to be called on. In response to the question, "What do you know about water?" Hector offers the first idea, "You could swim in a swimming pool."

Claire repeats Hector's contribution, "You could swim in a swimming pool." She calls the children's attention to how they will keep a record of their ideas, saying, "Okay. Ms. Derrick is going to write your ideas down so that we remember them and we can come back to it."

Ashley adds, "You could swim with sharks."

After repeating Ashley's suggestion, Claire probes further by asking, ". . . would anybody here like to swim with sharks?"

Hector expresses his feelings and rationale about that idea. He responds, "Not me. Because they bite people."

Ariel adds a category, stating, "You could drink water."

Claire reinforces Ariel's response by repeating it and adding, ". . . we drink water every day."

Jacob suggests another use for water, saying, "You need water for the hoses." Then he answers Claire's direct question, ". . . what do you use water coming out of the hose for, Jacob?" with an activity that he probably has experienced. He replies, "To clean the driveway."

Jesse adds another dimension to the use of water from hoses, "to clean the fire out."

Again in response to the direct question, ". . . did you use water today?" Christopher says that water can be used "in the bathtub."

Claire also includes the child who does not speak English. The child's contribution to the discussion is translated by an aide: "She helps her mom wash dishes."

Claire acknowledges the addition and tells the children, "So we'll put that in the washing category."

Phillip, the eighth child to contribute, is then called upon: "Okay, Phillip has an idea."

He says, "We need water for flowers."

Claire acknowledges his comment by saying, "Yes, that's a new idea. We need water for flowers. Does anybody have another idea of, for what we need water for?"

Hector says, "Dogs could go in the water." In response to Claire's question, "Do dogs need water for other things?" he says that dogs need water "to take a bath" and "to swim."

Claire repeats Hector's ideas and asks, "Any other ideas why a dog might need water?"

Phillip expresses his need to talk and says, "Let me. I was thinking about it, too."

Ariel says, "To drink."

Claire recognizes that more than one person wanted to talk: "I heard it. I heard it, let, from someone I don't think had a chance. Okay, Ariel, what do dogs need water for?"

"To drink," responds Ariel.

The conversation begins to wind down when Claire repeats, "To drink. Do all animals need water?"

The children respond in unison, "Yes."

"All animals," says Claire. "Do we need water?"

Again in unison the children respond, "Yes."

Claire summarizes the discussion by saying, "Yes. I wanted to talk about what some of the children said, which was very important. Plants need water. People need water. Firefighters need water. Animals need water."

At her invitation, "Let's go to our water song," the group begins to sing the water song to the tune of "Bingo."

Friends Play with Words

Standard 1: Habits
Talking a Lot

◆ Playfully manipulate language

Kate, Danielle, Ashley and Zora are in a preschool class that is studying water. After the teacher tells a story about the beach, the girls are inspired to draw rainbow fish. When one of their teachers, Ms. Derrick, gets the conversation started, the girls begin to playfully manipulate language, first with sounds and then with a repetitious sentence using their own and their friends' names.

The teacher explains to Jesse, off camera in an adjacent dramatic play area, that "they're making rainbow fish."

Kate asks, "Are you going to get rainbow fish at the sea?"

Jesse does not answer.

The teacher calls her attention to the question, saying, "Jesse, Kate asked you a question."

Kate then repeats her question, "Are you going to get rainbow fish at the sea?"

Jesse's answer is not audible.

"Uh-oh. They're going to catch our fish," continues Kate.

Zora begins the first word play, "Yep. Ya-oh."

"Ya-oh? What does ya-oh mean?" asks Kate, recognizing that she has not heard this word before.

Danielle comments about her picture, "I like blue 'cause my brother's favorite color is blue."

Kate then announces, "I like pink and yellow. That's why I'm making a rainbow fish."

This statement touches off a series of playful "I likes" among the girls.

Zora says, "I like my friend Kate. I like my friend Kate. I like my friend."

Danielle chimes in, "I like my friend Zora."

Zora replies, "I like my friend Danielle."

Ashley joins the chorus, "I like my friend Zora."

Danielle chants, "I like my friend Kate. I like my friend Kate."

Ashley changes the refrain by naming herself, "I like my friend Ashley."

There is a brief moment of laughter. Zora's comment is inaudible.

Kate puts herself back into the chant, saying, "I like my friend Kate."

And so the word play continues, with all four children using their own names.

Ashley says, "I like my friend Ashley."

Zora says, "I like my friend Zora."

And Danielle says, "I like my friend Danielle."

Research Perspectives

"Why do children talk? Beyond being biologically designed to do so, children talk to share thoughts and feelings, to ask for things they need, to question new ideas, and just to enjoy speaking. There are as many reasons that children talk as there are children. It is for functional and social reasons that we all learned language."

From Christie, J., Enz, B. and Vukelich, C. (1997). *Teaching Language and Literacy, Preschool through the Elementary Grades.* Addison-Wesley Educational Publishers Inc., 22–23.

Talking to One's Self

Preschoolers begin to use language to monitor their social behavior, verbalize goals, talk themselves through a task, remember steps in a newly learned skill or emphasize their intentions. This behavior is a precursor to the valuable self-monitoring skills used later in reading and should be encouraged. Specifically, we expect preschool children to:

- begin to make spontaneous and audible corrections to their own behavior, actions or language (for example, "Hoppy, I mean happy!" or "I said, 'two,' I meant, 'three!' "); and

- talk to themselves out loud to make plans, guide behavior and actions, or monitor thinking.

Preschool Standards

Standard 1: *Habits*
- Talking a Lot — pg. 48
- Talking to One's Self — pg. 58
- Conversing at Length on a Topic — pg. 60
- Discussing Books — pg. 64

Standard 2: *Kinds of Talk and Resulting Genres*
- Narrative — pg. 74
- Explaining and Seeking Information — pg. 82
- Getting Things Done — pg. 90
- Producing and Responding to Performances — pg. 94

Standard 3: *Language Use and Conventions*
- Rules of Interaction — pg. 100
- Word Play, Phonological Awareness and Language Awareness — pg. 104
- Vocabulary and Word Choice — pg. 112

How Children Exhibit Talking to One's Self

Some talking aloud involves simple, subvocal corrections of speech or action. Other instances allow children to verbalize their intent or the steps in a process. For example, a child playing blocks might say to no one in particular, "I'm going to build a bridge now. Over the train!" Still other examples of talking to one's self are attempts to guide behavior. One four-year-old girl was glaring across the room at her younger sister, who was playing with a doll. The four-year-old said to herself, "No, I won't take the doll away from her. I don't want time out." The girl was learning to use language to control her own impulses, a critical aspect of socialization.
— adapted from McCabe, 1992

Stephen Spells *Volcanoes*

Standard 1: Habits
Talking to One's Self

◆ Talk to themselves out loud to make plans and guide behavior

Kathy, the teacher, has asked a small group of children to theorize about why dinosaurs are extinct. Earlier, Stephen offered this definition of extinct: "It means they died." In response to Kathy's query, Stephen has theorized that volcanoes caused dinosaurs to die. "It died from the volcano," he says.

She asks, "Who? Which died from the volcano?"

"What?" he asks.

"What died from the volcano?" she asks.

"My dinosaur," Stephen responds.

Kathy notes that Stephen is giving more details about his theory, saying, "Ohhh, because before you just said they started dying, now you're saying they died because of the volcano."

Stephen has drawn a picture to illustrate his theory. As he writes, he talks to himself, subvocalizing the letters he thinks spell the word *volcanoes*, "*v-o-l—c-a-n-o—s.*" Stephen meets the standard for talking to one's self as he guides his writing behavior by talking out loud to himself. Stephen surpasses the standard for word play for preschool because his speech-to-print transition includes a high-level ability to sound out and spell the word *volcanoes*. He leaves out the letter *e*, which is silent. Stephen demonstrates that he understands the meaning of the plural form of the word when he says, "There was a bunch of dinosaurs."

Conversing at Length on a Topic

Daily conversations with others are critical if children are going to develop their language skills. Preschoolers begin to advance from simple yes or no answers to lengthier exchanges on a single, familiar topic or experience. Specifically, we expect preschool children to:

◆ initiate and sustain a conversation with comments or questions through at least four exchanges;

◆ recognize the topic of the conversation and make topic-relevant responses (for example, "I know Ernie. Yeah, on *Sesame Street*, but I like Bert better.");

◆ recognize invitations to converse versus questions intended to elicit a brief response; and

◆ listen to others and avoid "talking-over."

Preschool Standards

Standard 1: *Habits*
- ◆ Talking a Lot — pg. 48
- ◆ Talking to One's Self — pg. 58
- ◆ Conversing at Length on a Topic — pg. 60
- ◆ Discussing Books — pg. 64

Standard 2: *Kinds of Talk and Resulting Genres*
- ◆ Narrative — pg. 74
- ◆ Explaining and Seeking Information — pg. 82
- ◆ Getting Things Done — pg. 90
- ◆ Producing and Responding to Performances — pg. 94

Standard 3: *Language Use and Conventions*
- ◆ Rules of Interaction — pg. 100
- ◆ Word Play, Phonological Awareness and Language Awareness — pg. 104
- ◆ Vocabulary and Word Choice — pg. 112

Preschool: Standard 1/Commentary on Student Performances

Evie Lifts Dirt Clods

Standard 1: Habits
Conversing at Length on a Topic

- Initiate and sustain a conversation with comments or questions through at least four exchanges

- Recognize the topic of the conversation and make topic-relevant responses

- Recognize invitations to converse versus questions intended to elicit a brief response

Evie meets the standard for sustaining a conversation as she answers questions posed by Jerri, an adult visitor, about things that are too heavy to lift.

"Like big clods of dirt, so big," Evie begins, making stretching motions with her hands. She solicits Jerri's attention, saying, "And do you know what?" and then she adds a topic-relevant detail to the conversation: "One time I picked it up with a shovel."

During the next three exchanges, Evie stays on topic as she answers the question, "Oh, did that [the shovel] make it easier?"

"But I was . . . I picked up heavy rocks," Evie says.

"Heavy rocks," Jerri repeats.

"With clods of dirt," Evie adds.

"Okay," Jerri says. "Using the shovel? Oh, that's a pretty good idea."

Evie concludes, "And it was hard."

"It was hard work. Yeah," Jerri adds.

Again, Evie recognizes Jerri's invitation to continue the conversation when she responds to the question, "Why were you moving the rocks? Tell me about that."

Evie explains, "Because we were making our yard bigger. That's what we had to do."

Jerri responds, "Oh, so you had to move the rocks out of the way?"

Evie interrupts Jerri to tell her, "And there were lots of worms."

"There were worms?" Jerri asks. "Where were they?"

Evie is not sure at first, saying, "I don't know." But after thinking about it, she responds, "They were in the dirt."

Jerri asks, "After you moved the rocks, then what did you do?"

Evie's briefly answers, "We left them." But Evie signals a shift in the conversation by saying, "And you know what? . . . There were birds, and they were looking for worms. One was in the dirt, and one was in the grass."

Jerri asks, "Oh yeah? Did they find the worms?"

"I don't know," says Evie. "I don't know."

In this conversation, Evie has recognized the invitation to converse rather than give brief responses to questions. She stays on the topic, telling about moving big clods of dirt and heavy rocks with a shovel to make her yard bigger. She also talks about seeing lots of worms in the process as well as two birds that were looking for worms. Evie surpasses the standard for sustaining a conversation by more than doubling the number of exchanges expected of a preschooler.

Fredric's Cat

Standard 1: Habits
Conversing at Length on a Topic

◆ Initiate and sustain a conversation with comments or questions through at least four exchanges

◆ Recognize the topic of the conversation and make topic-relevant responses

◆ Recognize invitations to converse versus questions intended to elicit a brief response

In this sequence, Fredric recognizes Jerri's question, "Why would a cat be a good pet?" as an invitation to converse.

"I like . . . I like them rubbing my legs. Sometime cats rub my . . . sometimes . . . one of my . . . every time . . . sometime when I go over my neighbor's, my neighbor's house, we have fun and we eat dinner together and breakfast together. And, um, and my, and she has cats. Um, one, two cats. Two cats, yeah. One, one is afraid of people . . . ," he says.

"Um," Jerri injects.

Fredric continues, ". . . even me, um, my neighbor. One cat is . . . climb all over your neck and, and it rubs, and I like, and I like when cats rub your legs. . . . And I don't care if they scratch me. It don't hurt."

"Really?" Jerri questions.

Fredric offers proof: "I scratch myself hard, and it don't hurt."

Fredric seizes another opportunity to converse when he is asked, "If you had a cat, what would you name it?" "If I had a boy," he says, "I'd name him City. And if I had a little cat girl, I'd name her Leah."

Fredric meets the standard for conversing at length on a topic in this conversation about cats. He talks about what he likes about his neighbor's cats, which rub on his legs, climb on his neck and scratch. He explains why he doesn't mind being scratched. He tells what he would name male and female pet cats. Fredric stays on topic and sustains the conversation through four exchanges.

Research Perspectives

"Vocabulary, language skills, and knowledge about the world are acquired during interesting conversations with responsive adults. Talking about books, about daily happenings, about what happened at day care or at work not only contributes to children's vocabularies, but also increases their ability to understand stories and explanations and their understanding of how things work — all skills that will be important in early reading."

From Burns, M., Griffin, P. and Snow, C., eds. (1999). *Starting Out Right: A Guide to Promoting Children's Reading Success.* Washington, D.C.: National Academy Press, 8–9.

Discussing Books

Understanding the conventions of book reading is critical to the development of early reading skills. Discussing books should become an automatic companion to read-aloud sessions with preschoolers. Very young children relate texts primarily to their own experiences, but they also should be provided ample opportunities to discuss pictures, name and identify objects, and react to stories. Specifically, we expect preschool children to:

- gather around a book and pay attention to the reader and the book;
- know the front-to-back progression of a book and the left-to-right progression of print;
- know that words and pictures convey meaning;
- pose and answer specific questions about the text (for example, word meaning, recounting and recalling, describing, naming: *Q:* "What did Billy need to fix?" *A:* "His wagon. I have a red wagon, too.");
- recite familiar refrains from book(s) that have been heard several times;
- if asked, use the text to predict what might happen next (for example, *Q:* "What do you think happens next?" *A:* "He's going to miss the bus.");
- discuss character motivation (for example, "Kitty didn't go to the party because she was sad"); and
- identify a favorite book and tell why they like it.

Preschool Standards

Standard 1: *Habits*
- Talking a Lot — pg. 48
- Talking to One's Self — pg. 58
- Conversing at Length on a Topic — pg. 60
- Discussing Books — pg. 64

Standard 2: *Kinds of Talk and Resulting Genres*
- Narrative — pg. 74
- Explaining and Seeking Information — pg. 82
- Getting Things Done — pg. 90
- Producing and Responding to Performances — pg. 94

Standard 3: *Language Use and Conventions*
- Rules of Interaction — pg. 100
- Word Play, Phonological Awareness and Language Awareness — pg. 104
- Vocabulary and Word Choice — pg. 112

Collecting Touchstone Books

"Touchstone books" are the stories found in high-quality literature for children. A collection of 10 or so of these books can take a group of preschoolers through months and months of book discussions and exploration. Children never tire of rereading their favorites. Several books by one author (such as Jane Yolen or Cynthia Rylant) or several books on a particular theme can be read over and over again. Through discussion, children learn to make connections across texts by different authors or to identify common themes in a single author's work.

Preschool: Standard 1/Commentary on Student Performances

Summarizing *The Little Red Hen*

Standard 1: Habits
Discussing Books

- Pose and answer specific questions about the text
- Discuss character motivation

In this segment, the teacher holds up a familiar book, one that has been read aloud several times. She asks, "Do you remember this story? What is this story about?"

"Chicks," a few students say.

When the teacher calls on Victoria specifically, the child gives a nice summary of the story: "The chicken who was making bread. And . . . in the story the chicken was, was doing the work to make the bread, and her friends wouldn't help her so she did it all herself, and when it was finally done she didn't let her friends, um, she didn't let her friends eat it with her because they didn't help her."

Victoria does an excellent job of talking about this book and may be considered above standard, since retelling or summarizing a story is not part of the standards until the end of first grade.

Note that other children definitely are paying attention; one child even comments on the moral of the story, saying, "And that's what they deserved."

Preschool Standards

Standard 1: *Habits*

- Talking a Lot — pg. 48
- Talking to One's Self — pg. 58
- Conversing at Length on a Topic — pg. 60
- Discussing Books — pg. 64

Standard 2: *Kinds of Talk and Resulting Genres*

- Narrative — pg. 74
- Explaining and Seeking Information — pg. 82
- Getting Things Done — pg. 90
- Producing and Responding to Performances — pg. 94

Standard 3: *Language Use and Conventions*

- Rules of Interaction — pg. 100
- Word Play, Phonological Awareness and Language Awareness — pg. 104
- Vocabulary and Word Choice — pg. 112

The Importance of a Literacy-Rich Environment

Quality schools and day care centers provide daily opportunities for small groups of three to four children working with the teacher to read and talk about books. Teachers and caregivers should encourage children to ask questions and make comments about books as they are read. A single high-quality storybook is a rich resource. It can be used to encourage awareness of language and rhythm, stress the power of illustration, anticipate or predict story lines, identify themes, or elicit related personal experiences. Rereading favorite texts helps students develop language fluency. The best preschools are filled with interested listeners and animated talkers. Both teachers and children recognize books as a touchstone for this talk.

Accomplished teachers talk *with* rather than *at, down to, in front of* or *above* children. They listen to and talk about text-related or text-inspired comments, and they give considered feedback to both. Children should be encouraged to share their favorite books at home, talk about the ideas they inspire and see that family members are also readers. It is important that children see the connection between all kinds of print and reading: newspapers give information, shopping lists give reminders, recipes give ingredients, signs give directions, etc.

Preschoolers begin to gain print awareness and might sing the alphabet song daily by rote. Lots of talk and attention to books and print of all kinds reinforces letter recognition. At this age, discussion of the alphabet is best embedded in ongoing activities (for example, learning to write one's name, finding one's book or lunch based on the initials in the front, identifying a favorite burger restaurant by its first letter).

Preschool: Standard 1/Commentary on Student Performances

"He Was Still Hungry"

Standard 1: Habits
Discussing Books

- Gather around a book and pay attention to the reader and the book

- Recite familiar refrains from book(s) that have been heard several times

Arona, the teacher, reads to a small group of children during the reading time that begins each school day. Each child in the class can make a choice to look at books in pairs, in small groups or individually. This small group of children meets two of the discussing books standards.

The children and Arona are gathered around the book and are paying close attention to the words and pictures. Arona is reading *The Very Hungry Caterpillar* by Eric Carle, a book the children have heard many times before. As she reads each line, the children repeat after her the refrain, "still hungry." By the third line, she waits for them so that they all say the refrain together.

Arona: "On Monday, he ate through one apple. But he was still hungry."

Children: "Still hungry."

Arona: "On Tuesday, he ate through two pears. But he was still hungry."

Children: "Still hungry."

Arona: "On Wednesday, he ate through three plums. But he was . . ."

Children and Arona: ". . . still hungry."

New Standards

Telling the Story

Standard 1: Habits
Discussing Books

- Gather around a book and pay attention to the reader and the book
- Know the front-to-back progression of a book and the left-to-right progression of print
- Pose and answer specific questions about the text
- Recite familiar refrains from book(s) that have been heard several times

Students in this class have daily opportunities to listen to read-aloud stories, share ideas and answer questions related to the text. This discussion, in which the students focus on the picture and then talk about its relation to the story, precedes a Writers Workshop mini-lesson on detail. In the mini-lesson, students are encouraged to think about details in their own writing. Of course, the mini-lesson is age appropriate; detail for many preschoolers means adding more descriptive *elements* to their drawings, rather than descriptive *words*.

The teacher begins by holding up a page and saying, "Look at the picture very carefully. What is this picture about?"

Kendall is able to respond to this two-page spread of a familiar picture book, giving specific examples of what goes on in the story at this particular point. She answers, "Um, there's, um, some chicks, and a momma, and a momma chick, and she found some, um, some things on the floor . . ."

"Seeds," one of the group interjects.

Kendall continues, ". . . seeds on the floor. And then she buried them and then, and then she said, 'Who will help me water these?' to her friend. And then, and then she, and then they said, 'Nobody.'" Kendall goes on to recount the action, quoting specific characters in the story: "And then, and then the cat said, 'Not me.' And, and the pig said, 'Not me.' And uh, the duck said, 'Not me.' And then she said, 'I'll . . . I'll water them myself!' " Kendall obviously is capable of reciting repeated refrains from familiar books.

The teacher agrees, "That's right. You know that she is watering because there's what in the picture?"

The children identify the watering can. The teacher then focuses the children's attention on setting when she asks, "Where does this story take place? Where is this story? Is it in the desert?"

The children identify the barn, and then the teacher goes on to add more specificity, saying, "In a barn in a . . . farm." She asks the children to point out more picture details that support the story: "We see the barn right here, we know that this is a farm because of the barn. We see the watering can, and we see . . . what else do we see?"

"The chicks!" someone offers. "And we know she's gonna, she's gonna, um . . . plant them to make the weed, because there's the . . . the thing to put the weed in, and you can tell that she's gonna, she's gonna . . . plant 'em because there's the, thum . . . that, she's gonna plant 'em because there's the . . . what're they called again?"

"The hoe?" the teacher prompts.

"Yeah, the hoe. And then, um, she's gonna, she's gonna water the weeds, because there's the watering can," says the child.

The teacher ends the segment by stressing the word *details*, the topic of her upcoming mini-lesson: "All of the things that you see in this picture are details. Can you say that word?"

Discussing Eric Carle Favorites

Standard 1: Habits
Discussing Books

- Pose and answer specific questions about the text

- Recite familiar refrains from book(s) that have been heard several times

- Identify a favorite book and tell why they like it

This preschool class has been engaged in a study of books by author Eric Carle. Preceding the teacher's rereading of *The Very Busy Spider*, one child readily answers a question about what the spider is doing. As the teacher rereads the story, the children are actively engaged and recite familiar refrains. They join in spontaneously, quoting the horse, "Neigh, Neigh."

When the teacher prompts, "Help me," the children begin to say the words of the story as the teacher continues to read, holding up the book for the children to follow along and see the progression of words. At times, the teacher pauses, allowing the children to supply the next word in the story.

The teacher reminds the children they have read many Eric Carle books, pointing to a chart the class has made that compares the books. She then says, "What I want to know is, which is your favorite book and why?"

Ricky replies, *"The [Very] Hungry Caterpillar."* When asked why it is his favorite he states, "Because he got fat." When asked what he did to get fat, Ricky is able to explain that he got fat by "eating the, all the food."

Christina offers *The Quiet Cricket* as her favorite "because he made the sounds at the end."

Daniella says her favorite is *The Very Busy Spider*. She also is able to give a reason, saying, " 'Cause there's a fly on every page."

These preschoolers have developed the habit of discussing books as an automatic part of enjoying books read aloud to them. They also have learned to be accountable for their opinions by stating reasons specific to the text of the books.

Preschool: Standard 1/Commentary on Student Performances — 71 —

Adam's Favorite Part of the Book

Standard 1: Habits
Discussing Books

◆ Identify a favorite book and tell why they like it

In this segment, Adam is very animated as he talks about a book his dad is reading to him in the evenings at home. His class also is reading the book at school. The book, *James and the Giant Peach* by Roald Dahl, is an unlikely selection for preschoolers because it is a chapter book with almost no pictures. It is also, however, the end of the school year in a program where adults regularly read aloud to children. The book has caught Adam's and some of his classmates' imaginations.

Adam laughingly and with sound effects explains his favorite part of the book, "I like the part where the peach falls on the Empire State Building. The peach falls into the needle that's on the top part. And all the bugs and James are like, 'Yike!' "

He answers his teacher's direct query about the additional setting in which he is hearing the story: "I want to hear who's reading the story to you."

"My Dad," Adam answers.

"When does Dad read the story?" the teacher asks.

"Every single night," says Adam.

The teacher queries, "Every single night?"

Adam nods. When she asks, "So do you guys read a chapter or many chapters a night?" he answers, "Um, chapters and chapters and many chapters." He agrees not to tell the ending since he and his dad probably will finish the book before the class.

The segment ends with Raymond sharing a part that he liked, saying, "I remember when the, when the peach, when they tied the seagulls around the peach so the seagulls could fly the peach."

Adam starts over again telling about his favorite part: "But remember the part when the peach fell on the Empire State Building?"

New Standards

Standard 2:
Kinds of Talk and Resulting Genres
Introduction

Talk serves different purposes, and children need ample opportunities to speak and listen in the different genres. Standard 2 identifies four genres: narrative, explaining and seeking information, getting things done, and producing and responding to performances.

For children to feel comfortable sharing a narrative, the teacher must remain stationary and attentive. Preschool narratives come in a variety of models: personal memories, stories made up in response to pictures or story or television retellings, or stories made up entirely from the child's imagination. Children also may use narratives to share knowledge; these stories are precursors to informational writing. When preschoolers reminisce about shared experiences, adults can help extend the narrative by asking open-ended questions ("And then what happened?") or repeating phrases that show their attentiveness ("You 'broke the stool.' I remember how upset you were.") On the other hand, when children volunteer to an adult a narrative about an unshared experience, they tend to tell a longer narrative.

Kindergartners' language performance, like the breadth of their knowledge about the world and their early literacy skills, reflects their earlier chances to learn from family and preschool interactions. Exchanging personal narratives at the dinner table, reading and discussing books with

---

Preschool Standards

Standard 1: *Habits*

- Talking a Lot — pg. 48
- Talking to One's Self — pg. 58
- Conversing at Length on a Topic — pg. 60
- Discussing Books — pg. 64

Standard 2: *Kinds of Talk and Resulting Genres*

- Narrative — pg. 74
- Explaining and Seeking Information — pg. 82
- Getting Things Done — pg. 90
- Producing and Responding to Performances — pg. 94

Standard 3: *Language Use and Conventions*

- Rules of Interaction — pg. 100
- Word Play, Phonological Awareness and Language Awareness — pg. 104
- Vocabulary and Word Choice — pg. 112

> Public speaking is valued in adult life yet undervalued in modern classrooms, so [this] genre is very important.

adults at home or preschool, and talking with adults about why things happen and how things work all contribute to children's language and knowledge. Telling personal narratives also helps children master the kind of language they will need for writing later on.

When explaining information, preschoolers may continue to use personal narratives; therefore, the distinct genre emerges later in the year. Teachers can offer linked experiences that build children's knowledge — for instance, a unit on rocks that involves collecting local samples, sorting by physical qualities, learning the names, visiting museums, etc. By the end of the project, children are more prepared to offer a clear explanation, for example, of certain types of rocks.

Most preschoolers need adult assistance in getting things done, and their ability to plan activities is very limited. They can, however, give directions related to a simple task or situation that is visible. They are much more successful giving and following directions if they are physically engaged in the task at the time — baking in the kitchen, playing with blocks or building a model. Young children also begin to use language to negotiate their time for work and play — disagreeing, collaborating, taking turns or sharing as needed.

Public speaking is valued in adult life yet undervalued in modern classrooms, so the last genre is very important. Children benefit from giving language performances as early as ages three to four. Finger plays, action verse, nursery rhymes and songs all fit the bill. Sharing simple verbal responses prepares children for the more critical literature responses in later grades.

Narrative

The spoken narrative is a precursor to the forms of fiction and nonfiction narrative accounts that children eventually will read. In addition, relating past experiences is a prerequisite for transitioning from speech to print. Preschool children can produce longer narratives if adults extend the production with questions that increase structure, such as "Tell me more" or "What was the dog doing?" or "Was the bike broken?"

Though typically more successful with factual accounts of personal experiences, preschoolers may produce some combination of fact and fiction.

Specifically, by the end of preschool we expect children to:

◆ give a simple narrative (with adult prompting if necessary), recounting two or more events that are not necessarily in chronological order (for example, "Puppy chase me, and he lick my knee" or "We rided the merry-go-round. Mommy took us. We got our tickets."); and

◆ recount knowledge gained through observation, experience or text.

Preschool children should learn to include these elements for telling more complete and varied narratives:

◆ orient the listener by giving some setting information about people, objects, and where and when events occurred (for example, "I had a shot once. With a needle. He [doctor] gave me a big hole in my arm.");

◆ describe information and evaluate or reflect on it (for example, "I went down the blue slide. It was real fun.");

◆ include quotations (for example, "He went, 'Get out of here,' and I said, 'No, I won't.' "); or

◆ mark the end of the story directly or with a coda (for example, "That's what happened.").

Preschool Standards

Standard 1: *Habits*
- ◆ Talking a Lot — pg. 48
- ◆ Talking to One's Self — pg. 58
- ◆ Conversing at Length on a Topic — pg. 60
- ◆ Discussing Books — pg. 64

Standard 2: *Kinds of Talk and Resulting Genres*
- ◆ Narrative — pg. 74
- ◆ Explaining and Seeking Information — pg. 82
- ◆ Getting Things Done — pg. 90
- ◆ Producing and Responding to Performances — pg. 94

Standard 3: *Language Use and Conventions*
- ◆ Rules of Interaction — pg. 100
- ◆ Word Play, Phonological Awareness and Language Awareness — pg. 104
- ◆ Vocabulary and Word Choice — pg. 112

Anna Is Jealous

Standard 2: Kinds of Talk and Resulting Genres
Narrative

- Give a simple narrative (with adult prompting if necessary), recounting two or more events that are not necessarily in chronological order
- Recount knowledge gained through observation, experience or text
- Orient the listener by giving some setting information about people, objects, and where and when events occurred
- Describe information and evaluate or reflect on it
- Include quotations

The images and commentary in this section refer to performances available on the accompanying CD-ROMs.

Anna meets and exceeds the preschool narrative standard as she recounts playing a game with her brother. Anna orients Shari, who is her teacher and the listener, by establishing the time frame and what she was doing. She says, "Once when Molly's family came over to stay with us for dinner, I played Huckle."

She describes the next sequence of events, saying, "And when I was, and when I let Huckle through the secret door, oops! There we go again." She motions with her hands to indicate which direction Huckle went and then says, "Ben laughed so hard, his chair tipped over." She quotes her brother in her description of the next series of events: "And he went to Mommy and said, 'Mommy can you rub my head?' "

Shari asks, "Did she?"

Anna nods.

Shari continues, "Did she put anything on his head?"

Anna adds evaluation to her detailed response, saying, "Well, a little bit of ice. . . . She put it in a bag and put it on his head where he bumped it."

"And guess what he said?" Anna asks as she continues her eventful story. She quotes her brother again when she says, " 'Anna, can I have a turn?' "

She continues, "And I moved to his chair. We had, we started playing. And then it happened to me when he let Huckle through the trap door." She evaluates and reflects on the events when she says, "I laughed so hard. And I, my chair fell over. . . . And I went to Mommy and bumped my head."

Shari's statement, "You just wanted an ice pack on your head," offers Anna an opportunity to explain herself as a character in the narrative. She shares the motive for her actions and her goal, saying, "No, I was jealous that Ben got the attention from Mommy, so I got fall down."

Anna's ability to develop herself as a character in the narrative by describing her feelings (jealousy) and goal (more attention) is evidence that her narrative skills exceed the preschool narrative standard.

Preschool Standards

Standard 1: *Habits*

- Talking a Lot — pg. 48
- Talking to One's Self — pg. 58
- Conversing at Length on a Topic — pg. 60
- Discussing Books — pg. 64

Standard 2: *Kinds of Talk and Resulting Genres*

- Narrative — pg. 74
- Explaining and Seeking Information — pg. 82
- Getting Things Done — pg. 90
- Producing and Responding to Performances — pg. 94

Standard 3: *Language Use and Conventions*

- Rules of Interaction — pg. 100
- Word Play, Phonological Awareness and Language Awareness — pg. 104
- Vocabulary and Word Choice — pg. 112

Developmental Sequence of Early Narratives

At age three and a half, children generally combine only two events in their longer narratives, called a "two-event narrative." By age four, children's narratives consist of more than two events, but the events often are told out of sequence in what is called a "leap frog narrative." In these narratives, omissions often make it difficult for the listener to make sense of the story. By age five, children rarely have trouble sequencing events in oral narratives. However, they usually end their narratives prematurely, dwelling on a climactic event at the end of their narration in what is called an "end-at-high-point narrative." Six-year-olds tell a well-formed story that orients the listener to who, what and where something happened. They narrate a sequence of events that builds to some sort of climax and then goes on to reach a resolution and tell how things turn out. This is the form of narrative that is most commonly presented in early storybooks and that teachers expect children to produce in the primary grades.

— Peterson & McCabe, 1983

Charles's Trains

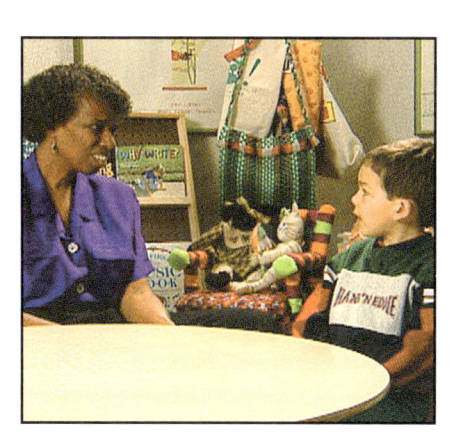

Standard 2: Kinds of Talk and Resulting Genres

Narrative

- Give a simple narrative (with adult prompting if necessary), recounting two or more events that are not necessarily in chronological order
- Recount knowledge gained through observation, experience or text
- Orient the listener by giving some setting information about people, objects, and where and when events occurred
- Describe information and evaluate or reflect on it
- Include quotations

Charles, for whom English is a second language, is talking to Jerri, a visitor to his preschool. The conversation evolves into a chronological narrative based on his experience playing trains with his grandfather.

The segment begins with the prompt, "Is there somebody that you play with? Um, that you play trains a lot with? What kinds of things do you do with the trains? When you play?"

Charles responds in detail, indicating his knowledge and experience with trains. He answers, "Poppie has like, like a lot of bar train trains. It has, it has mail cars, and coaches, and even has, has tank cars, orange tank cars. Even it has a diesel, has two diesels."

Jerri asks, "When you and Poppie use the trains, do you ever pretend?"

Charles provides some evaluative information, answering, "Um, of course, a lot." He continues, orienting the listener to the people involved as well as the situation by saying, "When my sister and me . . . we don't, we don't play with the big diesels, Poppa's. Because last time . . . I told Poppa, 'Poppa, turn the switch!'"

He gives the listener insight into his grandfather's thinking when he says, "Then Poppa saw that the diesel was going next to the switch." Charles directly solicits the listener's attention for the climax of the story, saying, "And you know what happened?"

Jerri asks, "What happened?"

Charles delivers the climax and reflects on it when he says, "The train crashed because Poppa didn't turn the, the switch straight. I told him one time, and he didn't listen."

"Oh, and so it crashed," Jerri repeats.

Charles goes on to resolve the story, "Yeah, and you know who fixed it?"

"Who?" she asks.

"Uncle Al," announces Charles.

Jerri responds, "So he knows something about trains too."

"Yeah," says Charles.

Charles's narrative meets the preschool standard for narrative. He is able to orient the listener to the people involved (sister, grandfather, uncle and himself), the objects (diesel engine and switch) and the time (the last time). He includes evaluative information and quotes himself. Charles actually goes beyond the preschool standard when he includes a climax and a resolution.

Preschool Standards

Standard 1: *Habits*
- Talking a Lot — pg. 48
- Talking to One's Self — pg. 58
- Conversing at Length on a Topic — pg. 60
- Discussing Books — pg. 64

Standard 2: *Kinds of Talk and Resulting Genres*
- Narrative — pg. 74
- Explaining and Seeking Information — pg. 82
- Getting Things Done — pg. 90
- Producing and Responding to Performances — pg. 94

Standard 3: *Language Use and Conventions*
- Rules of Interaction — pg. 100
- Word Play, Phonological Awareness and Language Awareness — pg. 104
- Vocabulary and Word Choice — pg. 112

Encouraging Narratives

To encourage preschool children to launch into a narrative, it is essential to stand still, look at them and listen. They need a willing and interested listener who is sending attentive signals. It is important that they not feel rushed, and response is critical. No response is a response. Children who receive no response are likely to say very little. Responses that are less leading encourage narration without directing the narrative. Useful strategies include:

- repeating the exact words of the children when they pause;
- simply nodding and saying "uh-huh"; and
- asking for more information (for example, "Tell me more" or "And then what happened?").

— Peterson & McCabe, 1983

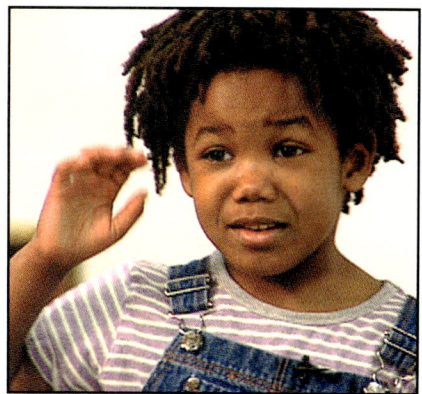

Preschool: Standard 2/Commentary on Student Performances

Evie's Lost Ball

Standard 2: Kinds of Talk and Resulting Genres
Narrative

- Give a simple narrative (with adult prompting if necessary), recounting two or more events that are not necessarily in chronological order
- Recount knowledge gained through observation, experience or text
- Orient the listener by giving some setting information about people, objects, and where and when events occurred
- Mark the end of the story directly or with a coda

Evie is chatting with Jerri, a visitor to her preschool classroom. Evie tells a simple narrative, recounting several events that she experienced involving a ball that she thought was lost.

"Do you know what?" Evie asks, soliciting Jerri's attention. She then gives some setting information, "One time when I couldn't find that ball for Zany's birthday . . . do you know what?"

"What happened?" Jerri asks.

"I put my jacket on when it was time to go because we were having a sleepover," says Evie, adding more details to the recounting of her experience. "Do you know what happened?" she asks once more.

"What happened?" Jerri asks.

"When I put my coat on, the ball went, popped out of my sleeve," exclaims Evie.

Jerri laughingly makes sure that she has understood the punch line, asking, "It was in the sleeve? That's pretty good. I'll bet you were surprised."

Evie appears to end the story directly by saying, "That's what really happened."

Jerri repeats, "That's what really happened. That's a surprising thing."

Evie goes on, "And I couldn't find it and I looked everywhere. And when I went running down the stairs, it went . . ."

"Went bouncing down the stairs?" anticipates Jerri.

But Evie says, "When I looked in Zany's closet, I didn't see it."

Evie meets the preschool standard for narrative. She orients her listener by sharing why the ball was important and where she was positioned. She appears to end the story, but instead she extends it, giving the story greater effect. In fact, Evie goes beyond the preschool standard when, at the beginning and several times during the telling of the story, she solicits the attention of the listener.

New Standards

More Complete Narratives

A complete narrative includes describing information and evaluating or reflecting on it. Both narratives below have more than two past events or action words. Both are about being stung by a bee, which has temporal sequence in the real world. Both unfold in the order the events happened.

Narrative One, however, does not have a high point. It is a simple list of unevaluated events. There is no emotional heart of the story. In contrast, Narrative Two does have a high point. The child uses repetition, evaluating her response to the sting.

An evaluation doesn't disclose information about what happened. Rather, it reveals the event's meaning for the narrator. There are many kinds of evaluation. Some are obvious; others are more subtle, such as changing tone of voice, repetition or an unusual vocabulary choice. Note that the listener models appropriate ways to encourage narratives.

Narrative One
(eight-year-old girl)
Listener: Have you ever gotten jabbed by something?
Child: By a bee.
Listener: By a bee? Oh, tell me about it.
Child: It got kind of cool one day, and my grandma came. She called me, and she wanted to know where Dennis was.
Listener: Where Dennis was?
Child: Yeah, and I ran outside to tell her and I was running and I stepped on a bee.
Listener: You were running, and you stepped on a bee. Ah. Then what?
Child: Nothing. I just went in the house and had to have something on it.

Narrative Two
(five-year-old girl)
Listener: Have you ever gotten jabbed by something?
Child: Uh-huh. I got jabbed with a bee.
Listener: By a bee? Oh, tell me about it.
Child: See, I got jabbed on my foot. I was barefooted. I screamed and I screamed and I cried and I cried. I screamed and I screamed. Until my next door neighbor came out and my Dad came out and my brother came out. And they all carried me into the house, but after that happened I got to sleep overnight with my neighbor.

— Peterson & McCabe, 1983

Preschool Standards

Standard 1: *Habits*
- Talking a Lot — pg. 48
- Talking to One's Self — pg. 58
- Conversing at Length on a Topic — pg. 60
- Discussing Books — pg. 64

Standard 2: *Kinds of Talk and Resulting Genres*
- Narrative — pg. 74
- Explaining and Seeking Information — pg. 82
- Getting Things Done — pg. 90
- Producing and Responding to Performances — pg. 94

Standard 3: *Language Use and Conventions*
- Rules of Interaction — pg. 100
- Word Play, Phonological Awareness and Language Awareness — pg. 104
- Vocabulary and Word Choice — pg. 112

Preschool: Standard 2/Commentary on Student Performances

Angel's Computer Game

Standard 2: Kinds of Talk and Resulting Genres
Narrative

◆ Give a simple narrative (with adult prompting if necessary), recounting two or more events that are not necessarily in chronological order

◆ Recount knowledge gained through observation, experience or text

◆ Orient the listener by giving some setting information about people, objects, and where and when events occurred

◆ Describe information and evaluate or reflect on it

Angel, a preschool student, is using a computer to write her own alphabet book. When asked, "Do you work on a computer every day?" she tells about her home computer, how she got it and even the disadvantages of old technology, saying, "It doesn't teach you that much science."

Angel begins, "I always work on my computer at my house 'cause I have a computer that's really old, and it doesn't teach you that much science." Angel has answered the question directly, explaining that she always does work on the computer at home. She continues with the story of how her mother surprised her with a new computer.

As is typical for preschool children, she stops midstream, shifting to tell about an interesting part of the computer having to do with numbers, possibly a game she plays. She says, "And, and now for my, my mommy, she had a surprise for me and I have, and I have a big, um, like, it's a computer that, um, you have to . . . do you know that, um, I have a, um, computer that when you like, um, you first, when you see the number on the, I mean, the letter on the computer, then when it says the letter, every time, I don't even know where it is and my mommy shows me, and you have to click it, and you have to, um, type the letter before the letter goes off the computer."

This is the type of narrative we expect from a preschooler. With adult prompting, she relates information involving at least two events (she works on a computer, her mother surprised her with it and her mother helps her "click" the numbers). She gives an accurate accounting of her own experience and observations. She orients the listener to the people (mommy), setting (home) and objects (the computer). Angel's comments about the old computer even offer some evaluative information — the newer computer is better because the old one "doesn't teach you that much science."

Explaining and Seeking Information

Children who experience daily read-alouds and conversation with peers and adults are likely to turn to books to seek information. In later years, children are expected to organize information in essays and reports, the preschool version of which is explanatory talk. Though preschoolers still may use personal narratives to provide information, explanatory talk should begin to appear. Specifically, we expect preschool children to:

◆ seek or provide information by observing; looking at books; or asking teachers, parents and peers;

◆ request or provide explanations of their own or others' actions, speech or feelings;

◆ explain their own or others' intentions and thinking when asked (for example, *Q:* "Why is the milk out?" *A:* "For cereal. I want some cereal.");

◆ give simple, one-sentence explanations, with supporting details or evidence (for example, "I cut my knee because I fell.");

◆ request or provide explanations of word meanings (for example, "What's 'your highness'?");

◆ use all their senses to describe physical characteristics of objects, self and others;

◆ describe objects, self and others in terms of location and position; and

◆ use gestures and sounds when they don't have descriptive words (for example, describing an accident scene, "They took him in that . . . that . . . RRRR-RRRR. It was LOUD!").

Preschool Standards

Standard 1: *Habits*
- ◆ Talking a Lot — pg. 48
- ◆ Talking to One's Self — pg. 58
- ◆ Conversing at Length on a Topic — pg. 60
- ◆ Discussing Books — pg. 64

Standard 2: *Kinds of Talk and Resulting Genres*
- ◆ Narrative — pg. 74
- ◆ Explaining and Seeking Information — pg. 82
- ◆ Getting Things Done — pg. 90
- ◆ Producing and Responding to Performances — pg. 94

Standard 3: *Language Use and Conventions*
- ◆ Rules of Interaction — pg. 100
- ◆ Word Play, Phonological Awareness and Language Awareness — pg. 104
- ◆ Vocabulary and Word Choice — pg. 112

Preschool: Standard 2/Commentary on Student Performances — 83 —

Jacelyn Finds Some Bugs

Standard 2: Kinds of Talk and Resulting Genres
Explaining and Seeking Information

- Seek or provide information by observing; looking at books; or asking teachers, parents and peers

- Request or provide explanations of their own or others' actions, speech or feelings

- Give simple, one-sentence explanations, with supporting details

- Describe physical characteristics of objects, self and others

In this science lesson, a small group of children is examining the contents of a stocking the class had buried the previous fall. Jacelyn observes, "Oh! There's a bug in it!"

"Where?" asks Shari, the teacher.

Jacelyn points, "Right there. See it?" She adds a description: "Yeah, there's a white bug."

The teacher wonders if it is really so, urging the children to "look closely."

In response, Jacelyn emphatically focuses the others, exclaiming, "Look! See! See all them!" She summarizes her discovery simply, explaining, "See those white things? Those are bugs."

Jacelyn meets the standard for explaining information. She observes closely and then describes and labels what she sees as bugs.

New Standards

Philip Talks about the Orchestra

Standard 2: Kinds of Talk and Resulting Genres
Explaining and Seeking Information

◆ Seek or provide information by observing; looking at books; or asking teachers, parents and peers

◆ Give simple, one-sentence explanations, with supporting details or evidence

◆ Explain their own intentions and thinking

◆ Describe physical characteristics of objects, self and others

◆ Describe objects, self and others in terms of location and position

◆ Use gestures and sounds when they don't have descriptive words

Following a class visit to Heinz Hall, the home of the Pittsburgh Symphony Orchestra, Philip drew a picture of what he saw. In this sequence, Philip explains his picture of the orchestra and its various sections: percussion, brass, woodwinds and strings. Philip goes into great detail about the conductor's role, including how he directs the orchestra standing on his stool. Philip also explains the meaning of the conductor's gestures with the baton.

Jerri, a visitor to Philip's preschool classroom, requests, "Tell me about your picture."

"Well," he explains, "this is a percussion section. This is a brass section, and this is where the conductor stands." He continues his explanation by describing his intentions, "This is, was, this is gonna be, um, this is gonna be woodwinds, and this is gonna be strings."

Jerri then asks, ". . . tell me about a conductor. Is the conductor somebody who helps in some way? Does he help the orchestra?"

Philip gives a simple explanation that provides detail about how the conductor helps the orchestra, "He helps the orchestra. He, he helps the, he tells the orchestra which way to play."

After Jerri shares, "You know, the other day I was in Heinz Hall where the concert is. I was there," Philip seeks additional information by asking, "Did you hear the music, though?"

Jerri responds, "No, I didn't get to hear the music, but I was going to ask you, would you tell me about your visit?"

Philip explains what he observed, "Well, well, well, at the symphony it didn't just have a tuba." He continues the simple explanation of his actions with supporting detail, "I just drew a tuba, though. That's all that, that would fit."

Philip expands on his explanation of the orchestra when prompted by Jerri's question, "What else happened at the concert?"

He begins with a question, "Well, do you know what the conductor uses is, is, to get, so the orchestra, so the people all the way in the back can see him?"

"What does he use?" Jerri asks.

Philip gives a simple, detailed explanation of his observations, locating the conductor's position and his actions. He says, "He uses a little stool to make him higher and I, and he uses a baton so the, um, orchestra can see him."

Jerri asks for more details: "Oh. Well, how does he use the baton? What does he do with it?"

Philip uses gestures to help his explanation: "He goes like this [waving arms in and out]. And if he does it like this [waving arms in and out higher in the air], they have to play big and loud." He continues as he lowers his waving arms and speaks more quietly, "When he goes like this, they have to play soft and quiet."

Philip continues, "And if they go, and if he goes like this [raising his waving arms slightly], they have to play medium."

Anna Explains the Body Alphabet

Standard 2: Kinds of Talk and Resulting Genres

Explaining and Seeking Information

- Request or provide explanations of their own or others' actions, speech or feelings
- Use gestures and sounds when they don't have descriptive words

Anna is explaining to Shari, her teacher, how she and a few of her classmates used their bodies to make letters on the gym floor earlier in the day. Shari had not been in the gym at the time. Anna uses gestures as she describes the *H*, *A* and *N* that she, Emily and Annie made. Jacelyn helped them make a *W*.

Anna begins, "In the gym, me and Annie were going to make an *H* today, but in a surprise, we said, we yelled, 'Shari, Shari,' and we noticed you weren't here."

Shari tells Anna, "I was, I was up here talking to my friends [preparing for the videotaping]."

"Oh," Anna replies.

Shari asks for more information, saying, "So you made an *H*. What kind of *H* did you make? Did you make it with your bodies, or did you make it with blocks?"

Anna, using gestures as well as words, explains, "Bodies. Annie was right here on the green rug [gestures], and Emily was right here, but I was right on this. So it was like this, Annie, Emily and me [gesturing the shape of an *H*]."

"Oh," says Shari, "so it took three of you to make the *H*."

"Yeah," Anna responds.

"Did you make any other letters?" Shari inquires.

Anna begins to explain how the children made the *A*, again using gestures to shape the letters. She says, "Uh, we made a *A*. Annie . . . [gesture]"

Shari asks, "How many people did you need for that?"

". . . me and Emily," Anna continues, gesturing.

Shari summarizes, "The same three people made two letters. Did you do anything else?"

Anna explains with gestures, "Well, we made a *N*. Annie, Emily and then me."

Shari had moved one of her fingers toward Anna's hand motions but pulls it back. She says, "I thought you were going to need another finger. That's great!"

Shari once again asks, "What else did you do in the gym?"

"Well," Anna responds using gestures and words, "we decided to ask another person to play with us. We were making an *M*. So we decided to make a *W*. So, it was Emily, me, Annie . . . and Jacelyn."

"And Jacelyn," Shari says. "You needed to ask some other people to help you."

Anna meets the standard for explaining information. She is able to explain, using words and gestures, how she and several classmates used their bodies to form letters of the alphabet.

Crickets

Standard 2: Kinds of Talk and Resulting Genres
Explaining and Seeking Information

- Seek or provide information by looking at books or asking teachers, parents and peers

- Give simple, one-sentence explanations, with supporting details or evidence

- Request or provide explanations of word meanings

- Describe objects, self and others in terms of location and position

- Use gestures and sounds when they don't have descriptive words

These two children are discussing some of the insects that are characters in the books they have been reading. First, the teacher asks Ricky, "How about you, Ricky, which one's your favorite?"

He answers that it is the crickets "because the crickets jump a lot."

Christina volunteers to describe the cricket. "And, and these are the wings," she says. She holds up the model and continues, "And when they open, then this thing right there, that looks like a tongue, it's a thing."

The teacher helps her out, saying, "Oh, it's called an abdomen."

Christina repeats, "The abdomen."

Ricky offers that crickets have a distinct sound: "And then, and then they do that sound . . . with their feet." When the teacher asks Ricky to describe the sound, he makes a little squeak.

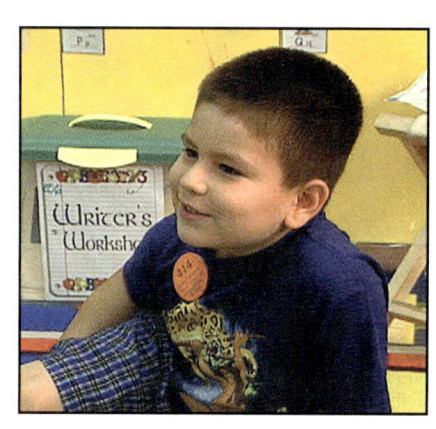

Christina remembers that the class has a book that can be used to demonstrate the sound and says, "I'll show you what it sounds like."

After a brief struggle over who might have the honor of finding the cricket sound, both children open the book to the correct page, and the electronic noise is heard.

Thorny

Standard 2: Kinds of Talk and Resulting Genres
Explaining and Seeking Information

◆ Request or provide explanations of word meanings

This brief segment is an excellent example of a preschool student explaining the meaning of a word and its opposite. When asked what he notices about the paintings, Spencer says, "I notice that some of the flowers are kinda a little bit thorny, and some aren't."

The teacher asks him to define *thorny:* "Thorny, what does that mean?"

Spencer is able to explain what the adjective means. Note that he makes a "smart mistake" when he adds *un* to *thorny* to describe its opposite. This shows that he is becoming aware of grammatical constructions and is beginning to attempt the irregular forms of words almost unconsciously. "That means that they have thorns. And, and, um . . . and unthorny means that they don't have thorns."

Research Perspectives

"The more a child hears of one or another aspect of the language, the greater the opportunity the child has to learn it. Opportunities for learning are enhanced when children engage in many and varied interactions with other people..."

From Hart, B. and Risley, T. (1995). Meaningful Differences in the Everyday Experience of Young American Children. Paul H. Brookes Publishing Co., xi.

Getting Things Done

At the preschool level, children are able to give and follow directions on simple tasks that are visible, familiar or close at hand. Their ability to plan step by step is limited; however, they may articulate future goals or actions. And, with assistance, they can complete projects that span several days. Their sharing and negotiating skills are just beginning to mature. Specifically, we expect preschool children to:

◆ listen to, comprehend and carry out directions with three to four simple steps (for example, "Go to the cubby, hang up your sweater and bring your lunch back.");

◆ give directions that include several sequenced steps;

◆ ask for clarification to carry out more complicated directions (for example, while baking, "What comes next?");

◆ use actions or pictures to augment language (for example, demonstrating how to cut the paper or open a container); and

◆ engage in brief conversation (three to four exchanges) to negotiate sharing, planning and problem solving.

Preschool Standards

Standard 1: *Habits*
- Talking a Lot — pg. 48
- Talking to One's Self — pg. 58
- Conversing at Length on a Topic — pg. 60
- Discussing Books — pg. 64

Standard 2: *Kinds of Talk and Resulting Genres*
- Narrative — pg. 74
- Explaining and Seeking Information — pg. 82
- Getting Things Done — pg. 90
- Producing and Responding to Performances — pg. 94

Standard 3: *Language Use and Conventions*
- Rules of Interaction — pg. 100
- Word Play, Phonological Awareness and Language Awareness — pg. 104
- Vocabulary and Word Choice — pg. 112

Philip Knows How to Solve a Conflict

Standard 2: Kinds of Talk and Resulting Genres
Getting Things Done

- Give directions that include several sequenced steps

- Engage in brief conversation (three to four exchanges) to negotiate sharing, planning and problem solving

Philip, along with other students in his preschool class, has learned a four-step process for solving problems. He tells about a problem he helped solve, recounting when "Mitchell and Michael Patrick were tickling Sam, and Sam didn't like it."

He recounts the first three steps, saying, "We, we already got everybody together, we already knew what the problem [was] and then we had to figure out a solution." He later adds, "Ah, ah, ah, and the fourth step is called the go step." When asked about the go step, he replies that it "means you do the solution that you chose."

Philip clearly was able not only to state the steps in the problem-solving process but also to use it to negotiate a solution for a problem his classmates were having.

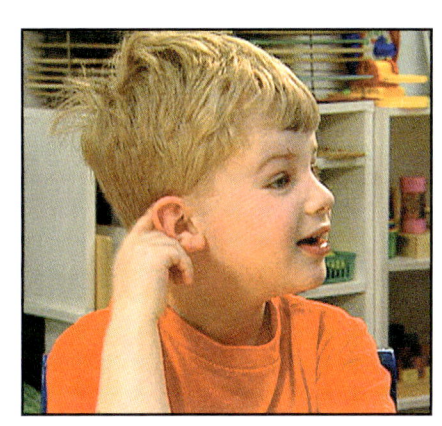

Evie Knows How to Feed Her Dog

Standard 2: Kinds of Talk and Resulting Genres

Getting Things Done

◆ Give directions that include several sequenced steps

◆ Use actions or pictures to augment language

Evie explains the four steps involved in feeding her dog. When asked if the food comes in a can, she uses her hands to draw the distinction as she says, "One kind does, and one kind doesn't." She explains that her dog "likes it mixed up with water, together." She clarifies that the other kind of food comes in something shaped like a garbage can. She explains, "But it's white, and that's what the other kind of food comes in. And the other kind of food is one scoopful, then put water in, first put the dry food in, then the second food, then the wet." When asked if she has to mix it up, she replies, demonstrating with hand movements, "Uh-huh, with a, with a spoon, and then it's all right." She concludes her description of the steps in feeding her dog, claiming, "Then she likes it."

Preschool: Standard 2/Commentary on Student Performances

Block Play

Standard 2: Kinds of Talk and Resulting Genres

Getting Things Done

◆ Engage in brief conversation (three to four exchanges) to negotiate sharing, planning and problem solving

These preschoolers work as a team as they engage in block play. They talk to solve the problem of how to build a boat into which they all can fit. After Josh suggests, "We need these," Evie, wanting to use the large, open blocks, counters, "But they're not open."

Merinda, moving a large, open block into the play area, suggests, "Yeah, let's put it like right here."

Evie moves the planning forward with her suggestion: "We could use these for a big paddle."

As other children put paddles in the boat, Josh adds, "Let's get some more paddles."

With the boat nearly complete, Merinda and Nadia start to put baby dolls and blankets in the boat. The discussion then turns to the question of where they will sit. Nadia argues, "But then we won't have any room for us."

The children discuss this problem, suggesting, "We can put these [blankets] down so we can sit on them."

Josh suggests, "We can stand to make sure."

Merinda offers a choice, saying, "Okay. You can have it all, or we can stand."

Nadia accepts the solution, saying, "We can sit on the blocks."

This group of preschoolers has learned how to communicate to get things done during block play. They listen to each other, make suggestions to move the planning forward and share possible solutions to a problem they encounter.

New Standards

Producing and Responding to Performances

When preschoolers respond to a performance (whether it's a live storyteller, video or play) they are taking the first tentative steps toward what eventually will become reflection and critique of works of art, music or literature. Offering polite attention, giving a simple reaction or asking thoughtful questions is a sufficient start at this age.

By three or four years of age, children are very ready to produce brief performances, especially in small groups accompanied by music, rhyme or body movement. This is an excellent entree into acquiring the skills needed for reading aloud, giving reports and public speaking in later years. Specifically, we expect preschool children to:

◆ attend to a performance (for example, watching and listening to a performance 10 or more minutes long);

◆ describe the experience and/or their reaction to the performance (for example, "I was scared" or "I liked the clown. He was funny.");

◆ ask questions about things that they don't understand (for example, "Why is Tiny Tim so sad?");

◆ join in appropriately;

◆ draw from a rehearsed repertoire to give a brief performance (for example, in highly practiced forms like the "ABCs," "Itsy-Bitsy Spider" and "I'm a Little Teapot");

◆ as performers, look at the audience as appropriate;

◆ speak, sing or act in a loud-enough voice; and

◆ speak, sing or act out a few sentences.

Preschool Standards

Standard 1: *Habits*
- Talking a Lot — pg. 48
- Talking to One's Self — pg. 58
- Conversing at Length on a Topic — pg. 60
- Discussing Books — pg. 64

Standard 2: *Kinds of Talk and Resulting Genres*
- Narrative — pg. 74
- Explaining and Seeking Information — pg. 82
- Getting Things Done — pg. 90
- Producing and Responding to Performances — pg. 94

Standard 3: *Language Use and Conventions*
- Rules of Interaction — pg. 100
- Word Play, Phonological Awareness and Language Awareness — pg. 104
- Vocabulary and Word Choice — pg. 112

Responding to Performances

This standard places slightly more focus on *producing* performances. However, the first three criteria clearly refer to how preschoolers might respond to a play, musical performance, painter's exhibition, or visit from a police officer or firefighter.

The most common performance preschoolers experience is the teacher reading aloud or a performance by a visiting storyteller. In fact, preschoolers should be read to and have an opportunity to respond to stories *daily*. Listening, describing reactions and asking questions are all ways of responding to a storyteller or read-aloud session. For more information on appropriate ways to respond to and discuss stories, refer to page 64.

Preschool: Standard 2/Commentary on Student Performances

Philip Wonders about Sheet Music

Standard 2: Kinds of Talk and Resulting Genres

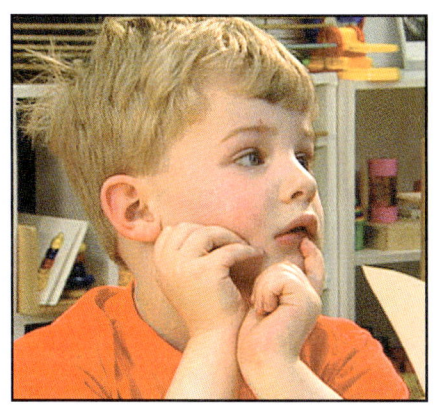

Producing and Responding to Performances

◆ Attend to a performance

◆ Ask questions about things that they don't understand

Philip and Jerri, a visitor to the classroom, have been discussing the visit his class made to the symphony the previous week. See pages 84–85 for Philip's explanation of the orchestra. In this segment, he asks a question about something he did not understand.

Philip has just been asked, "What else happened at the concert?" He takes the opportunity to seek information about something that he did not understand by asking a question of his own: "Well, I, this, I've never asked this question. Um, what, how, how do the people in the orchestra know, know to play, know to, know, know, know what song to play?"

Jerri repeats the question, "Oh, how do they know what song to play? You know what? That is a very good question. Did you see anything, uh, up in front of them when they were playing the music? Did they have anything up in front of them, maybe sitting up like this in front of them [holds paper up]? Did you notice that? Did you notice anything like that? Well, they probably had stands in front of them with pages that they turned."

Philip's facial expression indicates that he is listening carefully, trying to understand. "Oh, oh, so, oh, so that's how they know," Philip exclaims.

"That's it," Jerri responds. "They have sheet music in front of them."

Philip recalls, "So does the conductor."

Chavez "Reads" a Familiar Poem

Standard 2: Kinds of Talk and Resulting Genres

Producing and Responding to Performances

◆ Draw from a rehearsed repertoire to give a brief performance

◆ Speak, sing or act in a loud-enough voice

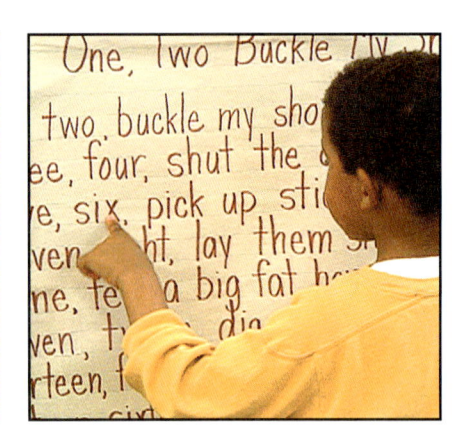

A small group of children is gathered around an easel on which a familiar rhyming poem is printed. Earlier, the children read the poem in unison while Arona, the teacher, pointed to the words. Individual children are enthusiastically taking turns reading the poem by themselves.

"Can I do it?" asks Chavez.

"You'd like a turn, Chavez?" Arona asks. "Okay."

Marcus wants to know, "Can I do it with Chavez?"

"No," Arona reminds him, "you had your turn. Let him have a turn now."

Chavez points to each word as he reads. He starts with the title: "One, one, two buckle my shoe." Then he continues, "One, two, buckle my shoe. Three, four, shut the door. Five, six, pick up sticks." He reads "seven" but points to the wrong line.

The teacher points to help him make the correction and says, "Here's seven down here."

Chavez then continues to the end of the poem: "Seven, eight, lay them straight. Nine, ten, a big fat hen."

Preschool: Standard 2/Commentary on Student Performances — 97 —

Five Fishies

Standard 2: Kinds of Talk and Resulting Genres

Producing and Responding to Performances

◆ Draw from a rehearsed repertoire to give a brief performance

◆ As performers, look at the audience as appropriate

◆ Speak, sing or act in a loud-enough voice

◆ Speak, sing or act out a few sentences

The following example is the type of performance expected of preschoolers. They have learned a short rhyme by heart and can perform it independently, along with gestures. They act together in unison, speak loudly and look at the audience as they perform. Other children in the class enjoy the performance by joining in. They recite:

Five little fishies swimming in the pool.
First one said, the pool is cool.
Second one said, the pool is deep.
Third one said, I want to sleep.
Fourth one said, let's dive and dip.
Fifth one said, I spy a ship.
Fisherman's pole lands with a splash!
Away the five little fishies dash!

New Standards

Standard 3: Language Use and Conventions
Introduction

Standard 3 outlines important aspects of language use and conventions. It is a three-part standard, including: rules of interaction; word play, phonological awareness and language awareness; and vocabulary and word choice. An understanding of how language should be used in social settings is just as important as learning the conventions of vocabulary and grammar. The first part of Standard 3, rules of interaction, addresses these important social conventions.

Word play, phonological awareness and language awareness are all important to the development of strong readers and writers. At this age, children begin to display a dawning understanding of the conventional nature of language. They delight in books that turn the world topsy-turvy, such as the ones written by Dr. Seuss. They begin to notice and wonder about words. They experiment with the conventional use of words by producing playful or nonsensical phrasing. And they often display a literal understanding of common idioms, such as "put to sleep." When children experiment with language, they gain an awareness of the sounds of words, word parts and even grammar.

As they learn to talk, children become more aware of the rhythm and cadence of our language. Eventually, children understand that words are made up of component sounds — the phonemic awareness that both enables and reflects

Preschool Standards

Standard 1: *Habits*
- Talking a Lot — pg. 48
- Talking to One's Self — pg. 58
- Conversing at Length on a Topic — pg. 60
- Discussing Books — pg. 64

Standard 2: *Kinds of Talk and Resulting Genres*
- Narrative — pg. 74
- Explaining and Seeking Information — pg. 82
- Getting Things Done — pg. 90
- Producing and Responding to Performances — pg. 94

Standard 3: *Language Use and Conventions*
- Rules of Interaction — pg. 100
- Word Play, Phonological Awareness and Language Awareness — pg. 104
- Vocabulary and Word Choice — pg. 112

> Word play, phonological awareness and language awareness are all important to the development of strong readers and writers.

emerging literacy. Phonological awareness activities are both a precursor and a support to phonemic awareness. In preschool, it begins with listening — to environmental sounds, words and word parts, and clapping or beating to the rhythm of language.

Phonological awareness is not centered on the level of the individual phoneme. It encompasses such things as rhythm, rhyme, patterns, and onsets and rimes. Rhyming is a strong predictor of success in reading and writing. Rhythm, also an important part of language play, helps children attune their ears to sounds of words and word parts. Overall, the focus is on *playing* with language rather than on producing specific words.

Even grammar shows up in preschool. Children develop a facility for combining words, producing complete and longer sentences more frequently. Eventually, they become aware of rules governing such combinations and are able to recognize violations of word order. Certain "smart mistakes" such as "I falled" instead of "I fell," though incorrect, do indicate the development of a grammatical system.

Vocabulary development is directly linked to academic achievement. Vocabulary size and the kinds of words children know depend at least in part on experience. By age five, most children will know about 5,000 words (Anglin, 1993), often the most frequent words in their native language. Having an adequate vocabulary does not imply knowing a particular set of words but rather learning a sufficient *number* of words to represent the various concepts that are age and setting appropriate. Children also must learn the concepts behind the words. To do so, they need opportunities to expand their familiarity with vocabulary domains and to understand the relationships of words in those domains.

Language for use in social interaction, word play, phonological awareness and a growing vocabulary all support the development of fluency and accuracy in speaking, listening, reading and writing.

Rules of Interaction

Preschoolers need to feel confident speaking, whether they use standard English, a nonstandard dialect of English or some other language. Appropriate and expected modes of speaking and listening may differ widely from school to home and may be complicated further by cultural differences. A general respect for language differences and social rules of school interaction is critical for children's willingness to talk — and talk is critical to academic success. Specifically, we expect preschool children to:

◆ know and be able to describe rules for school interactions (for example, using "inside" voices, taking turns, raising a hand to speak); and

◆ learn rules for polite interactions (for example, saying "please" and "thank you").

Preschool Standards

Standard 1: *Habits*
- Talking a Lot — pg. 48
- Talking to One's Self — pg. 58
- Conversing at Length on a Topic — pg. 60
- Discussing Books — pg. 64

Standard 2: *Kinds of Talk and Resulting Genres*
- Narrative — pg. 74
- Explaining and Seeking Information — pg. 82
- Getting Things Done — pg. 90
- Producing and Responding to Performances — pg. 94

Standard 3: *Language Use and Conventions*
- Rules of Interaction — pg. 100
- Word Play, Phonological Awareness and Language Awareness — pg. 104
- Vocabulary and Word Choice — pg. 112

Preschool: Standard 3/Commentary on Student Performances — 101 —

Are Dinosaurs Extinct?

Standard 3: Language Use and Conventions
Rules of Interaction

◆ Know and be able to describe rules for school interactions (for example, using "inside" voices, taking turns, raising a hand to speak)

In a small-group setting, these preschool children are talking about what they remember about dinosaurs. The children are eager to share what they remember, and the teacher has to remind them to listen to each other. The conversation continues in a free-wheeling fashion. Later on, Evie, with her back to the camera, responds to the teacher's question about whether or not mammoths are extinct, too. She says, "Yeah, my mom said they are, and I saw one in a picture, and do you know what I saw? A mammoth with . . ." when she is interrupted by Alex, who is sitting to her right.

As Alex says, "I was watching it on TV because they were trying to get . . . ," Evie objects, reminding Alex of the rules of interaction when she says, "I'm talking."

The images and commentary in this section refer to performances available on the accompanying CD-ROMs.

New Standards

Alex's Spill

Standard 3: Language Use and Conventions

Rules of Interaction

- Know and be able to describe rules for school interactions

When he has an accident at the snack table, Alex indicates that he is aware of the school rule regarding cleaning up spills. He gets some assistance from Jeffrey, a classmate. Children in this room clearly are learning polite rules of interaction when, at the beginning of this segment, an unknown child can be heard making a request, "Please pass the water."

In the process of reaching for cookies on the snack tray, Alex spills his juice. He turns toward his teacher, telling her, "Kathy, I spilled my juice."

Kathy responds with the question: "What do we do when we spill the juice?"

Alex replies, "Clean it up."

Another child gives the details of the routine, saying, "Get a paper towel, and clean it up."

As Alex wipes up the spill, Jeffrey lifts the cookie tray out of the way.

One of the children says, "Jeffrey, don't take that."

Alex explains Jeffrey's actions when he responds, "Yeah, because I spilled, and I have to clean it up still."

"All by yourself," pronounces the child.

"Well, I need help," Alex responds.

Research Perspectives

"Preschools should help children to learn, think and talk about new domains of knowledge."

From Burns, M., Griffin, P. and Snow, C., eds. (1999). *Starting Out Right: A Guide to Promoting Children's Reading Success.* Washington, D.C.: National Academy Press, 44.

Word Play, Phonological Awareness and Language Awareness

Children's enjoyment of language and capacity to play with language enrich their lives as preschoolers and offer opportunities to learn things about language that will be helpful to them later on with formal reading and writing. The focus of this standard is on *play*—playing with sounds, words and word meanings rather than on *producing* particular words. While children play and experiment with words, they develop foundation skills for reading and writing. Specifically, we expect preschool children to:

◆ listen for and play with the rhythm of language (for example, clapping to the words in a chant or rhyme);

◆ recognize and enjoy rhymes (for example, nursery rhymes);

◆ play with language through songs, alliteration and word substitution (for example, "Ring Around the Rosy," "Five Little Monkeys");

◆ play with words and their meanings (for example, a three-year-old changes the expected to the unexpected, "Daddy, doggie meow!");

◆ experiment with unconventional uses of words (for example, "soda in my arm" for an arm falling asleep);

◆ recognize and enjoy metaphorical language;

◆ in a string of sounds or words, listen for and identify the first, middle or last sound or word in the string;

◆ in a string of sounds or words, listen for and identify the missing sound or word;

◆ try oral blending of familiar word parts (for example, "If I say 'hop . . . scotch,' 'butter . . . fly,' or 'valen . . . tine,' what do I have when it comes together?");

◆ build letter recognition (names and shapes only);

◆ recognize violations of word order;

◆ engage in sentence play; and

◆ transition from speech to print (for example, provide the words or label for a picture, dictate words of a story, or begin to use letters and words).

Preschool Standards

Standard 1: *Habits*
- ◆ Talking a Lot — pg. 48
- ◆ Talking to One's Self — pg. 58
- ◆ Conversing at Length on a Topic — pg. 60
- ◆ Discussing Books — pg. 64

Standard 2: *Kinds of Talk and Resulting Genres*
- ◆ Narrative — pg. 74
- ◆ Explaining and Seeking Information — pg. 82
- ◆ Getting Things Done — pg. 90
- ◆ Producing and Responding to Performances — pg. 94

Standard 3: *Language Use and Conventions*
- ◆ Rules of Interaction — pg. 100
- ◆ Word Play, Phonological Awareness and Language Awareness — pg. 104
- ◆ Vocabulary and Word Choice — pg. 112

Research Note

Children's knowledge of the regularities of language is revealed by their performance on various tasks. Dr. Jean Berko Gleason, using a set of made-up terms like *wug*, demonstrated that children who have heard only the singular nonsense form applied to a picture spontaneously produce the regular plural form *wugs* if shown two such pictures. Children formed this construction even though they could not possibly have heard this plural before.

Preschool: Standard 3/Commentary on Student Performances

"Buckle My Shoe"

Standard 3: Language Use and Conventions

Word Play, Phonological Awareness and Language Awareness

- Listen for and play with the rhythm of language (for example, clapping to the words in a chant or rhyme)
- Recognize and enjoy rhymes (for example, nursery rhymes)

Vocabulary and Word Choice

- Learn new words daily from what is being explored or read aloud
- Show a general interest in words and word meanings, asking adults what a word means or offering definitions
- Use some abstract words and understand that these words differ from concrete things, places or people

Like preschool children everywhere, these children enjoy repeating a familiar nursery rhyme, "Buckle My Shoe." In this instance, the teacher has printed it as a poem on a chart and points to the words as the children recite. She asks the children what rhyming words are. Fredric defines the term when he says, "It almost sound like the same sound."

She then asks the class to repeat the poem, this time by saying the rhyming words in each line in a louder voice, "One, **two,** buckle my **shoe.**" The class proceeds to read along as she directs their attention to the words on the chart. To give them more practice playing with rhyming words, the teacher then asks the children to whisper the rhyming words in each line. These preschool children have taken the first steps toward phonemic awareness.

Preschool Standards

Standard 1: *Habits*
- Talking a Lot — pg. 48
- Talking to One's Self — pg. 58
- Conversing at Length on a Topic — pg. 60
- Discussing Books — pg. 64

Standard 2: *Kinds of Talk and Resulting Genres*
- Narrative — pg. 74
- Explaining and Seeking Information — pg. 82
- Getting Things Done — pg. 90
- Producing and Responding to Performances — pg. 94

Standard 3: *Language Use and Conventions*
- Rules of Interaction — pg. 100
- Word Play, Phonological Awareness and Language Awareness — pg. 104
- Vocabulary and Word Choice — pg. 112

Smart Mistakes

Children's informal acquisition of grammatical rules has a surprising and endearing consequence called "smart mistakes." For example, when children understand that the past tense usually is marked by an *-ed,* they become more logical than the language itself. They overapply such rules, producing such forms as "hided," "goed" and "drinked." Eventually, children come to know the exceptions to regular application of English rules — but it's a process that will take years. In the meantime, adults can use an indirect form of correction, repeating the child's utterance with the correct form (for example, "You hid from Sammy?").

Generally, preschool children remain more interested in meaning than in form. They are more likely to notice a sentence is wrong because it makes a silly claim than because it is grammatically incorrect. (A child might correct "Cookies is yucky" to "No! Cookies is yummy!)

Grammatical Awareness in Preschool

Children will acquire numerous grammatical rules naturally, without formal instruction. They use many basic sentence types: simple declaratives ("The dog ate my lunch."); interrogative forms ("Did the dog eat my lunch?"); negatives ("The dog didn't eat my lunch."); negative interrogative forms ("Didn't the dog eat my lunch?"); and truncated passives ("My lunch was [or got] eaten.")

Preschoolers use basic English inflections, also without formal instruction. They can make plurals of words they've never heard before and form possessives, past tenses and the progressive tense *(-ing).* They make up new words using suffixes they have learned the typical meaning of, such as the agentive *-er* (a person who types is a "typer") or the adjective ending *-ly* ("lightly" or "darkly" as an analogy to *dirty*). They also make up new words by producing compounds ("plate egg" and "cup egg" for *fried egg* and *boiled egg*).

— Clark, 1993

It's So Chocolate

Standard 3: Language Use and Conventions

Word Play, Phonological Awareness and Language Awareness

- Play with words and their meanings
- Recognize and enjoy metaphorical language

During the fall, while engaged in a unit on decomposition of matter, the class had combined food scraps in a nylon stocking and then buried it in the ground. Now it is spring, and after digging it up, these preschoolers are examining the decomposed mass. When the teacher asks, "What do you see?" one child predictably replies, "Ucky and dirty."

However, another child, delighting in the experience, responds, "It's so chocolate . . . and brown."

This stimulating experience encourages use of descriptive language, in this case producing a metaphor.

The Importance of Word Play

Singing, chanting, and playing with the sounds and rhythm of language are the first steps toward phonemic awareness. Such play gives children a sense that language is made of words, that words are made of separate parts and that those parts are made of separate sounds. Preschoolers' enjoyment of and their willingness to play with silly verses, rhymes and alliterative phrases (for example, "big bad bears burp berries") indicate their awareness of language. When children feel comfortable generating their own word play, they are more likely to take the kinds of risks that reading and writing require. These risks include, for example, sounding out words or drawing on experience with words to guess the meaning of new words in unfamiliar texts. Such risks also include trying to spell words they can say but have never written before.

Preschool Standards

Standard 1: *Habits*
- Talking a Lot — pg. 48
- Talking to One's Self — pg. 58
- Conversing at Length on a Topic — pg. 60
- Discussing Books — pg. 64

Standard 2: *Kinds of Talk and Resulting Genres*
- Narrative — pg. 74
- Explaining and Seeking Information — pg. 82
- Getting Things Done — pg. 90
- Producing and Responding to Performances — pg. 94

Standard 3: *Language Use and Conventions*
- Rules of Interaction — pg. 100
- Word Play, Phonological Awareness and Language Awareness — pg. 104
- Vocabulary and Word Choice — pg. 112

Preschool: Standard 3/Commentary on Student Performances

The Water "Bingo" Song

Standard 3: Language Use and Conventions

Word Play, Phonological Awareness and Language Awareness

◆ Listen for and play with the rhythm of language (for example, clapping to the words in a chant or rhyme)

◆ In a string of sounds or words, listen for and identify the first, middle or last sound in the string

◆ Build letter recognition (names and shapes only)

A unit on water has been the focus of study for this preschool class. The teacher adapted the lyrics of the song, "Bingo," to fit the topic:

> *There is something we all need*
> *And water's what it's called*
> *W-a-t-e-r*
> *W-a-t-e-r*
> *W-a-t-e-r*
> *And water's what we need.*

In this lesson, the teacher's objective is to develop phonemic awareness. The teacher asks children to clap instead of saying the name of the letter *w*. Some children are able to do this. As the teacher increases the difficulty of the task by asking the children to clap instead of saying the first two letters, *w* and *a*, more children catch on and are able to clap instead of saying the letter names. The teacher continues to increase the difficulty of the task until the children are asked to clap instead of saying the names of all five letters, *w, a, t, e* and *r*.

The teacher then reprimands herself for making a mistake and singing the wrong word because she forgot to follow along and read the words on the chart. She noted they had sung "and water's what it's called" when the words on the chart actually said, "And water's what we need."

This focus on the text leads Jacob to notice two words on the chart that are the same. He points to the word *we* in the line, "There is something **we** all need," and to the word *we* in the line, "And water's what **we** need." He says, "These are the same." Jacob demonstrates print awareness, distinguishing individual words from all the letters on the chart.

New Standards

Preschool: Standard 3/Commentary on Student Performances

What I Wrote

Standard 3: Language Use and Conventions

Word Play, Phonological Awareness and Language Awareness

◆ Transition from speech to print

This is an excellent example of preschool children transitioning from speech to print. Ricky has drawn a picture — note that his name is written across the top of the page. The first step in the transition is allowing children to "tell the story" of their pictures, as Ricky does with the teacher. He begins, "When the caterpillar was outside, he looked at the clouds and the sun."

Note that the teacher encourages him to continue by asking, "And what else was he doing?"

"He was looking for food," Ricky replies.

Next, Alysa dictates a story to go along with her picture in response to the teacher's prompt: "Now tell me about your picture. Tell me your story."

The teacher writes down her words on the page as Alysa speaks, "It was raining, and then the ladybug wanted to fly. Then he landed in a house."

Note that the teacher asks, "Then what happened?" This type of open-ended question — "And then what happened?" "What else?" "Then what?" — is the correct phrasing for encouraging children to continue their narratives.

Alysa ends, "Then when it was raining, the flower was growing."

The children in this preschool class are all at different levels of transition from speech to print. Some draw pictures only, others add their names, and still more are able to approximate words with initial and ending consonants. All are aware of themselves as "writers" and are given daily opportunities to transition from speech to print.

Preschool: Standard 3/Commentary on Student Performances

The Restaurant Sign

Standard 3: Language Use and Conventions

Word Play, Phonological Awareness and Language Awareness

◆ Try oral blending of familiar word parts

◆ Build letter recognition

◆ Transition from speech to print

In this segment, the children are engaging in pretend play. They are operating their own restaurant and taking orders when they decide they need more customers. Angel suggests, "Maybe we can make a sign everywhere and then they . . . and then like if they see it then the teacher can read it and then they'll come over."

The teacher does not miss the opportunity to assist the children in their sign-making and help them identify letter sounds: "All right. What do you need for your sign?" The children say paper, and she asks, "What type of paper would you like? Do you want big paper, do you want small . . . okay. Let's go get it."

Though she is ready to help, the teacher allows the children to remain in charge: "Okay. So let's do it. You guys decide. Now, what do you want to write on your sign?"

"Um, we can maybe write, um, please come to our restaurant, we need more customers."

When they are settled, the teacher asks, "Angel, what word would you like to start with?"

She identifies the initial consonant for *please*, and then the next child attempts to identify the second sound, "/Pl/, /pl/, /pl/, /l/." Then they successfully add the *e* and the *z* to represent the final sound. The group continues, with the teacher guiding them, "Okay. Paheli, how do you, how would you write the word *come*? What do you think it starts with?" Paheli replies, "Um, *c*."

Before they begin, they pause to consider spacing between words. The teacher guides, "You know what, between words, you know what you do?"

"You put a space," one child volunteers.

The teacher agrees, "You put a space, so let's use two fingers. Do you see my fingers? So you can start right . . . after my fingers and that will tell us, you know, what'll tell us? That these are two different words." This type of growing awareness is just what you would expect of children transitioning from speech to print. They understand that words stand alone, that they are separated with spaces and that individual sounds combine to make words.

The children continue to sound out the words, segmenting individual sounds and then identifying each letter representation. These children actually are above the standard. Note that they have advanced beyond oral blending of word parts to segmenting and blending of phonemes. The teacher helps them break down the individual phonemes in words and then write the letters for the sounds. They identify the middle sound, the last and so on and blend them back together aloud to make sure they have a phonetic spelling of the word. This type of "sounding out" is above standard for preschoolers. Also note that the teacher does not attempt to correct the children's phonetic spellings, as in "plez."

These children clearly are transitioning from speech to print. When taking orders on their little tablets, the girls write letters or scribbles; however, their finished sign is quite readable and accomplishes their advertising goal.

New Standards

Vocabulary and Word Choice

There is a direct correlation between vocabulary development and academic success, so students' acquisition of new words should be emphasized from the start. Learning new words and the ideas and concepts associated with those words should occur daily. The most effective way to increase children's vocabulary at this age is by reading to them — reading (and rereading favorite books) every day. Specifically, we expect preschool children to:

- add words to familiar knowledge domains;

- sort relationships among words in knowledge domains;

- add new domains from subjects and topics they are studying (for example, in math, shapes like circle and triangle or in science, reptiles like snake and lizard);

- learn new words daily in conversation;

- learn new words daily from what is being explored or read aloud;

- show a general interest in words and word meanings, asking adults what a word means or offering definitions;

- recognize that things may have more than one name (for example, "Fluffy is a cat, the cat is a pet, the pet is an animal");

- categorize objects or pictures and tell why they go together (for example, group the following objects into toy or food categories: ball, skates, grapes, kite, bread, milk);

- increase vocabulary of verbs, adjectives and adverbs to exercise options in word choice;

- use some abstract words and understand that these words differ from concrete things, places or people; and

- use verbs referring to cognition, communication and emotions.

Preschool Standards

Standard 1: *Habits*
- Talking a Lot — pg. 48
- Talking to One's Self — pg. 58
- Conversing at Length on a Topic — pg. 60
- Discussing Books — pg. 64

Standard 2: *Kinds of Talk and Resulting Genres*
- Narrative — pg. 74
- Explaining and Seeking Information — pg. 82
- Getting Things Done — pg. 90
- Producing and Responding to Performances — pg. 94

Standard 3: *Language Use and Conventions*
- Rules of Interaction — pg. 100
- Word Play, Phonological Awareness and Language Awareness — pg. 104
- Vocabulary and Word Choice — pg. 112

Preschool: Standard 3/Commentary on Student Performances

Charles's Train Vocabulary

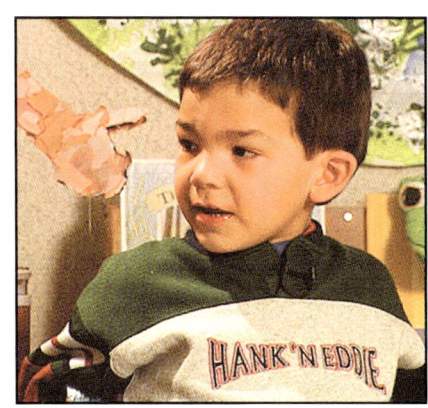

Standard 3: Language Use and Conventions

Vocabulary and Word Choice

◆ Add words to familiar knowledge domains

◆ Sort relationships among words in knowledge domains

◆ Add new domains from subjects and topics they are studying

◆ Use verbs referring to cognition, communication and emotions

Charles and Jerri, a visitor to the classroom, are engaged in a conversation about one of Charles's special interests, trains, a subordinate of the domain of transportation. Charles demonstrates his extensive train vocabulary by naming a variety of types of train cars: hopper, box, tank, automobile and coach. He indicates that in school they have begun a study of transportation and another subordinate of the domain, cars. Charles clearly recognizes trains as part of the transportation domain when he gives the example of having "seen" transportation on a television show. When he talks about the activities on the show, Charles uses a verb referring to cognition, *pretend*. Other interesting words in Charles's vocabulary include *collection* and *connect*. English is Charles's second language.

The conversation begins when Jerri asks Charles, "Tell me about trains. I don't know anything about trains. What can you tell me about trains?"

Charles begins to list different kinds of train cars, saying, "There are hopper cars . . . even, even box cars, even tank cars, even automobile cars."

Jerri asks, "In the block corner at school, do you sometimes pretend and use trains?"

"Oh, yeah," he says. "Sometimes we have trains, and now we don't use trains. Because, 'cause we learned about cars and transportation."

He continues, "I saw, I saw the transportation on *Sesame Street*. Because I saw them, I saw Big Bird and Snuffy pretend that them, them was trains."

"They were pretending that they were trains?" Jerri asks.

"Yeah," says Charles.

"How did they do that?" she wonders.

"Oh, them just got a train, a little train collection. And them connect the cars in the train. Then them see that them can play. And then them pretend that them can be a train," Charles says. But he warns, "And even, even, there's something wrong."

"What's wrong?" Jerri asks.

"Snuffy and Big Bird, them had a wagon for them coaches," he says.

Jerri laughs and asks, "Why did they need a wagon?"

"Because, because there was, was a little girl and boy was, was, was pretending that them wanted to go on the train with Snuffy and Big Bird was playing," Charles explains.

"Okay," she says.

Charles resolves the story by saying, "So them got a wagon for them coaches."

Building Knowledge Domains

A knowledge "domain" encompasses a set of words that may be classified further into categories with subordinate terms. For instance, a knowledge domain might be transportation, while a subordinate within that might be boats. "Object-level" terms for boats might be *ferry, canoe, rowboat* or *tanker*. It is important for children to develop a lexicon that includes many different domains or kinds of words. Some of these were acquired by children when they were infants or toddlers, such as the typical sounds made by animals (*moo* and *baa*). Children arrive at preschool typically knowing terms in the following domains:

People: babysitter's, relative's, teacher's and own name; *doctor; cowboy; clown*; etc.

Animals: typical pets (*cat, dog*) as well as zoo animals and farm animals

Games or routines: greetings (*hello, hi*); farewells; polite phrases (*please, thank you, no thanks*); games like *hide and seek* and *peekaboo*

Body parts and functions: common body parts, some still in baby talk (*tummy*) or euphemisms (*tinkle*)

Clothing: clothing worn, as well as manipulatable parts (*buttons, zippers,* etc.)

Food: vegetables (*corn, carrot*); fruit (*apple*); drink (*milk, juice*)

Household: rooms, parts of rooms (*ceiling, wall*), appliances, furniture, objects, toys

Classroom: *cubby, snack, mat, playdough*

Outside world: destinations (*the beach, downtown, gas station*), as well as typical outside objects (*sand boxes, trees, snowmen, sprinklers, sidewalks,* etc.)

Descriptive words: colors, common adjectives (*hot, cold, hungry, thirsty*)

Sound effects: *moo, quack, vroom, woof*

Grammatical words: The child can connect utterances using words like *and* and *because* and use the basic pronouns and reflexive pronouns (*myself*), helping verbs (*did, could*), a variety of prepositions (*about, inside*), question words, articles, and quantifiers.

Verbs: common verbs related to everyday activities (*smile, jump, run, pretend, kiss*)

Time words: *tomorrow, yesterday, later*

Vehicles: *airplane, helicopter, truck*

— Pan & Gleason, 2001

Preschool: Standard 3/Commentary on Student Performances

Philip's Orchestra Vocabulary

Standard 3: Language Use and Conventions

Vocabulary and Word Choice

◆ Add new domains from subjects and topics they are studying

Philip's preschool class recently visited the Pittsburgh Symphony Orchestra. He and a visitor to his classroom are discussing a picture he has drawn about what he saw there. As he gives the explanation of his picture, Philip uses the words from the new domains that he has been learning about.

Responding to the prompt, "Tell me about your picture," Philip explains, "Well, this is a percussion section. This is a brass section, and this is where the conductor stands." He continues his explanation by describing his intentions: "This is, was, this is gonna be, um, this is gonna be woodwinds, and this is gonna be strings."

Anna's Feelings Vocabulary

Standard 3: Language Use and Conventions
Vocabulary and Word Choice

◆ Use verbs referring to cognition, communication and emotions

Anna's vocabulary allows her to express a wide range of emotions and states of mind. In this segment, several brief clips from a long conversation with her teacher, Shari, are used to demonstrate her word choices. She talks about how amazed she was when her father pulled her brother Ben's tooth. Anna describes several different instances during which she felt jealous of, frustrated by and angry with Ben. She talks about being embarrassed when she confused Molly's mom for her own. And finally, Anna describes how she and Ben confused their mother.

"Know what?" Anna begins.
"What?" asks Shari.
"My brother lost his baby teeth," says Anna.
Shari asks for more information, "He did? What did he, what did you do with it after he lost it?"

Anna continues her narrative, concluding with her state of mind, "It was, it was loose. And Kim told me that Daddy put, took the tooth out right now. And I was so amazed."

In the next segment, Anna has just described how her brother fell out of a chair and was comforted by their mother. She is able to express the emotion she felt at the time and why. Anna also tells Shari what she did about it: "I was jealous that Ben got the attention from Mommy, so I got fall down."

Next, Anna describes an instance when she mistook Molly's mom for her own. She says, "And I was so embarrassed. It wasn't my mommy. My mommy's over there. It was Vickie, Molly's mommy. And I was so embarrassed and ran over to my mommy and went behind her back." Both Anna's description of her actions and her animated retelling indicate that she understands what being embarrassed means.

Anna describes the highs and lows of playing with her brother: "It kind of makes me frustrated so I tell Ben to stop it when he says, 'Okay.' He says, 'Can I make something for you?' and I said, 'Sure.' "

Shari draws on her previous conversations with Anna when she says, "Yeah, you like to play with your brother. I know that."

Anna responds, expressing another emotion she has felt in these situations, "Sometimes it's like I don't. It's like I, sometimes I'm angry at him, and sometimes I don't feel like playing with him."

In the final segment, Anna describes how she and Ben played a trick on their mother, leaving her confused. She says, "And then I went into my box, and he went into his box. Ben dressed up in my clothes in his box. Me dressed up in Ben's clothes in my box. And when Mommy said, and she was so confused. I mean, we jumped out of our boxes and then again, but this time she didn't get a bump."

"Oh, my goodness!" Shari replies.

Preschool: Standard 3/Commentary on Student Performances

Insects and Spiders

Standard 3: Language Use and Conventions

Vocabulary and Word Choice

- Add words to familiar knowledge domains

- Sort relationships among words in knowledge domains

- Add new domains from subjects and topics they are studying

- Learn new words daily from what is being explored or read aloud

- Show a general interest in words and word meanings

- Recognize that things may have more than one name

The children in this preschool class are completing an author study of Eric Carle. Many of the books chosen have insects and spiders as their main characters. Through their readings, the children are learning new words in familiar knowledge domains.

The teacher asks, "What does Eric Carle like to write about?"

The children reply, "Crickets, ladybugs, caterpillars."

And when she asks them to give the domain name, "What were all those called though, the cricket, the ladybug, the caterpillar, what were they?" they clearly understand that ladybugs and crickets are insects.

The students also have added a new domain because of their reading. Note that one child in the group makes an important distinction, "except the spider." The teacher agrees and asks for more information: "Except the spider, the spider wasn't an insect. Do you remember what the spider was?" As the children try to recall the difficult word, she gives them a hint when she pronounces the first vowel and consonant sound, "/ar/."

With this help, the children recall the word instantly, "Arachnid."

New Standards

Benjy's Science Journal

Standard 3: Language Use and Conventions

Vocabulary and Word Choice

- Add words to familiar knowledge domains
- Sort relationships among words in knowledge domains
- Learn new words daily from what is being explored or read aloud
- Show a general interest in words and word meanings

Benjy is in a literacy-rich preschool environment and is on standard for vocabulary development and word choice. His initial writing attempts are age appropriate and include the usual scribblings and phonetic spellings, with an occasional word standing out that has clear sound-letter correspondence. The curriculum is so well integrated at this school that the opportunity for seamless rather than isolated concentration on vocabulary is possible.

For instance, the class is engaged in a long-term study of the life cycle, which crosses many disciplines, showing up in their science activities, reading materials, writing and even artwork. Their fiction and nonfiction read-alouds include stories about honeybees and pollination, they observe flowers and bees in the play yard, they make notes and scientific drawings in their journals, they enjoy and imitate the work of Georgia O'Keeffe, and they have even had a "honey-tasting" in which they sampled several varieties and labeled them with descriptive words.

Here Benjy is looking over several O'Keeffe watercolors of flowers and explaining some of his own work in his science journal. When looking at a particular print, the teacher asks, "This is a beautiful one, too. Do you think that's the inside of a flower, too?"

Benjy agrees, and when asked to identify the close-up of the flower part, he replies, "That would be the color inside the flower. That could be the pollen."

When the teacher asks about a colored diagram with flower parts, Benjy explains, "Yeah. And this is, these are all the parts."

Then Benjy turns to a page in his science journal to show another flower: "And this, I drawed this flower all by myself."

The teacher takes a closer look and asks him to identify some parts, "Can you show that to me? Tell me some of the parts that you drew."

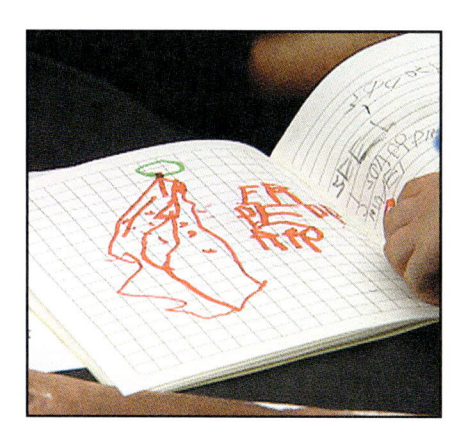

In a soft voice Benjy identifies "the, the needle" and says, "And the, um, these are the leaves, and these are the thorns." The teacher sees where he has written *t* and *h,* and then he goes on, "And, um, these are the petals."

Benjy then turns a few pages to show some of his favorite drawings, many of them germs. He explains, "This is a germ, too. This is a germ, too. This is a germ." Next, he comes upon a seed taped to his book, saying, "This is a kind of a seed," and explaining that he "digged it." After he points out "another germ," Benjy is confused when he comes across a new entry. He's not sure what it is at first, "What is that . . . ?" but soon identifies it. "Oh, that's a pepper!" he says. "That's a red, hot pepper!" Note that though out of order, Benjy has labeled his drawing successfully with all the letters for the word *pepper.* When it comes to sound-letter correspondence, this performance is above standard.

A rich, integrated unit of study has allowed Benjy to reach the expected standard for vocabulary development and word choice. He is adding words to familiar knowledge domains and learning new words daily from what is being explored and read in class. In addition, his science activities are allowing him to sort relationships among words in knowledge domains.

Defining *Busy*

Standard 3: Language Use and Conventions

Vocabulary and Word Choice

- Learn new words daily in conversation
- Learn new words daily from what is being explored or read aloud
- Show a general interest in words and word meanings

In this preschool class, the teacher takes every opportunity to talk about word meanings. Here, she gives the students practice in defining words such as *busy*, part of the title of an Eric Carle book they are reading aloud. She also asks them to explain what an author and illustrator actually do.

To begin, the teacher asks, "Whose books have we been studying this past week?"

The students immediately chime in, "Eric Carle."

Next, the teacher asks the group, "And what do we know about Eric Carle?"

One child answers, "He's the author and the illustrator."

When asked for more information, "What does an author do?" another child explains, "He writes the words."

The teacher then asks, "And what does the illustrator do?"

She is told that "he draws the pictures."

The discussion continues when the teacher suggests they revisit one of Eric Carle's stories. When asked to remember the title, the children are quite familiar with it, and all shout, *"The Very Busy Spider."*

The teacher asks, "And do you all remember what the word *busy* means?"

Brianna explains that it is "when you are working hard." When asked what the spider was doing, she says, "He was making the web."

This is a quality preschool-level book discussion. The children obviously have become familiar with this author, know the title of his book, know the main character and story line, and can explain the vocabulary they have learned.

Kindergarten & First Grade

Kindergarten & First Grade

Speaking and listening are important academic and social skills in their own right — and they help children become good readers and writers. Reading, writing, speaking and listening are integrated, connected skills that build one upon the other.

Discovering New Words and Concepts

Most kindergartners and first graders come to school bursting with energy and eager to please. Their sense of self is well developed by this age. Five- and six-year-olds seem to know who they are — and they plunge into their days with a breezy confidence. They try mightily to figure out the new game of school, the classroom rules and the teacher's expectations of them. With eyes and ears keenly attuned to the world around them, they are more than ready to begin school.

A milestone for kindergartners, in fact, is that they learn to work independently for some stretch of time. They can, in effect, put their natural need for attention from a caring adult on hold for up to 15 or 20 minutes — a long time for kindergartners, particularly in a group setting where so much is going on. They increasingly are able to focus their attention on a learning project or task, such as drawing a picture story, looking at a book with a partner or manipulating math cubes. This capacity to focus opens up the possibility of structuring classroom time so that some children can work on their own or in small groups while others get one-on-one or small-group instruction from the teacher.

At play, children at this age often roam together in small herds; kindergartners tend to play in groups of four or five children, while first graders tend to cluster in groups of six or eight. Children at this age still revel in dramatic play, elaborating on the familiar themes of family and adult activity and adding swashbuckling adventures of the latest blockbuster superheroes and heroines. The scenarios typically are more elaborate now than they were in the preschool years. Playing house is perennially popular as well; within the boundaries of play, children love pretending to be grown-ups. Outdoors, kindergartners and first graders play vigorously — participating in running and chasing games; swinging, sliding and jumping rope; shooting basketballs; and kicking soccer balls. This cooperative play replaces the more solitary play of earlier years.

These play groups don't necessarily function as teams. Kindergartners and first graders often jockey for position to play the best part or get the most chances to shoot the ball, for example, rather than cooperating for a common goal. They also explore and test relationships with their peers within their play groups. A typical example: "If you're going to be her friend, you can't be my friend."

At this age, children are beginning to be aware of how they compare with their classmates. They know who is the most popular, the most aggressive, the best athlete. At the same

New Standards

time, children at this age are getting better at thinking of people by more than a single characteristic of "the most . . ." or "the best . . ." They understand that people have more than one dimension.

Speaking and Listening: What to Expect

The most significant feature of language development among kindergartners and first graders is the enormous growth in vocabulary. Their eager and alert minds literally are picking up words and absorbing knowledge like sponges.

Kindergartners and first graders are more detailed in their talk because they are learning more and more words. They enjoy — and are very capable of — learning specific words related to particular domains, or knowledge areas. For example, *buildings* can be *arcades, cafes, churches, clinics, galleries, libraries, mosques, museums, offices, row houses, stadiums, synagogues, theaters* or *towers*, to name a few. By first grade, children begin making deliberate word choices to make their meaning clear; they ponder whether to use *backhoe* or *bulldozer*, for example, which is an important development. They like big, impressive and unusual words.

Like younger children, kindergartners and first graders continue to talk a lot about topics that are engaging and immediate to them. They talk about family activities and other topics that are important in their lives, such as pets, toys, sports and television programs. They also talk excitedly about new things they're

New Standards

learning to do and plans they're making with friends. They talk about topics they feel strongly attached to, such as their pets, toys or hobbies, and about new topics that ignite their interests or imaginations.

By this age, children can tell stories that make sense. They tell not only what happened, but also about the other people who took part. No longer do their stories seem jumbled and confusing, as the stories of preschoolers often are. Now, they can recount five or six well-sequenced events — although kindergartners, especially, are apt to stop at the climax rather than wind down to a true ending. "The nurse gave me a shot, and it really, really hurt!" This is where their attention frays and their bodies wriggle — a very predictable point. They often leave their listeners in the lurch, wondering how it all turned out. By the end of first grade, children can build to a climax and then resolve it.

By this age, children can define new words and explain all sorts of things to other students. They speak in longer, compound sentences. For example, a kindergartner may say, "I want to go outside 'cause it's hot," thus explaining his motivation.

Kindergartners and first graders are starting to understand the rules of socializing with others. Some know the social graces of saying "excuse me" and "I'm sorry," for example, while others still need to learn. Children at the younger end of this age range often do not know how to build a conversation with a shared focus; their exchanges sometimes seem disjointed. For example, one child may say, "Last night, we had a party at my aunt's house for her birthday." Another child will add, "My brother had a party, and we had helium balloons . . ." And the conversation will take off with the balloons until it veers away somewhere else. Children at this age often don't directly acknowledge or build on or connect to what other children say, although they clearly are listening and pick up the gist or a snippet. The transitional glue that holds conversations together is yet to be discovered. And indeed, first graders are better at responding to the topic than kindergartners are.

Most children at this age are comfortable speaking in small, familiar groups, although many still hide behind their mothers' skirts or their fathers' trousers when their parents are present. Familiarity does matter; like preschoolers, children at this age continue to talk more to people they know and are comfortable with. In kindergarten and first grade, though, children bond more readily with interested adults in any environment that feels safe. Teachers, instructional aides and parents in classrooms all qualify.

Kindergartners occasionally come up with startlingly good metaphors in their attempt to describe the world, but this ability begins to fade among first graders as their language proficiency expands. As they add more and more words to their working vocabulary, children have less need to use metaphors to make their meaning clear. In fact, they start to want to express their ideas with the "correct" words, rather than with made-up language. Kindergartners and first graders also should be able to produce rhyming words.

Most children speak very intelligibly by the time they reach kindergarten. While they sometimes slur their /r/s or mix up their /f/s and /th/s, as in "I'm firsty" for "I'm thirsty," this type of error is normal and not a cause for concern. These kinks in pronunciation even out by first grade. In fact, learning to read improves pronunciation. Many children experience "ah-ha" moments when they sound out words and make the letter-sound connection; for them, spelling makes pronunciation visible.

Developing Oral Language

Physically, kindergartners and first graders embody a lively awkwardness that, unchecked, can turn a classroom to chaos in a matter of minutes. Children need to learn the rituals, rules and routines that enable them to channel their buoyancy productively — without making a mess. This is not to imply that teachers should curtail hands-on learning activities. Rather, teachers can incorporate more active learning activities into their instruction if students know how to use and care for materials effectively.

Procedural talk, then, takes on great importance at the beginning of the school year and beyond. Teachers organize their classrooms very purposefully before the children arrive — and they should talk to children about how to use the room. This is housekeeping talk, to be sure, but it is also a good way to build speaking and listening skills. Teachers model these skills as they explain how to clean the paint brushes, care for the fish tank, set up the puppet theater, put away the books and writing materials, file their work in a portfolio, insert a CD in the computer, and so on. These conversations can introduce new words and concepts to children. Sometimes, teachers will want to talk through the procedures with two or three children — and then have these children teach others. Teachers don't have to — and shouldn't — do all the talking. Children develop speaking and listening skills by asking questions and teaching something they know to others.

In preschool, oral language development is the main academic focus. In kindergarten and first grade, students start learning to read and write — *but speaking and listening continue to be equally important skills.* Speaking and listening are important academic and social skills in their own right — and they help children become good readers and writers. Reading, writing, speaking and listening are integrated, connected skills that build one upon the other. Telling stories aloud, for example, helps children make the transition to writing a story. Acting out stories helps children understand why characters act the way they do. Engaging in book talks helps children learn to comprehend text. Hearing and using new words in everyday talk helps children add these words — and the concepts they represent — to their working vocabularies and working knowledge.

Teachers, then, should get children talking — *and give them core academic content to talk about.* Children talk more about topics with which they are familiar, but not yet bored. So, for example, a lively book talk is likely to result after children have read a good book two or three times and, perhaps, done an author or genre study with it as well. And children talk more about topics that interest them. Extended conversations are likely to occur, for example, as children create habitats for tadpoles and observe them as they develop into frogs over the course of several weeks.

And teachers should seed these conversations with challenging vocabulary words and concepts that are immediately — and repeatedly — useful to children for a sustained period of time. Nurturing frogs, for example, suggests *algae, amphibian, aquatic, croak, environment, gills, habitat, lungs, oxygen, swamp, tadpole* and *wetlands,* to name a few. Teachers can point out that *frog* has multiple meanings and uses, such as "frog in the throat" and "to go frogging."

In short, teachers should create opportunities every day for children to discover something new and make sense of it by talking to others. And teachers' own descriptions and remarks should spur the conversations. Open-ended questions and comments generate the most talk: "Why do you think the tadpole's tail is getting smaller?" "Tell me more about what you see." These kinds of questions also lead children to explore new concepts deeply.

Kindergartners and first graders should be learning challenging vocabulary in more than one knowledge domain. Through extended, intensive curriculum units on amphibians, transportation or the weather — or any other meaty, engaging topic — teachers can help children acquire handfuls of new, domain-specific words every day. And indeed, without a solid academic curriculum and purposeful instruction, many children are unlikely to encounter these kinds of words in their everyday conversations.

Teachers also can enrich children's dramatic play, a favorite pastime among kindergartners and first graders, with new ideas, experiences and words. For example, teachers can take children to visit a restaurant or two and talk with them in detail about the food, service and decor. Back in the classroom, teachers can model a different kind of play-acting with these new situations, characters and settings (and, of course, words): ordering from a menu, serving customers, cooking food, paying the server and so on. Students also can discuss and write a menu with descriptions of the food, create recipes and publish a cookbook, plan and create the decor for a restaurant, and discuss the calculations for determining food prices. With a little imagination and careful planning, any excursion can be fodder for play, conversations and learning.

Teachers can nudge dramatic play forward by modeling situations that children then can use in their own play. These situations require no extravagant sets or expensive props, merely imagination. For example, simply by holding a tissue over each hand, a teacher can create two puppetlike characters that enact a little drama, a scene in a book or a classroom situation. She can use different voices for each character, modeling for children how to use language creatively. Most children don't do this on their own; it's not an intuitive kind of play. But they pick it up quickly and go on, as children will do, to make it their own.

As in preschool, all kindergartners and first graders need many opportunities to talk. Teachers should build these opportunities into the school day in many ways, beyond the curricular activities. During the morning routine, snack time, break time, lunch time and other transition points in the day, teachers should make time to talk to children personally, informally, casually. They should be thoughtful about these exchanges and encourage children to talk. For example, teachers can comment on a wonderful drawing one child is finishing up or a new hair ribbon another is wearing. These comments may spark stories about a trip to the ball park or a shopping excursion.

Finally, teachers should pay particular attention to children who, for whatever reason, have a hard time talking or fitting in with their classmates. Shy children can shine in a special, private conversation with a teacher. Boisterous children can have the floor to themselves in an individual chat with a caring adult. All children care deeply about something — and in talking about that something, they come off as bolder, gentler or more kind than they do at any other time. It's up to teachers to discover that special something and give children a chance to talk about it regularly.

Full-Day Kindergarten? Yes!

These standards assume a full-day kindergarten class. Children in half-day kindergarten will take longer to meet the standards. Full-day kindergarten tends to allow more extended time for reading, writing, speaking and listening than half-day kindergarten does. In fact, a recent study, which is described in the book *Meaningful Differences* (Hart and Risley, 1995), found that children in full-day kindergarten achieve almost twice as much as children in half-day kindergarten.

Standard 1: Habits
Introduction

Standard 1 describes the kind of habits that children should develop to improve their speaking and listening skills. Talking in a variety of situations and for different purposes is important as children are beginning to write because their early writings are very dependent on their oral language. Children need to talk on a daily basis, learn to carry on longer conversations, self-monitor as needed and discuss books regularly. At this age, as at earlier ages, personal differences and cultural norms affect children's behavior. Personal differences mean that some children volunteer readily in whole-class discussions, while others prefer structured situations in which the appropriate type and length of talk is clear. Cultural variations also result in different speaking and conversation behaviors. For instance, interruptions are quite acceptable for some groups but not for others; some groups value brevity while others value embellishment and detail. (For a detailed discussion of cultural differences in narrative styles, see page 231.)

Children's spontaneous talk about topics of interest should be encouraged. Children can be expected to listen much more attentively now, and they may begin adapting their speech for dif-

---

Kindergarten & First-Grade Standards

Standard 1: *Habits*
- Talking a Lot — pg. 130
- Talking to One's Self — pg. 138
- Conversing at Length on a Topic — pg. 140
- Discussing Books — pg. 144

Standard 2: *Kinds of Talk and Resulting Genres*
- Narrative — pg. 152
- Explaining and Seeking Information — pg. 158
- Getting Things Done — pg. 168
- Producing and Responding to Performances — pg. 174

Standard 3: *Language Use and Conventions*
- Rules of Interaction — pg. 181
- Word Play, Phonemic Awareness and Grammatical Awareness — pg. 182
- Vocabulary and Word Choice — pg. 190

> Children can be expected to listen much more attentively now, and they may begin adapting their speech for different audiences.

ferent audiences. For instance, talking to a grandparent at the dinner table is different from talking to a friend on the playground. Talk begins to move beyond one-on-one situations and informal small groups. In kindergarten and first grade, children should take part in regular reading and writing response groups. Children engage in longer turns of conversation now, although their exchanges might seem somewhat disjointed to the adult observer. This falls within developmentally appropriate expectations. At this age, children's ability to talk at length on a topic still exceeds their ability to write about it. Most children have discovered how helpful talking aloud can be and make spontaneous corrections. Children should not be discouraged from talking out loud as they work their way through difficult assignments such as solving problems in mathematics.

Discussing books is an important part of children's literacy and is linked inextricably to their improved reading and writing skills. Reading and rereading favorite books is vitally important at this stage and allows students to study the way a particular author uses language. Since they are reading more on their own and being read to daily, students' discussions are deeper in content as well as more polished lexically and grammatically. They begin discussing longer and more challenging texts as well as comparing two or more books by the same author or in the same genre. All this questioning, predicting and summarizing works to improve their speaking skills as well as their reading and writing fluency.

Talking a Lot

In kindergarten and first grade, children's talk — which once primarily took place in one-on-one or small-group settings — now encompasses larger groups and audiences, especially in the classroom. In addition, children's comments and questions become more specific than the expression of basic ideas, needs or feelings. Language play continues to be an important part of their development. Specifically, by the end of first grade we expect children to:

- talk about their ideas, experiences and feelings;

- listen to others, signaling comprehension by clarifying, agreeing, empathizing or commenting as appropriate;

- playfully manipulate language (for example, deliberate rhyming, intentional or unconscious use of metaphor, name games like "Sue, Sue, bo-boo. Banana Fanna fo-foo");

- listen to and engage in sentence play (for example, manipulate and combine sentence structures at the syntactic level);

- negotiate how to work and play (for example, "Can I have the shovel? You can use the scoop.");

- ask or answer focused questions for the purpose of learning something; and

- share and talk about what they're reading or learning (for example, reactions or focused discussions after read-alouds or book talks).

In kindergarten and first grade, children transition from speech to print and begin writing daily. Sharing and soliciting responses to their writing should be a regular part of the writing process. We expect children to:

- share and talk about their writing daily (for example, in response groups during the Writers Workshop); and

- give and receive feedback by asking questions or making comments about:

    truth — "Is that true, what you wrote, about driving a hundred miles an hour?"

    clarity — "I don't get why you broke the bat. You didn't tell why."

    extent — "Okay, but you already told me about Snow White's evil stepmother once. What happened next?"

    relevance — "What's that got to do with a circus clown?"

Kindergarten & First-Grade Standards

Standard 1: *Habits*
- Talking a Lot .... pg. 130
- Talking to One's Self .... pg. 138
- Conversing at Length on a Topic .... pg. 140
- Discussing Books .... pg. 144

Standard 2: *Kinds of Talk and Resulting Genres*
- Narrative .... pg. 152
- Explaining and Seeking Information .... pg. 158
- Getting Things Done .... pg. 168
- Producing and Responding to Performances .... pg. 174

Standard 3: *Language Use and Conventions*
- Rules of Interaction .... pg. 181
- Word Play, Phonemic Awareness and Grammatical Awareness ...... pg. 182
- Vocabulary and Word Choice .... pg. 190

New Standards

Kindergarten & First Grade: Standard 1/Commentary on Student Performances

Tessa on Being Jealous

Standard 1: Habits
Talking a Lot

- Talk about their ideas, experiences and feelings
- Share and talk about what they're reading

The early readers in this group are asked to remember what it was like when they did not know how to read. They have just listened to a book about a grandfather who has decided he wants to learn how to read. Tessa answers a focused question that relates the topic of the book to her own experience. She expresses her feelings comfortably, complete with justification, when she says, "I got jealous of some people because I know somebody in this classroom that was a pretty fast reader . . ." She also paraphrases her own self-reflection at the time: ". . . why am I not just getting the hang of it?" Her response focuses on the topic of the book and the challenges of learning to read, and it is personal, unembarrassed and articulate. The K–1 students in this classroom have daily opportunities to discuss what they read.

The images and commentary in this section refer to performances available on the accompanying CD-ROMs.

Kindergarten & First-Grade Standards

Standard 1: *Habits*

- ◆ Talking a Lot — pg. 130
- ◆ Talking to One's Self — pg. 138
- ◆ Conversing at Length on a Topic — pg. 140
- ◆ Discussing Books — pg. 144

Standard 2: *Kinds of Talk and Resulting Genres*

- ◆ Narrative — pg. 152
- ◆ Explaining and Seeking Information — pg. 158
- ◆ Getting Things Done — pg. 168
- ◆ Producing and Responding to Performances — pg. 174

Standard 3: *Language Use and Conventions*

- ◆ Rules of Interaction — pg. 181
- ◆ Word Play, Phonemic Awareness and Grammatical Awareness — pg. 182
- ◆ Vocabulary and Word Choice — pg. 190

Encouraging Talk

Research shows that children who are corrected a lot talk less often than, and not as well as, children whose parents respond to *what* they are saying rather than *how* they are saying it. Children eventually will sort out the exceptions to the rules of grammar, often the source of their mistakes. Parents and caregivers can encourage talk by simply repeating what children say using the correct form, rather than telling them they have said something wrong.

Almost everyone feels encouraged to talk when they have an attentive listener. It's important to help children feel relaxed when they begin to talk; don't rush them, and remain stationary whenever possible if they are speaking to you. Quality "ear time" that includes thoughtful feedback is a must for young children who are just beginning to articulate their needs and feelings.

It is important to remember that many normal children have pronunciation difficulties until the ages of seven or eight. Pronunciation is important, but being concerned about pronunciation is *not* the same as being concerned about language development — especially not in preschool. Some children begin to stutter between the ages of two and five years. For some unknown reason, stuttering is three to eight times more likely to happen with boys. If you notice stuttering, do nothing. The worst thing you can do is to worry about a child's stuttering and let him know you are worried about it. More than 50 percent of all stutterers recover by the time they reach puberty without any treatment at all, and 80 percent of all child stutterers recover by their late teens. Teachers and caregivers also may encounter some children who are silent for a time. Some may have hearing impairments, which may interfere with the pace of their language acquisition. Other children new to a second language environment may observe silently for a period. These children's silence need not be a cause for concern as long as they are attending to the talk of others and are participating in activities while their own language begins to blossom.

Kindergarten & First Grade: Standard 1/Commentary on Student Performances

Cane's Beehive

Standard 1: Habits
Talking a Lot

◆ Talk about their ideas, experiences and feelings

◆ Listen to others, signaling comprehension by clarifying, agreeing, empathizing or commenting as appropriate

The beginning of the day in this first-grade classroom includes time for talk. Children are invited to answer the question "What's new?" When called upon, they have an opportunity to share a piece of news while the teacher writes out their responses on the board. It is somewhat surprising — given such an open-ended question — that all the children called upon give a brief and interesting highlight of their day. These responses demonstrate awareness of different types of conversational settings, as well as understanding of appropriate length and topic.

In this example, Cane relates his interesting observations of a bee in a nearby beehive. Though this anecdote is brief, Cane orients the listener to the setting as if he were beginning a narrative, even backing up from "yesterday I saw this . . ." to add ". . . there's this beehive." He then relates his experience of trying to shoo a stray bee outside. The other children in the group listen appropriately, signaling their comprehension with amused laughter and comments such as "I think he likes that screen door."

A second child gives a topic-relevant response, suggesting that Cane get a beekeeper's protective suit. "I think you should get some kind of suit so that you can block it from the bees," the child says, and he taps his forearm to indicate protection from stings. He goes on to explain that "then you can start getting honey from that hive."

Mariah's Writing

Standard 1: Habits
Talking a Lot

- Listen to others, signaling comprehension by clarifying, agreeing, empathizing or commenting as appropriate

- Share and talk about their writing daily

In this brief example, Mariah reads a story she is working on. The piece is about Cassie, who wants a cat, and Mariah speaks clearly, adding appropriate inflection to denote a new speaker. Her writing response partner then comments on a favorite part: "I liked the part where, um . . . because you saw you running home. It's like you see yourself running." The partner's response is keyed in to Mariah's work. At one point, he shuffles through her pages, and it looks like he is searching for the specific point in the story that he is referencing. These students clearly are in the habit of sharing and talking about their work daily.

Kindergarten & First Grade: Standard 1/Commentary on Student Performances

Austin's Planets

Standard 1: Habits
Talking a Lot

◆ Share and talk about their writing daily

As a part of their science curriculum, Austin's class is researching each of the nine planets. Even though Mercury is not his assigned planet, Austin is interested in Mercury and makes it the topic of a fictional story he is working on. In this segment, Austin demonstrates his ease with sharing and talking about his writing daily. He begins sharing his story by stating, "This one's the first page." He then reads his story about Tommy, who is visiting Mercury, "one of the hot planets." Austin stops reading just after we find out that Tommy has left his water gun in the spaceship and is now defenseless and trapped by fire. Austin shows his familiarity with the structure of books when he explains that his story is "dedicated to my mom," even noting that "I wrote 'mom' on this side because I didn't have enough room." Austin shares his illustration, which contains all nine planets, but when asked if his character will visit them all, he clarifies, "No, just Mercury."

New Standards

Sherry Analyzes Her Poem

Standard 1: Habits
Talking a Lot

◆ Share and talk about their writing daily

Sherry describes her plans for the poem she intends to write and then discusses the completed poem, "Flowers," with her teacher. Even though first graders increasingly are able to use written language to communicate, their ability to talk about their ideas still far exceeds their ability to write about them.

Purposeful talk between Sherry and her teacher helps Sherry focus her thoughts before she begins to write by directly articulating her plan to use descriptive words representing "the five senses and feelings." More specifically, she intends to have a "feeling" ending to her poem. (Following is the full text of Sherry's poem with her minor misspellings.)

Flowers
Little flowers
Pretty, soft flowers
Orange flowers
Diffrent flowers,
Old flowers,
New flowers
I love flowes!

When the poem is written, Sherry has another opportunity to talk with her teacher, who challenges Sherry to demonstrate that she followed her plan for the poem. Sherry replies, "Um, I used some of the colors, um, and I used all kinds of flowers, like different flowers." She reads the specific sentence that is her feeling ending, "I love flowers," and, with the teacher's help, identifies the senses of sight and touch in the line "Pretty, soft flowers."

Daily conversations about their writing help children grasp the link between their thoughts, spoken words and written words. Talking about their writing goals and their efforts to meet those goals gives children ownership of the process and a stake in working toward success.

Kindergarten & First Grade: Standard 1/Commentary on Student Performances

Talk about /ch/ Sounds

Standard 1: Habits
Talking a Lot

- Talk about their ideas, experiences and feelings

- Listen to others, signaling comprehension by clarifying, agreeing, empathizing or commenting as appropriate

- Ask or answer focused questions for the purpose of learning something

This class of K–1 students is making notes on the aspects of informational writing. They are working as a group while the teacher is typing in their notes on a big screen. The teacher pauses to discuss the word *character*. Michelle immediately offers the expectation that the word would be pronounced "/ch/aracter." When the teacher asks why, Michelle recalls that they have learned that *c-h* usually is pronounced "/ch/." When asked what this letter pairing is called, Zoe ventures, "Consonant blend," but when others disagree, Tatiana correctly answers, "Digraph." These children clearly are meeting the standard for talking a lot. They signal their comprehension by agreeing or disagreeing and offer examples when asked.

Now the group works on the distinction between consonant blends and digraphs (neither of which explains the /ch/ in *character*). Alex, Chelsea, and others give examples of digraphs and the sounds they make: "/sh/," "/th/," "/wh/," "/ph/" and so on. The teacher points out the difference — a digraph has *two* consonants that make *one* sound; a consonant blend has *two* letters that make *two distinct* sounds. She then asks for examples of consonant blends, and the children offer: "/br/," "/fr/," "/cr/" and so on.

The students in this group are able to talk about their ideas and explain their thinking, even on a somewhat abstract topic. They are able to follow the discussion and answer focused questions to learn the distinctions between different sounds. The teacher takes time to note that not all words fit into the rules of English — there are, in fact, some exceptions. Michelle, who is bilingual, compares the use of the silent *h* in *character* to the use of *h* in Spanish. She notes that it "doesn't make any sense" that in her native language the *h* is silent, and she gives an example: "Como en huevo."

This level of daily talk prepares students to be accomplished readers and writers. In addition, this segment exemplifies the type of self-monitoring that children eventually do independently in reading. As readers, children are expected to monitor their comprehension at the word and sentence levels, often talking aloud and self-correcting. In effect, the children in this discussion act as a group to talk aloud and monitor their reading at the word level.

New Standards

Talking to One's Self

By kindergarten, children begin to recognize the value of talking aloud. They move from a nearly unconscious use of language to purposefully articulating problem-solving strategies and self-correcting while reading aloud.

Specifically, by the end of first grade we expect children to:

◆ make spontaneous corrections to their own behavior, actions or language (for example, "John say, I mean *said*, 'I want a double scoop.' ");

◆ talk to themselves out loud to make plans, guide behavior or monitor thinking (for example, "No, no. Start over, not round enough for a circle."); and

◆ mimic the language of adults.

While they are reading we expect children to:

◆ monitor themselves at the word and sentence levels; and

◆ use a variety of self-correcting strategies (see *Reading & Writing grade by grade*).

Kindergarten & First-Grade Standards

Standard 1: *Habits*
- ◆ Talking a Lot — pg. 130
- ◆ Talking to One's Self — pg. 138
- ◆ Conversing at Length on a Topic — pg. 140
- ◆ Discussing Books — pg. 144

Standard 2: *Kinds of Talk and Resulting Genres*
- ◆ Narrative — pg. 152
- ◆ Explaining and Seeking Information — pg. 158
- ◆ Getting Things Done — pg. 168
- ◆ Producing and Responding to Performances — pg. 174

Standard 3: *Language Use and Conventions*
- ◆ Rules of Interaction — pg. 181
- ◆ Word Play, Phonemic Awareness and Grammatical Awareness — pg. 182
- ◆ Vocabulary and Word Choice — pg. 190

Research Perspectives

"... spoken language is the medium by which much teaching takes place, and in which students demonstrate to teachers much of what they have learned."

From Cazden, C. (1988). *Classroom Discourse, The Language of Teaching and Learning.* Heinemann, 2.

Conversing at Length on a Topic

By kindergarten, children know the difference between questions requiring brief responses and invitations to converse. In addition, their ability to make topic-relevant responses and their attempts to initiate and sustain conversation result in lengthier exchanges. Specifically, by the end of first grade we expect children to:

Kindergarten & First-Grade Standards

Standard 1: *Habits*
- Talking a Lot — pg. 130
- Talking to One's Self — pg. 138
- Conversing at Length on a Topic — pg. 140
- Discussing Books — pg. 144

Standard 2: *Kinds of Talk and Resulting Genres*
- Narrative — pg. 152
- Explaining and Seeking Information — pg. 158
- Getting Things Done — pg. 168
- Producing and Responding to Performances — pg. 174

Standard 3: *Language Use and Conventions*
- Rules of Interaction — pg. 181
- Word Play, Phonemic Awareness and Grammatical Awareness — pg. 182
- Vocabulary and Word Choice — pg. 190

◆ initiate conversations by bringing up topics that are likely to interest others (for example, a child approaches a girl playing Barbies: "Do you have Skipper? I do.");

◆ initiate and sustain a conversation with comments or questions through at least six or seven exchanges (for example, ask questions that extend the topic: *Child 1:* "Yesterday was my birthday." *Child 2:* "What did you get as a present?" *Child 1:* "A bike.");

◆ occasionally ask for or provide clarification (for example, *Child 2:* "What color bike?");

◆ solicit others' contributions (for example, *Child 1:* "A blue bike. And I got a helmet. Do you wear one?"); and

◆ mark new topics explicitly (for example, *Child 2:* "Do I wear a helmet when I ride my bike? Yes, so I don't hurt my head if I fall." Or, in a new conversation, simply, "Guess what happened on the slide?").

Topic-Relevant Responses in Conversation

Children in kindergarten and first grade recognize the value of continuing a conversation, as displayed by their willingness to contribute to conversations even when they have not been asked specific questions. Children often make their contributions in the form of comments that are rather loosely associated with the topic — sometimes resulting in a type of conversation that may seem slightly disjointed, for example:

Child 1: Me and my dad went fishing.

Child 2: We saw fish at the aquarium. Have you seen the jellyfish? I liked the really jumbo one.

Or, alternatively —

Child 2: Me and my dad go skating. We skate in the park on Tuesdays.

An adult would see "I went fishing" as the conversation topic, but a kindergartner might consider it to be "fish."

Teachers should encourage students to continue and extend conversations by asking questions and modeling topic-relevant responses.

Kevin on Bees

Standard 1: Habits
Conversing at Length on a Topic

- Initiate and sustain a conversation with comments or questions through at least six or seven exchanges

- Occasionally ask for or provide clarification

- Solicit others' contributions

Kevin's K–1 class is engaged in an extensive study of life cycles. The class has been focusing on bees, including observing beehives, researching and reading about bees, writing reports, making models, and performing a play about pollination. In this segment, Kevin demonstrates his ability to converse at length. He is very vocal and knows quite a lot about bees. However, he is socially adept as well — moving with the flow of conversation, answering direct questions, posing questions or musing aloud, and allowing others to contribute.

The conversation, mainly between Kevin, Brendan and the two teachers, lasts for at least six or seven exchanges. When the teacher asks which type of bee the students are to be modeling, Kevin offers some information: "And drones don't have stingers." Kevin also clarifies a difference with the queen bee's stinger: "Yeah. They, they can pull it back in because it's straight."

The teacher adds, "That's right. And the worker bees have the barbs."

Kevin shows his understanding when he agrees, "Yeah, the barbs."

When asked, "Can somebody describe a worker bee?" Kevin answers and solicits others' contributions by reasoning, "They're the only ones that can visit flowers and pollinate. Though we're not really sure if they're the only ones that can pollinate. Maybe the bees, and maybe the queen bees could pollinate?" The students continue with a discussion of the roles of the different bees.

Later, Kevin shows the importance of seeking clarification when he asks, "Oh, so you mean like they, they go to new, to another queen after . . . after the mate flight, the flight where they do the mate?"

At one point Kevin and Brendan disagree about the relative importance of the bees' activities. Kevin decides flying is most important: "The most important part of being bees, actually."

Brendan disagrees, "Not the most important, the food!" This then moves into a consideration of a bee's life span.

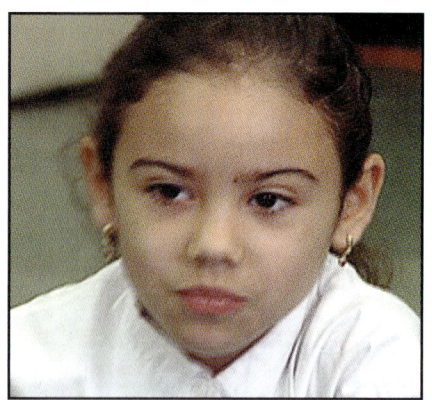

Talking Buddies Discuss What They Want to Learn

Standard 1: Habits
Conversing at Length on a Topic

- Initiate and sustain a conversation with comments or questions through at least six or seven exchanges
- Ask for clarification
- Solicit others' contributions
- Mark new topics explicitly

First-grade students in this segment are involved in a shared reading of the book *The Wish,* by Becky Winter. With the teacher, the children read aloud that portion of the story in which a wheelchair-bound character, Ellen, expresses her wish to join her classmates in a game of softball.

The teacher checks for literal comprehension when she asks, "What was Ellen's wish?"

Tavish replies correctly, "To play the game of softball."

In an activity designed to provide the children with practice in both conversing and exploring the deeper meaning of the text, the teacher says, ". . . think now of something you would like to do. Something that maybe you would like to learn or something you know how to do and want to do better. And you're going to talk to your talking buddy [about it] for a little while."

After repeating the instructions for the boys in her group, Kaila says, "I know how to do basketball."

Tavish says, "I can do basketball really good."

To extend the conversation and stay on topic, Kaila asks Tavish, "Is there another game that you want to learn to play?"

Tavish boasts, "Right, I can beat you [Nirjhar] in basketball. I can beat everyone except my brother, sometimes."

Nirjhar says, "I want to learn baseball because I don't want to play basketball. But I want to play baseball. I want to learn baseball and . . . basketball too."

In response to Nirjhar, Tavish says, "You know what you should do at the beginning?" Using gestures to accompany his words, Tavish continues, "You should bounce the ball and then hit. But then, when you get really good at it . . . you can play the real game of it. You play the real game. Then, if you have a sister or a mother you can throw it. But then you play the real game."

Nirjhar interrupts, "But T-ball is so easy!"

Seeking the information she lacks to understand the conversation, Kaila asks, "What is T-ball?"

Speaking with authority, both boys give a definition in unison using swinging gestures and words. "[T-ball is] where you have the stand and you put the ball [he indicates] and you hit [the ball] with a bat [he swings his arms]."

"Oh yeah," says Kaila, indicating that she understands.

Soliciting her participation, Nirjhar says to Kaila, "So, when you wanted to learn, um, basketball, was it hard for you?"

Kaila shakes her head.

Nirjhar pushes for more information from Kaila: "Was it hard for you? What did you do? In basketball, what did you do the first thing?"

Kaila asks for clarification: "Baseball?"

Nirjhar repeats, "In basketball, what is the first thing?"

Tavish interjects, "Bounce the ball! Bounce the ball, first! Just bounce the ball."

Kaila answers, "Bounce the ball, and I threw it into the hoop."

Tavish continues, "Then you do tricks with the ball. Then you play the real game."

Nirjhar counters, "Yeah, but you have to throw to your teammates."

Tavish admits, "Yeah, but then you play the real game."

Kaila replies to Nirjhar, "I was bouncing the ball, but I was playing by myself."

The first graders in this segment meet the standard for conversing at length on a topic. If you listen closely, you can hear the children initiate and sustain a conversation on the topic of learning new games for at least six or seven turns. Kaila asks for clarification when she doesn't understand what the boys mean by T-ball and again when she's not sure which game they are talking about, baseball or basketball. Nirjhar encourages Kaila to share her experiences by directly soliciting information about them. Tavish is not yet conversationally sensitive. He interrupts and takes turns that aren't his. Nevertheless, he is able to stay on topic and contributes relevant information at appropriate times.

Discussing Books

By the end of kindergarten, children use newly learned vocabulary to discuss books that they have read. This includes books enjoyed in read-alouds, partner reading or independent reading. In book discussions, end-of-year kindergartners use their own experiences to make sense of and talk about texts and to make predictions. They can give their reactions, listen carefully to others and offer related comments, and ask for clarification when needed.

Depending upon the complexity of the text, kindergarten children retell or reenact events in sequence, respond to simple content questions, and create artwork or written responses that show their comprehension.

By the end of first grade, we also expect children to:

◆ compare two works by the same author;

◆ talk about several books on the same theme (for example, "This book is like the last one. The kids are fighting, and the grown-ups want them to get along.");

◆ refer explicitly to parts of the text when presenting or defending a claim (for example, "No, he doesn't *like* his brother. He didn't want to take him, but his mom made him.");

◆ politely disagree when appropriate (for example, "Yes, he does, because they had fun after all.");

◆ ask each other questions that seek elaboration and justification (for example, "When did you think they were having fun? He was crying on the roller-coaster.");

◆ attempt to explain why their interpretation of a book is valid (for example, "He *does* like him. At the end he says, 'You're okay for a mutt,' but he's just kind of teasing . . . like nice.");

◆ extend the story;

◆ make predictions and explain their reasoning (for example, "He's going to miss it [the bus]. He's late again because . . . he's always late.");

◆ talk about the motives of characters (for example, "She is so angry about him losing her doll.");

◆ describe the causes and effects of specific events (for example, "Her snake got lost. It disappeared because she forgot to shut the cage.");

◆ retell or summarize the story (for example, "It's a book about animals and all the different places they live."); and

◆ describe in their own words new information they gained from the text (for example, "Some animals sleep during the day, like owls.").

Kindergarten & First-Grade Standards

Standard 1: *Habits*
- ◆ Talking a Lot — pg. 130
- ◆ Talking to One's Self — pg. 138
- ◆ Conversing at Length on a Topic — pg. 140
- ◆ Discussing Books — pg. 144

Standard 2: *Kinds of Talk and Resulting Genres*
- ◆ Narrative — pg. 152
- ◆ Explaining and Seeking Information — pg. 158
- ◆ Getting Things Done — pg. 168
- ◆ Producing and Responding to Performances — pg. 174

Standard 3: *Language Use and Conventions*
- ◆ Rules of Interaction — pg. 181
- ◆ Word Play, Phonemic Awareness and Grammatical Awareness — pg. 182
- ◆ Vocabulary and Word Choice — pg. 190

Jeremiah Learns to Read

Standard 1: Habits
Discussing Books

◆ Refer explicitly to parts of the text when presenting or defending a claim

◆ Politely disagree when appropriate

◆ Make predictions and explain their reasoning

◆ Extend the story

In this example, a combined class of kindergarten and first-grade students is discussing the book, *Jeremiah Learns to Read*. When asked how old he thinks the main character is, first grader Alex explains, "I think in his, probably, 70s." When asked to explain why, Alex refers to the illustrations in the text, saying " 'Cause he has white hair . . ."

The teacher then goes on to discuss the novelty of such an old man learning how to read, asking, "Does it surprise you that, uh, he doesn't know how to read?"

Most of the group agrees that it is surprising. Alexander, however, is a kindergarten student who politely disagrees. He then justifies his claim, explaining that he has already heard of another similar case: "No, it doesn't . . . because my mom read in the newspaper that there was a person who didn't learn how to read until he was 98!"

The teacher goes on reading and then asks the children to surmise information about a secondary character based on what she has just read. She asks, "Does Julianna know how to read? What do you think, Carlos?"

Carlos answers, referring explicitly to the passage just read, paraphrasing the character's words and then explaining his own thinking. "Well, because she said that you could do it to me, so I'm thinking that she doesn't know how to read. She wants, she, she wants Jeremiah to read to him, **to her,**" he says.

After a few more pages, the teacher asks if anyone can predict one of the character's next steps. Jimmy does not state explicitly *why* the character might do as he predicts, but he clearly understands it is because Jeremiah wants to learn. When asked, "Any clue what his plan might be?" Jimmy suggests, "Maybe, maybe he can go to somewhere, and someone can teach him."

At the end of the reading the teacher asks for ideas: "What do you think might happen if Julianna learns to read?"

Carlos not only predicts what might happen next, but also extends the story out into the future and explains how the story might evolve if his prediction is correct: "She'll read to, um, his brother . . ."

The teacher asks, "She'll read to his brother, Jackson?"

Carlos explains the effect of Julianna doing this: "Yeah, and then he'll learn to read and he'll, she'll tell somebody else how to read . . . and it'll keep going on and on."

In this rich and varied book discussion, students relate the story to their own experience and prior knowledge, discuss character motivation, make interpretations based on the text, make predictions, and extend the story.

Emma on Title

Standard 1: Habits
Discussing Books

◆ Refer explicitly to parts of the text when presenting or defending a claim

◆ Make predictions and explain their reasoning

This snippet shows Emma, a first grader, discussing the possible content of a book the class is about to read. She meets the standard for discussing books when she refers explicitly to the title as she predicts what the cow might wish for. Emma explains that "since it's called *Minnie and Moo Go Dancing*, I think maybe the first wish when the star came out reminded her about going dancing."

Wish Books

Standard 1: Habits
Discussing Books

- Refer explicitly to parts of the text when presenting or defending a claim
- Politely disagree when appropriate
- Talk about several books on the same theme
- Retell or summarize the story

These three first graders are showing a visitor a display of books and explaining why they are grouped together. First, Carlos explains that they have not yet read all the books: "Well, we haven't read all these books, but we read a few of them like *Amazing Grace, The Rainbow Fish* . . ." Emma and Gracie chime in to add other titles they've read, such as *I Wish I Were a Butterfly, Three Wishes* and *Clever Sticks.*

When asked what the books have in common, all three children give a different but accurate response. These different responses show that they are listening to one another and so avoid repeating information. Gracie explains the common theme: "Well, they're all about wishes, and they're all nice to read."

Emma points out that they all have rich language and illustrations: "They all have luscious language in them and they're, um, they all have, um, beautiful paintings."

Carlos explains that "some help people, some help, like *The Rainbow Fish.*"

Emma sums up their comments when she says, "And wishing is a very good, um, very good thing to have in our life."

When asked to name their favorites, all three children are able to identify their favorite book and tell why they like it (a preschool-level standard for discussing books). Gracie names *Fanny's Dream* and in the process summarizes the story and compares it to the classic fairy tale *Cinderella.* Carlos names his favorite book, *I Wish I Were a Butterfly,* and begins to tell about the book. A disagreement arises over whether the book is about a cricket or a grasshopper. Carlos goes on to explain, "It was a cricket and he, he, um . . . yeah, he doesn't like being a cricket. He doesn't like being a cricket . . . so he wants to be a butterfly."

Emma decides to consult the text to be sure that they are right: "Let's just see."

When the visitor asks, "Emma, what are you going to do?" Emma replies, "I'm going to see." She turns to the correct page, and all three peer in to confirm that it is indeed a cricket.

These first-grade students clearly have met the standard for discussing books.

New Standards

Tess, Talia and Carina Analyze a Poem

Standard 1: Habits
Discussing Books

- Compare two works by the same author

- Refer explicitly to parts of the text when presenting or defending a claim

- Ask each other questions that seek elaboration and justification

- Attempt to explain why their interpretation of a book is valid

Tess, Talia and Carina give a thoughtful analysis of Eve Merriam's poem, "A Lazy Thought." To guide their analysis, the girls have a checklist that includes questions about meaning as well as rhythms. Talia reads the poem aloud:

A Lazy Thought
There go the grownups
To the office
To the store
Subway rush
Traffic crush,
Hurry, scurry,
Worry, flurry.
No wonder
Grownups
Don't grow up
Anymore.
It takes a lot
Of slow
To grow.

The group begins its analysis. Talia states, "I think what they are trying to get at is a list of all the things where they're rushing." She then asks for clarification: "Did anyone get what they mean by traffic crush?"

"Um, yeah, I know," offers Carina.

Tess offers the first interpretation: "Like traffic is stuck."

"Oh," says Talia.

Carina elaborates, "Like, um, like, and sometimes the traffic like . . . 'cause there's so much traffic the cars bump into each other."

"Yeah, but don't dent," adds Tess.

"Half crash, but . . ." begins Talia.

Tess suggests yet another general interpretation: "Almost like, it's like, like, um, it's like the poem is telling you what you're going to have to do when you grow up."

A new line of inquiry begins when Tess asks, "Can you catch the rhythm of this poem?"

Talia asserts, "I don't think there's much rhythm."

"There goes [sic] the grownups / To the office / To the store," says Tess. The three girls refer back to the text, reading part of it aloud to answer whether or not the poem has a rhythm.

Subway rush
Traffic crush,
Hurry, scurry,
Worry, flurry.
No wonder
Grownups
Don't grow up
Anymore.
It takes a lot
Of slow
To grow.

They eventually decide that the poem has no rhythm. They use the following logic to justify their answer.

"It doesn't really have a rhythm," offers Carina.

"No, I don't think it does," agrees Talia.

Carina continues, " 'Cause if it did, um, it would like, we would hear, we would hear it. Like . . ."

"We wouldn't, um . . ." interrupts Talia.

Carina continues, "We wouldn't like, we would, we wouldn't say, 'Oh, it doesn't have a rhythm.' We would say like . . . "

Tess seems to finish the thought: "We would have to, like, say it over and over again."

"It would have to say, it would have to say the rhythm," notes Carina.

"Yeah," agrees Tess.

Talia elaborates on the idea that the poem has no rhythm: "When you read it, um, when you read it, sometimes it would have to sort of have in every sentence have to have a rhyming, rhyming word to, um, get, sort of get the beat into it. Because usually when you read a poem, like, there's lots of, um, um, rhymes in it, and it has a beat. But sometimes they don't always have a beat to it because they don't have rhyming words in it."

The girls' decision is questionable. There is rhythm in the middle of the poem, but the rhythm of the poem is irregular, making it difficult for the students to recognize.

Talia shifts the conversation, implying a question as she gestures with her hands in a back-and-forth, swishing motion. She asks, "What are they, um, using the 'Subway rush / Traffic crush, / Hurry, scurry, / Worry, flurry?' Um, what are they, what are, they're, they're off to work or they're working at their jobs, or . . ."

"That's how they get to work," replies Tess.

"Yep," Talia agrees and continues, "it also reminds me of, do you remember when we went to the multimedia?"

Tess remembers: "Um-hum, yeah."

Talia continues, remembering the previous experience: "And, um, you know Luka?"

Tess indicates that she is following her, saying, "Yeah."

The poem has reminded Talia of a book on the same topic: "And Luka's mom came in, and she wrote that book *Rush Hour*?"

"Yeah, *Rush Hour*," says Tess.

Talia goes on, "And the words . . ."

Tess seems to quote the book, " 'Wake up, wake up,' you know."

"They were like rush, rush," concludes Talia.

Nirjhar Retells the Story

Standard 1: Habits
Discussing Books

- Retell or summarize the story
- Refer explicitly to parts of the text

Nirjhar, Sherry, Kaila and Vicki are reviewing *Best Wishes for Eddie,* by Judy Nayer. They discuss the relationships among the characters and make predictions about the ending because they have not yet read the final chapter. In this segment, Nirjhar begins their discussion by recounting the events of the first chapter. He knows the story well and is able to highlight the important events as he pages through the book. His retelling is made more specific by direct quotes from the text: "Then they, um, opened the door and Ben said, 'What's up?' and Eddie says, 'Buenos tardes, muchachos.' " He sets the stage for the party to celebrate the "30th anniversaries *[sic]* of Eddie's bodega," which is the focus of the plot in this book. This kind of retelling helps first-grade children both confirm and correct their comprehension of books they have read independently and expand their pool of ideas about the text.

Standard 2: Kinds of Talk and Resulting Genres
Introduction

In kindergarten and first grade, children engage in a variety of genres to manage their activities, school, playtime and social interactions. Standard 2 identifies four genres: narrative, explaining and seeking information, getting things done, and producing and responding to performances.

Kindergarten and first-grade children are able to tell longer stories with more events in chronological order orally than they can in writing. They should be able to recount personal experiences with a causally linked chain of events in an interesting manner. Fictional narratives, in general, are more difficult, and any judgment of these should be more forgiving. Dramatic play and formal sharing continue to be good settings for narratives.

Children also advance in their abilities to seek and explain information. For the first time, they may be asked to produce school reports on particular topics, so their efforts must be more organized and involve visits to the library. In these situations, describing and explaining things now requires children to leave out extraneous information, broaden their descriptions and include visual aids. Kindergarten and first-grade children can give and receive directions for simple tasks, but now they also can draw on their experiences and their conceptual ability to provide directions to a place out of sight. This requires memory and an understanding of space and distance concepts. When solving problems together, they give more elaborate reasons for their actions or opinions. And they may support their opinions or arguments, but usually in a one-sided fashion.

Producing and responding to performances is important at this age. Children's own performances might include acting a part in a short play or reciting a poem before the class. Performances also can focus on students' own writing as they give author readings and offer quality responses to others' readings.

Kindergarten & First-Grade Standards

Standard 1: *Habits*
- ◆ Talking a Lot   pg. 130
- ◆ Talking to One's Self   pg. 138
- ◆ Conversing at Length on a Topic   pg. 140
- ◆ Discussing Books   pg. 144

Standard 2: *Kinds of Talk and Resulting Genres*
- ◆ Narrative   pg. 152
- ◆ Explaining and Seeking Information   pg. 158
- ◆ Getting Things Done   pg. 168
- ◆ Producing and Responding to Performances   pg. 174

Standard 3: *Language Use and Conventions*
- ◆ Rules of Interaction   pg. 181
- ◆ Word Play, Phonemic Awareness and Grammatical Awareness   pg. 182
- ◆ Vocabulary and Word Choice   pg. 190

Narrative

By now, children should require little or no adult prompting to complete a narrative. Their ability to put events in chronological order increases, and their level of detail should go beyond basic information and response. At this age, children can learn techniques to make their narratives more interesting.

Kindergarten & First-Grade Standards

Standard 1: *Habits*
- Talking a Lot — pg. 130
- Talking to One's Self — pg. 138
- Conversing at Length on a Topic — pg. 140
- Discussing Books — pg. 144

Standard 2: *Kinds of Talk and Resulting Genres*
- Narrative — pg. 152
- Explaining and Seeking Information — pg. 158
- Getting Things Done — pg. 168
- Producing and Responding to Performances — pg. 174

Standard 3: *Language Use and Conventions*
- Rules of Interaction — pg. 181
- Word Play, Phonemic Awareness and Grammatical Awareness — pg. 182
- Vocabulary and Word Choice — pg. 190

By providing more orientation; marking a deliberate decision to tell an important event out of sequence; and including quotes, evaluation or reflection, and more references to motivation, they become more adept with narratives. They tend to end their narratives before the climax, so resolutions require special attention.

Specifically, by the end of first grade we expect children to:

- independently give a detailed narrative account of an experience in which the actual sequence of numerous events is clear.

Kindergarten and first-grade children should learn to include these elements for telling more interesting and varied narratives:

- solicit and/or engage the listener's attention directly or indirectly before going into the full account (for example, a five-year-old starts, "Know what?"; a six-year-old says, "I broke my arm" before beginning the account of the accident.);

- orient the listener to the setting (people, objects and events) using concrete details, transition words and time words (for example, "Last night my mom and me saw a fire!");

- describe information and evaluate or reflect on it (for example, "I reached up there and my thumb got caught in the mousetrap. It really scared me, and I jumped off the stool.");

- develop characters by portraying themselves as one or by talking about another character's goals and motivations (for example, "She wanted to go home, so she said, 'I'm sick.' ");

- include quotations (for example, "Dad said, 'That's a whopper!' ");

- build the sequence of events to a climax and comment on how things were resolved; or

- mark the end of the story directly or with a coda to bring the impact of the past experience up to the present time (for example, "Do you want to sign my cast? I have to have it on for six weeks.").

Story of a Play

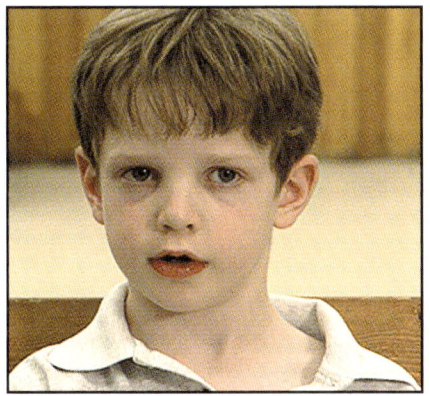

Standard 2: Kinds of Talk and Resulting Genres
Narrative

- Independently give a detailed narrative account of an experience

- Solicit and/or engage the listener's attention directly or indirectly before going into the full account

- Orient the listener to the setting

- Describe information and evaluate or reflect on it

- Develop characters by portraying themselves as one or by talking about another character's goals and motivations

- Include quotations

- Build the sequence of events and comment on how things were resolved

- Mark the end of the story directly or with a coda

The images and commentary in this section refer to performances available on the accompanying CD-ROMs.

Alex was asked to tell about the play he is rehearsing. In his response, he gives an excellent narrative account, which is actually a retelling of a play. This type of retelling is often more difficult than a narrative about a personal experience.

Alex begins with a one-sentence summary: "It's, um, about this flower that needs to be pollinated in a haunted house." This sentence engages the listener's attention and orients the listener to the setting. Alex accurately recounts the sequence of numerous events, including quotations from the characters.

"This little boy who has two friends, and they're on their way to the beach. And then they see this house, and they're surprised because they've never seen it before. So then they go inside, and the ghost opens the door and says, 'What do you want?' So then he says, 'May I use your bathroom?' And then he goes inside the bathroom, finds a flower, and the flower starts singing, 'Hallelujah.' So then he . . . the flower tells him his problem. Then he says, 'We . . . you are . . . I'm going to go out and find a flower just like him because he needs to be pollinated.' So then he sees some bats, so the bats say, 'Um, be careful,' and then the other one says, 'We'll be counting on you.' And then the ghost says, 'Stop.' So then he slides down the banister, and he tells his friends about it. And they go into a rain forest and find another flower and dig it out and put it in a box. Then they go back to the haunted house and put it inside, next to the other flower. And then the bees and the butterflies they found in the rain forest help pollinate."

Alex retells the events, concentrating the important information about the problem up front and even including the subjective response of the bats, "We'll be counting on you." Alex is able to build the sequence of events, explaining that after the flower was pollinated, they needed to get safely away from the house, despite the ghosts. He relates the trick of causing the ghost to sneeze with pollen and then aptly describes the resolution and the ghost's contrite response: "The ghost says, 'Stop, please, I . . .' and then the, and then, um, the little boy says, um, 'Okay, we'll stop if you promise to treat nature with care.' And then the ghost says, 'We promise.' " Alex then goes on to end the narrative by bringing the listener back to the present context, that of rehearsing the play: "And then everybody comes out for a bow, and we sing a few songs."

Emma's Fight with Her Brother

Standard 2: Kinds of Talk and Resulting Genres

Narrative

- Independently give a detailed narrative account of an experience

- Solicit and/or engage the listener's attention directly or indirectly before going into the full account

- Orient the listener to the setting

- Describe information and evaluate or reflect on it

- Include quotations

- Build the sequence of events and comment on how things were resolved

- Mark the end of the story directly or with coda

Emma independently gives an account of an experience with her brother. She begins by engaging the listener's attention and orienting the listener to the setting: "When I told my brother, one night when he was in my room and playing with me . . ." Emma builds the sequence of events, beginning with the banishment from her room, then moving to the resolution the next night: ". . . he was in my room and playing with me. . . . I told him to get out. . . . And I told him to, um, never come back or look at me again. . . . And then the next night I asked him if he could come back in my room and play. . . . And I promised that I wouldn't do that again. . . . And I said, 'Sorry.' "

She marked the end of her narrative by saying, "And I said, 'Sorry.' "

Kindergarten & First Grade: Standard 2/Commentary on Student Performances

Stephanie's Spider Story

Standard 2: Kinds of Talk and Resulting Genres

Narrative

- Independently give a detailed narrative account of an experience
- Solicit and/or engage the listener's attention directly or indirectly before going into the full account
- Orient the listener to the setting
- Describe information and evaluate or reflect on it
- Develop characters by portraying themselves as one or by talking about another character's goals and motivations
- Include quotations
- Build the sequence of events and comment on how things were resolved

Stephanie, a skilled narrator, recounts her adventures with spiders and slugs. She orients the listener to the setting in the den: "One time we had some spiders in our den. And we had flies. And, um, when I was looking up at our light, which the spider web, um, when they were there" (she circles her hand around). Stephanie does a good job of developing herself as a character who is not fond of insects. She pauses dramatically and gazes upward before quoting herself: "I was, like, 'Oh, my gosh!'"

She builds the sequence of events to a climax when we learn that the spider is rolling up its prey. The resolution, complete with graphic detail, comes when she calls for her father to bring paper towels because "some of the blood was dripping."

One child signals that she is listening by commenting that she too has had spiders, actually "two or three." Stephanie then relates another incident, this time with slugs: "My sister accidentally tried to kill them." She takes care to note that this was an earlier experience: "I was like a baby." Stephanie continues to develop her character along the same lines, describing the slugs with obvious distaste and quoting herself: "Agh!"

New Standards

When Chris Was Five

Standard 2: Kinds of Talk and Resulting Genres
Narrative

- Independently give a detailed narrative account of an experience

- Solicit and/or engage the listener's attention directly or indirectly before going into the full account

- Orient the listener to the setting

- Build the sequence of events and comment on how things were resolved

Chris has been invited to share a brief account with his classmates. This is a daily activity, and Chris knows that an appropriate response is a short narrative that interests the group. Chris orients the listener to the setting by explaining that he was outdoors "a long time ago when I was five." He builds the sequence of events: "I was like going to go inside the door to my house. And there was this wasp coming out of my bushes. Then me and my sister and my mom was by the wall. Then . . . and we were yelling, um, for my dad. Then he came with the keys and opened the door. Then we ran inside and then the wasp went and *banged* on the door!"

This narrative is a succinct and articulate story of an encounter with a wasp. Chris resolves the story by telling us that all were safe inside, but he still adds suspense by finishing with "the wasp went and *banged* on the door!" Chris meets the standard for delivering a narrative account.

Research Perspectives

"Children acquire language for expression and interpretation — to share with other people what their beliefs, their desires, and their feelings are about. Anyone who cares about children, therefore, has every reason to care about how they learn language."

From Hart, B. and Risley, T. (1995). *Meaningful Differences in the Everyday Experience of Young American Children*. Paul H. Brookes Publishing Co., ix.

Explaining and Seeking Information

Children's efforts to seek information from books or conversations with others become more focused and organized. Descriptions broaden from physical features, location and position to multiple characteristics.

In addition, children's descriptions extend beyond themselves to include the emotions, thinking and intentions of others. By the end of first grade, we expect children to:

- seek or provide information by observing; going to the library; or asking teachers, parents or peers;
- listen to information and exhibit comprehension;
- request or provide explanations of their own and others' intentions and thinking, especially when asked (for example, *Q:* "Why is your sweater on the table?" *A:* "I thought I was going back out.");
- describe things by focusing on multiple characteristics (for example, "My friend John is five. He loves his cowboy hat; every day he wears it.");
- describe things in more evaluative terms, giving reasons for evaluations (for example, "I don't like the mailman. He yells at my dog."); and
- share information (without extraneous details) that is organized on a topic and supported by a visual aid (for example, children bring in a picture — or draw one — of their pet — or one they'd *like* to have — and explain why it is a good pet for the family).

Kindergarten & First-Grade Standards

Standard 1: *Habits*
- Talking a Lot pg. 130
- Talking to One's Self pg. 138
- Conversing at Length on a Topic pg. 140
- Discussing Books pg. 144

Standard 2: *Kinds of Talk and Resulting Genres*
- Narrative pg. 152
- Explaining and Seeking Information pg. 158
- Getting Things Done pg. 168
- Producing and Responding to Performances pg. 174

Standard 3: *Language Use and Conventions*
- Rules of Interaction pg. 181
- Word Play, Phonemic Awareness and Grammatical Awareness pg. 182
- Vocabulary and Word Choice pg. 190

New Standards

Kindergarten & First Grade: Standard 2/Commentary on Student Performances

Reporting Research on Bees

Standard 2: Kinds of Talk and Resulting Genres
Explaining and Seeking Information

- Seek or provide information by observing; going to the library; or asking teachers, parents or peers

- Request or provide explanations of their own and others' intentions and thinking, especially when asked

- Describe things by focusing on multiple characteristics

- Describe things in more evaluative terms, giving reasons for evaluations

- Share information (without extraneous details) that is organized on a topic and supported by a visual aid

In this school, many classes are studying the life cycle and researching bees. The activities within each class vary, but all classes are focusing on pollination. In this segment, the teacher has invited a group of researchers from another class to share their information with her students. Her students had hit upon a stumbling block in their research, and the teacher suggested that they confer with students in another class. The teacher first explains, "Alex wanted to know whether one bee alone could build a hive or whether it takes, um, a lot of bees and whether it's important that they're . . . that bees have so many different jobs inside of a hive . . ."

With his answer to Alex's question, Daniel meets the standard for explaining information. Though his delivery is faltering and full of pauses and "ums," he answers the question clearly and gives reasons to back up his statements: "Um, one bee cannot build a hive because, uh, if, if it's not a queen it can't lay eggs and, and the colony that it, it makes will die because, uh . . . only one bee could, uh, go out and get pollen and get nectar and bring it back to the hives." Daniel focuses on the importance of the queen bee, noting that without her the colony would die out: "And, uh, when the bee is, uh, not, uh, getting . . . dies, and no other bee is there to, uh, in the colony the whole, uh, colony will just break down." Daniel describes the situation in evaluative terms, surmising what might happen if there were only one bee and predicting what the outcome would be. His reasoning is logical and based on solid information.

When Zane asks, "How do bees make hives?" Daniel explains the cooperative process the bees use to squirt out wax, soften it and press it into the hive: "Uh, they, um, make a big bee chain like this and, uh, uh, when . . . when they hang on to each other's legs, that way it makes, uh, the, the bee wax come out of its abdomen and the other bee chews it up, and, uh, when there's a hole in the, uh, hive, they just, uh, put it, they . . . they put the bee's wax on the, uh, uh, piece of the hive that's, uh, broken."

In this reply, Daniel describes several characteristics of the bees, including their anatomy, formation while making the hive and cooperative strategies. Daniel relates information pertaining only to the specific question and refers to a visual aid of the bee chain. Note the specialized vocabulary the student has learned and adopted for his own explanations: colony, pollen, nectar and abdomen.

New Standards

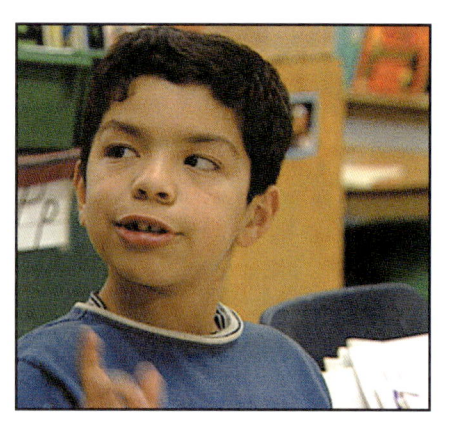

Carlos and Research

Standard 2: Kinds of Talk and Resulting Genres
Explaining and Seeking Information

- Seek or provide information by observing; going to the library; or asking teachers, parents or peers

- Listen to information and exhibit comprehension

- Request or provide explanations of their own and others' intentions and thinking, especially when asked

- Describe things in more evaluative terms, giving reasons for evaluations

- Share information (without extraneous details) that is organized on a topic and supported by a visual aid

In this segment, Carlos demonstrates his skill in explaining and seeking information. Carlos has been researching caterpillars and their transformation into butterflies. He is confused about some information that he has read about a certain type of caterpillar whose cocoon is poisonous. To clarify the information, he consults the original reference book and seeks help from his teacher. Carlos explains, "Now, this is where I got, I almost got all the cocoon information from this book."

The teacher asks, "This was your primary source of information?"

"For the cocoon," Carlos explains.

Carlos searches the book for the reference: "Not this page, not this page, ah-hah!" He points to the picture and stumbles a bit but then finally explains, "The queen caterpillar is the only one that's poisonous, and all the cocoons are not poisonous."

When the teacher asks, "And all the what are not poisonous?" Carlos attempts to explain his interpretation: "All the cocoons, only the queens' are poisonous, but all the cocoons are not poisonous."

The teacher tries to examine the text more closely, stressing that "the poison comes from the plant on which the caterpillar feeds in its Florida Everglades habitat."

Now Carlos understands and reiterates what the teacher has read. He describes what he knows in more evaluative terms, giving reasons for his thinking and checking to see if she agrees: "So, oh, like, so like . . . so I get it now . . . so like some, the caterpillar would eat poisonous plants and they get poisonous and the cocoon is poisonous, right?"

The teacher confirms his thinking: "That's right. For, like a bird or somebody who might think to . . . think they'd like to eat that chrysalis. Um, does that say here that's the only kind of chrysalis or the only kind of pupa [sic] that's poisonous?"

Carlos understands it now, stating, "Nope," and continuing excitedly, "No, I know more caterpillars that are poisonous."

Music for the Play

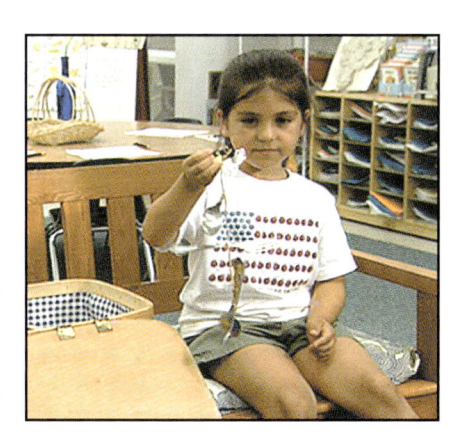

Standard 2: Kinds of Talk and Resulting Genres
Explaining and Seeking Information

◆ Request or provide explanations of their own and others' intentions and thinking, especially when asked

◆ Describe things by focusing on multiple characteristics

◆ Share information (without extraneous details) that is organized on a topic and supported by a visual aid

Tatiana meets the standard for explaining and seeking information. In this case, she is describing her own role as a stagehand and musician in an upcoming play. She does an excellent job of sharing information. She is organized, focuses only on the topic at hand and has brought instruments in to demonstrate. While Tatiana does not have a speaking part, she clearly has learned the story line of the play and knows when to accompany the action with sound effects.

Her presentation begins, "Well, we started on making sets in, for the backgrounds for the play and then we started doing the costumes and we're still working on the costumes right now."

When the visitor asks, "Are you going to wear any costumes?" Tatiana replies, "Um, not really, 'cause, 'cause, I'm not something that has lines really in the play."

Note that when asked about her role in the play, she uses vocabulary specific to theater arts: "I'm going to be a musician, a stagehand, and I'm, uh, going to do makeup on the people."

When asked to describe what the musicians will do, Tatiana gives a detailed description: "Well, we have different instruments that we made, like a triangle we made out of spoons and forks. And we also have this that we're going to use for flapping of bat wings. We have partners and we hit them and they sound like that. And the teacher that helps us with the music, she went to a nature store and got some things that sound like birds, like she got another kid a little, um, red thing and when you twist it, it sounds like a bird. And then this sounds like another bird, like. And there's one part in the play where a kid slides down the banister and we just got some blocks and I'm going to do that."

Tatiana focuses on several characteristics of the music element of the play. She names and shows instruments, tells how they were made or where they were purchased, demonstrates some tools for sound effects, and tells what they are meant to portray. Tatiana has shared the information in an organized and interesting fashion, without extraneous details and with visual aids.

The Neighborhood Jewish Community Center

Standard 2: Kinds of Talk and Resulting Genres

Explaining and Seeking Information

◆ Request or provide explanations of their own and others' intentions and thinking, especially when asked

◆ Describe things by focusing on multiple characteristics

◆ Describe things in more evaluative terms, giving reasons for evaluations

◆ Share information (without extraneous details) that is organized on a topic and supported by a visual aid

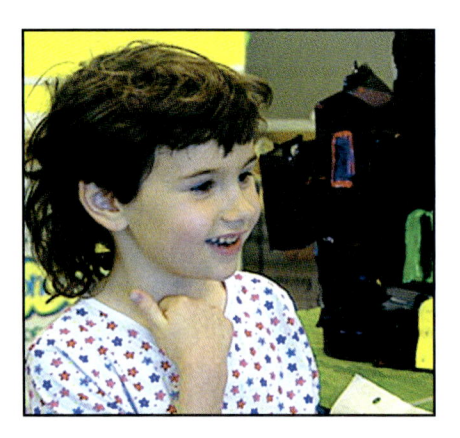

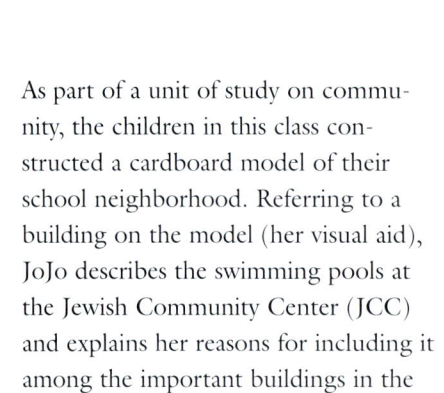

As part of a unit of study on community, the children in this class constructed a cardboard model of their school neighborhood. Referring to a building on the model (her visual aid), JoJo describes the swimming pools at the Jewish Community Center (JCC) and explains her reasons for including it among the important buildings in the neighborhood.

When asked what else might have been included in the model, JoJo describes what she thinks the JCC construction resembles: "To me it really looks like a swimming pool." When prompted to tell more about the swimming pool, JoJo describes multiple characteristics such as the size and temperature of the water in the various pools at the center: "Well, they have one for the grown-ups that's really cold. . . . I went in it . . . when I was in kindergarten. . . . And then we would have recess which we would go in the warm water. Once you jumped in, I'm like, 'Oh, it's burning hot!'"

JoJo provides listeners with a sense of time when twice she mentions that she is talking about a time long ago, ". . . when I was in kindergarten," and again when she says, "I did [go there a lot]. I went there ever since I was a baby for kindergarten."

When asked directly why she thinks the JCC is an important building for the community, JoJo communicates her point of view with words and inflection and provides reasons for her evaluation: "Yes, it is very important. . . . They make sure kids are safe and healthy. . . . They also set up programs for kids to go to. Like my sister goes to dance, and I go to karate there."

In this segment, JoJo meets the standard for explaining information at the first-grade level. When asked directly, JoJo reveals her thinking, describes multiple (two) aspects of the JCC and provides her evaluation of the JCC along with her reasons. Her information is organized, leaves out extraneous details and uses a visual aid to help her make her points.

Kindergarten & First Grade: Standard 2/Commentary on Student Performances

Handling Nervousness before a Class Play

Standard 2: Kinds of Talk and Resulting Genres

Explaining and Seeking Information

- Request or provide explanations of their own and others' intentions and thinking, especially when asked
- Describe things by focusing on multiple characteristics
- Describe things in more evaluative terms, giving reasons for evaluations
- Share information (without extraneous details) that is organized on a topic and supported by a visual aid

In this segment, Ariana reviews a photo journal of a class play with a visitor to the classroom. In response to the adult's direct question, Ariana explains her thinking about how to handle the challenge of memorizing lines and how to handle her nervousness before performing on stage. She describes multiple aspects of her experience when responding to a general question: "How did you practice for that play? It looks like it was a lot of work."

First, Ariana provides the listener with an orientation to the setting: "We practiced in the auditorium." Then she provides her evaluation of the experience: "And it was a little confusing, though." When asked why it was confusing, she gives a reason: "Because, I, um, just, sometimes I don't remember my part and stuff."

Ariana stays on topic and offers no extraneous details in this conversation. When asked what she did about feeling nervous, she provides her strategy and attributes it to her teacher: "I just took a deep breath. . . . That was my teacher's idea."

Ariana meets the standard for explaining information at the first-grade level. With the help of a visual aid to prompt her memory, she engages in a relaxed conversation with a new adult. She responds directly to questions, staying on topic without interjecting unnecessary information. She offers her subjective evaluation of the experience and provides reasons for her feelings. Ariana is able to name the strategy she employed to handle the situation and credits the teacher with helping her learn what to do in this situation.

New Standards

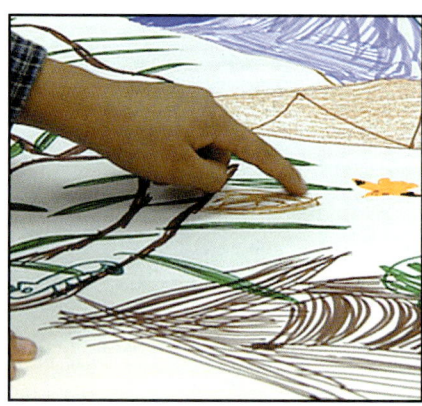

Lucas's Scenery

Standard 2: Kinds of Talk and Resulting Genres
Explaining and Seeking Information

- Request or provide explanations of their own and others' intentions and thinking, especially when asked

- Describe things by focusing on multiple characteristics

- Describe things in more evaluative terms, giving reasons for evaluations

- Share information (without extraneous details) that is organized on a topic and supported by a visual aid

In this segment, Lucas explains to his teacher why he included different types of Kenyan animal and plant life in the scenery he created to accompany a play he has written. Lucas meets the standard for explaining information because he thoroughly explains his thinking and intentions, describes multiple characteristics of Kenyan wild animal and plant life, and uses the visual aid he created to share information in an organized manner. His use of specialized vocabulary demonstrates a deep knowledge of the topic.

Lucas begins by describing his painting and pointing to various places on the large paper: "This is the dry grass because the sun is very hot and it dries out the grass." Moving to the other side of the painting he says, "This is Mt. Kilimanjaro with snow on top of it. Sometimes when I look at it, it looks sort of bluish and purplish, so I put different colors, different blues and purples." Starting at the base of the mountain and pointing to each level in turn, Lucas says, "Here is like very hot, and here, it gets cooler, then cooler, then cooler, then cold. . . . And then there's snow, and that makes it really cold!"

The teacher asks about the animals in Kenya. Lucas responds, "Here I have a chameleon in the tree. And this is a special kind of tree that only grows in Africa. It is a baobab tree. And this is a buffalo weaver and its nest. It weaves it and makes it like a circle. These two things are butterflies. They look sort of weird, but I made them to look like butterflies."

"Lucas, why are these things so important for your setting, these animals and these trees and this special grass?" asks his teacher.

Lucas replies, "Because if it just had the big animals that helped, that are in the story, it wouldn't, it would look weird without the little animals that it has in Kenya. . . . So it would look better."

"I see some ocean?" the teacher asks, pointing to a large blue patch.

He corrects her and elaborates, "That's a lake . . . with fish, shrimp and snails."

Lucas's teacher then challenges his reasons for including all these details in his scenery: "The one thing that I'm wondering is when you present your play, Lucas, and you have all these characters and your setting here, do you need these types of trees and the lake and Mt. Kilimanjaro there? Are those things all in your play?"

Lucas is able to answer, explaining, "No, but they look nice with the background to look more like Kenya. . . . And these are also a little important because they eat the leaves and without them they wouldn't be able to survive."

Lucas is deeply knowledgeable about the interdependence of animal and plant life in Kenya. This project and interaction with his teacher provide him with an opportunity to practice sharing what he has learned with his classmates and teacher. Lucas meets the standard for explaining information because he is able to describe his intentions, reasons and thinking for including specific details in the play scenery based on his knowledge of the topic.

Is It a Ladybug?

Standard 2: Kinds of Talk and Resulting Genres

Explaining and Seeking Information

- Request or provide explanations of their own and others' intentions and thinking, especially when asked

- Describe things by focusing on multiple characteristics

- Describe things in more evaluative terms, giving reasons for evaluations

Max incorrectly identifies an insect as a ladybug, but he does a good job of explaining his hypothesis. When asked, "How is that a ladybug? What would you expect to see if that was a ladybug, even a baby one?" he first explains his thinking based on common sense regarding size: "Well, um, they think that the size of it means how old they are." He then explains that this does not always hold true: "But on some creatures it isn't, that doesn't happen." Max then tries to compare the specimen to another creature whose life span and maturation he is familiar with: "And like a caterpillar, this, this is just like a caterpillar, but it . . . 'cuz you know how a caterpillar isn't, isn't, um, a butterfly." He repeats his reminder, stressing the question and waiting for understanding: "You know how a caterpillar isn't a butterfly? Well *this* isn't a ladybug! And the caterpillars form a chrysalis, and then . . . and then . . . and the caterpillars form a chrysalis to go into a butterfly and *these* form a chrysalis to go into a ladybug."

Max evaluates what he sees and explains his conclusion, based on his evaluation of the specimen's size, its position in the life cycle and prior knowledge. Though his assertions are incorrect, Max demonstrates skill in explaining somewhat complicated information, even referring to an illustrative example of the butterfly.

Kindergarten & First Grade: Standard 2/Commentary on Student Performances

Stephanie Lifting a Rock

Standard 2: Kinds of Talk and Resulting Genres
Explaining and Seeking Information

- Seek or provide information by observing; going to the library; or asking teachers, parents or peers

- Listen to information and exhibit comprehension

- Request or provide explanations of their own and others' intentions and thinking, especially when asked

- Describe things in more evaluative terms, giving reasons for evaluations

Stephanie demonstrates skill in explaining information, first providing her teacher guidelines for sensitively investigating under rocks and then taking it upon herself to inform her peers. The ability to speak with and explain things to peers confidently is important as students at this age begin to spend more time studying and researching collaboratively. Stephanie, who is not fond of insects (see her story about spiders on page 155), is mindful of respecting the habitats she is observing.

She begins one on one with her teacher: "Miss Gracie, um, when you, like, find something that lives under a rock, um, you should not, like, just drop it. You should, like, really just like, um, put it down slowly, or it'll maybe kill the animal, the little bug that's under it, or insect." Stephanie uses gestures to illustrate *placing* the rock back rather than simply dropping it. Miss Gracie is careful to show that she comprehends: "So you're talking about the rock? Oh, well that's something to be careful about."

With this affirmation, Stephanie is sure that her peers will benefit from the same information: "Um, guys, guys, guys! When you find . . . when you find a rock, um when you find something under a rock and you just drop the rock — don't do that, do it down slowly so it won't kill that animal, or bug."

Getting Things Done

In kindergarten and first grade, children argue an opinion, yet their viewpoint remains primarily self-centered. They can, however, consider the perspective and needs of another person, giving and/or receiving directions for a lengthier or more complicated sequence of steps. They continue to ask for clarification and take more responsibility for understanding information. Specifically, by the end of first grade we expect children to:

◆ listen to, comprehend and carry out directions with five or six simple steps;

◆ give directions that include several sequenced steps, explaining and elaborating when necessary (for example, explaining how to buy milk in the cafeteria or feed the class turtle);

◆ ask for clarification to carry out more complicated directions, persisting if necessary (for example, "How do I get the water bowl out? It's stuck in the cage.");

◆ use actions, writing or drawing to augment language (for example, the child draws a triangle and asks, "How can I get that on my tower? I want a pointy tower."); and

◆ engage in extended conversations (five or six exchanges) about a problem, with both sides presenting and listening to arguments and solutions.

Kindergarten & First-Grade Standards

Standard 1: *Habits*
- Talking a Lot — pg. 130
- Talking to One's Self — pg. 138
- Conversing at Length on a Topic — pg. 140
- Discussing Books — pg. 144

Standard 2: *Kinds of Talk and Resulting Genres*
- Narrative — pg. 152
- Explaining and Seeking Information — pg. 158
- Getting Things Done — pg. 168
- Producing and Responding to Performances — pg. 174

Standard 3: *Language Use and Conventions*
- Rules of Interaction — pg. 181
- Word Play, Phonemic Awareness and Grammatical Awareness — pg. 182
- Vocabulary and Word Choice — pg. 190

Kindergarten & First Grade: Standard 2/Commentary on Student Performances

Negotiate Recess Game

Standard 2: Kinds of Talk and Resulting Genres
Getting Things Done

◆ Engage in extended conversations (five or six exchanges) about a problem, with both sides presenting and listening to arguments and solutions

This segment shows two first-grade boys using language to get things done. In a spontaneous conversation around the work table, they negotiate what ball game they will play at recess, considering each other's perspective to come to a compromise.

Kevin begins by exclaiming, "Yeah, I can finally do dodge ball!"

But Brendan has other plans and attempts to solicit backers for his choice: "No, handball. Who wants handball raise your hand?"

In an attempt to influence Brendan, Kevin suggests that perhaps his finding the ball should carry some weight: "I found the dodge ball outside."

Brendan is ready to compromise: "Okay. Let's play dodge ball, but only one game."

Kevin seems intent upon the game all recess: "Why, why one game?"

Brendan gives in, "Fine, two."

But when Kevin pushes too far, saying, "Uh, yeah, 'cause, 'cause dodge ball's such a good game!" Brendan disagrees, "No."

Now Kevin tries to garner support: "Who likes, who likes dodge ball?"

Brendan decides that perhaps the way to solve this is with a friendly contest: "Actually, actually, whoever gets the dodge ball or handball first gets . . ."

And Kevin agrees, ". . . gets to decide which we do first."

Brendan then reiterates the rules: "But we're going to have a race, okay?"

These boys did an excellent job of advocating for their favorite game, while also agreeing to play both games at recess and even determining a friendly contest to decide which one is played first.

New Standards

How to Wear the Flower Costume

Standard 2: Kinds of Talk and Resulting Genres

Getting Things Done

- Give directions that include several sequenced steps, explaining and elaborating when necessary
- Use actions, writing or drawing to augment language

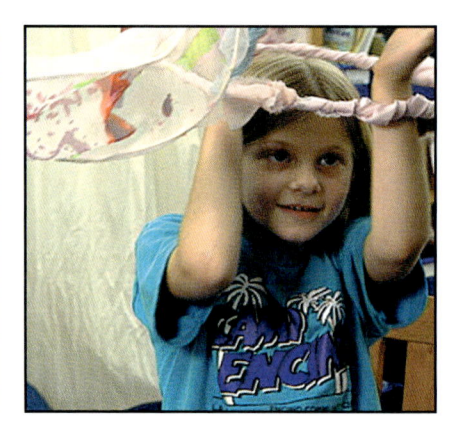

Zoe's first-grade class has done an extensive study of bees, including observing a beehive, reading books about bees, making clay models of bees, writing reports, and writing and performing a play about bees. In this segment, Zoe describes and demonstrates the steps for donning the "very magical" flower costume she will wear in the play.

Zoe meets the standard for first-grade children by being able to use language to communicate a sequence of instructions. She clearly knows the distinct steps of putting on the costume: "I'm going to put it through my arms. I'm going to go like this, then on the sides I'm going to split my arms like that and then I'm going to hold my arms like this and I'm going to look like a flower." Her accompanying demonstration is typical of first graders — they use writing or drawing to supplement their developing ability to communicate with words.

How to Write a Play

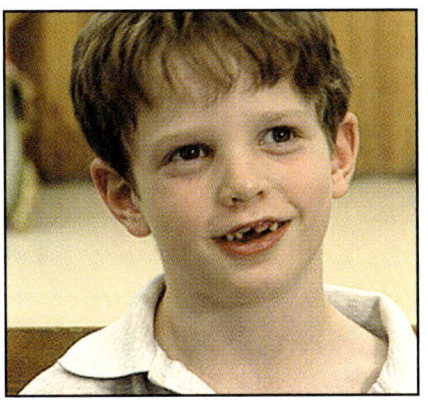

Standard 2: Kinds of Talk and Resulting Genres
Getting Things Done

- Listen to, comprehend and carry out directions with five or six simple steps

- Give directions that include several sequenced steps, explaining and elaborating when necessary

- Use actions, writing or drawing to augment language

Alex articulately explains how a group can work together to write a play. His explanation highlights not only his speaking abilities, but also the speaking and listening abilities of the entire group. As a whole, they listen to one another and share information, they use writing and drawings to help draft their play, they assign tasks, they complete sequenced activities, and they produce a long-term project resulting in a performance.

Alex explains how the play began as individual efforts, and then the group moved to consensus: "Um, I helped write it, but first we just started making . . . everybody was in a different group and started making their own play. So then we took a vote and whoever . . . and the haunted house was the one that, um, won."

Alex goes on to explain that there were different groups involved as well as different roles, such as directors and writers: "So then we started making that and I wanted to help them so the teacher that was helping them in that group said, 'I'm going to take a few more people to help me.' So then she picked me and a few other people, and we wrote the play."

Alex explains the next step, pausing to introduce the directors. He does it smoothly, without losing his train of thought: "And then we told, um, the directors — which are . . . one of them is Miss Rivera, my teacher, and the other is Miss Rosenthal, the other teacher, who is a very good friend of ours — so then, um, we gave the, all the script and everything to the teachers and they typed it out, made the, made a script for everybody, and we all have a script now." Off camera, Alex had mentioned that he was the narrator, and so he had to follow the script closely: "And right now I'm the only one who is using it. But everybody else knows their lines, and plus, I need to practice following the lines of people because . . . or else I'm going to be like, 'Whoa, where am I?' "

Alex gives an articulate description of how the group wrote the play: writing first drafts, voting on a story line, writing the story and making a script.

Conflict Resolution

Standard 2: Kinds of Talk and Resulting Genres
Getting Things Done

◆ Engage in extended conversations (five or six exchanges) about a problem, with both sides presenting and listening to arguments and solutions

In this conflict-resolution session, Shane and Dionicio each explain the problem, listen attentively to the other's interpretation of the argument and then reach a conclusion. While their comments are somewhat one sided and they lack the vocabulary to describe more complex emotions, Shane and Dionicio exhibit speaking and listening skills that meet the standard for first grade.

After agreeing to some ground rules, Dionicio begins, "When me and Shane were playing Reading Blaster 2000, um, when Shane . . . when Shane got the highest score and I got the lowest score, he, he always beated me on all the levels except for one and he said, um, he said, 'I win.' And I told him to stop, but every time when he got the highest score he, he kept on saying it, and, um, and he . . . and I, and I said to him, 'It's not fair to the other person who doesn't, doesn't win and the person that loses.' "

When asked how he feels about Shane's comments, Dionicio replies, "Kinda mad." Asked why, Dionicio lacks the vocabulary to describe the emotions of disappointment, envy and frustration. Instead he lapses into a retelling of the events: " 'Cuz, um, all the time he, um, always says that when he gets the highest score, 'cuz every time I want to . . . I want to play Reading Blaster 2000, and he keeps saying that he won 'cuz he got the highest score, and I got the lowest score."

When asked to tell his side of the story, Shane does his best to explain that he did respond to Dionicio's complaint: "Um, I stopped after he said, 'Stop.' " He then goes on to explain a somewhat complicated scenario of "who said what" involving a third party and missed communications.

In response to a question, Shane says he feels mad about it, too, and wrongly blamed: "Mad . . . because I stopped when he told me to stop."

These two boys obviously are ready to work out their disagreement. Shane suggests a solution might be "not be partners playing the game." And Dionicio concedes that perhaps they should put a little distance between themselves when he says, "Move away when he says that, that he gets the highest score and he says that 'I win.' "

Research Perspectives

"... teachers provide ideal language environments by engaging students in genuine conversations, conducting stimulating reciprocal discussions, and allowing children to converse with each other (at a moderate volume) during classroom learning activities."

From Christie, J., Enz, B. and Vukelich, C. (1997). *Teaching Language and Literacy, Preschool Through the Elementary Grades.* Addison-Wesley Educational Publishers Inc., 91.

Producing and Responding to Performances

In kindergarten and first grade, children's responses to performances of all kinds move beyond simple reactions to include more evaluative statements. Such questioning, responding and expressing of opinions mirror the skills needed for discussion of quality literature. Children's performances include rehearsal and memorization of a few lines of a play or poem. Producing performances begins to become more public. In addition to reciting a poem or singing a song, children also may take part in small school plays or presentations to parents. Children add to these memorized performances some read-alouds of their own writing, providing a strong link from speech to print. Specifically, by the end of first grade we expect children to:

◆ give simple evaluative expressions about a performance and explain their reasoning (for example, "I liked it because horses are my favorite animal.");

◆ critique a performance (especially their own) based on agreed-upon criteria;

◆ ask questions about things that they don't understand;

◆ draw from a rehearsed repertoire to give a brief performance (for example, "The Hokey Pokey");

◆ rehearse and memorize short poems or lines of a play (for example, memorize and present short speeches in the context of a class play or presentation prepared for parents or another class); and

◆ give a brief author performance or presentation of work.

Kindergarten & First-Grade Standards

Standard 1: *Habits*
- Talking a Lot — pg. 130
- Talking to One's Self — pg. 138
- Conversing at Length on a Topic — pg. 140
- Discussing Books — pg. 144

Standard 2: *Kinds of Talk and Resulting Genres*
- Narrative — pg. 152
- Explaining and Seeking Information — pg. 158
- Getting Things Done — pg. 168
- Producing and Responding to Performances — pg. 174

Standard 3: *Language Use and Conventions*
- Rules of Interaction — pg. 181
- Word Play, Phonemic Awareness and Grammatical Awareness — pg. 182
- Vocabulary and Word Choice — pg. 190

New Standards

Kindergarten & First Grade: Standard 2/Commentary on Student Performances − 175 −

Meagan's Portfolio

Standard 2: Kinds of Talk and Resulting Genres

Producing and Responding to Performances

◆ Give a brief author performance or presentation of work

Meagan, though only in kindergarten, meets the standard for producing a performance with a presentation of her portfolio. Speaking clearly and in an organized fashion, she does an excellent job of orienting the listener to the large body of work she is about to present. She begins by talking about reading: "Um, this book is what I did at the beginning of the year, and, um, so now I know how to read harder books. And, um, it's called *Rosie's Walk*. And, um, this is what I'm doing at the last of the year."

When asked to read the book aloud, Meagan shows her familiarity with the parts of a book, reading the cover title, title page and dedication page. She exhibits some good self-monitoring as well. Note that she is reading a very familiar book, and so she can lapse easily into reading by memory. She catches herself when she does this, however — she looks more carefully at the words and pronounces them slowly: "Around the pond, I mean, under . . . the . . . beehive."

When her father asks, "What happened to the bees?" she gives a succinct description: "The fox snucked [sic] them all down, 'cuz he couldn't jump that far, and then the bees got really mad and chased after him."

Meagan then moves on to show some of her best writing: "And then this is a response to my reading log, and I picked it for my best one because I have my title, 'One Day,' and a sentence and a picture. And it says, 'I like the part when the bee went on the flower, because I have seen a bee on a flower.' "

Now Meagan shares part of a story she wrote: "And this is the story that I did in writing, and it's called 'How to Take Care of a Kitten.' " Meagan begins to read: "One day my granny heard a bunch of noise. She started to look around. She did not find what was making the noise. Then daddy and mommy came home. My granny told them what happened. They looked in the closet. I asked them if I can keep the kittens." Skipping to the end of her story, she reads, "Good job, 'Yes, you may keep the cats.' "

New Standards

Retelling and Reenacting the Frog Fairy Dance

Standard 2: Kinds of Talk and Resulting Genres

Producing and Responding to Performances

- Give simple evaluative expressions about a performance and explain their reasoning
- Ask questions about things that they don't understand
- Draw from a rehearsed repertoire to give a brief performance
- Rehearse and memorize short poems or lines of a play
- Critique a performance (especially their own) based on agreed-upon criteria

In this segment, a group of first-grade children recalls and then performs a dance they produced earlier in the year in which they combined a story with movement. The teacher prompts them to recall the movements in the story by asking, "How did we do this dance?" The children collectively reconstruct what they did. With the help of a few props used in the dance (to jog their memory), the children describe the dance in sequence and then reenact it with their teacher.

Maria begins, "First we were playing around, and then you saw out your window . . ." Several children join in and continue the story by reminding the teacher that she played the part of an old lady. Peter and Karolina then tell the plot.

Peter starts, "And then you put, you put, um . . ."

And Karolina chimes in, ". . . a magic spell! . . . and then," she says, taking the hat and putting it on her head, "and then you put that on you."

The teacher tries to slow the group down and calls on Peter to explain. Peter begins by correcting the group, establishing the setting and one character: "That wasn't it. Um, we were dancing around, like, like dancing first and then, and then, you were the old lady, and then . . ."

Dominic finishes Peter's sentence and tells part of the plot: "And cast a spell on us."

Peter continues with important details and the resolution to the story: ". . . and then, you went over there [pointing to the corner of the gym]. We didn't see you, and then you put the hat on and then you had, um, a wand and then you bring us back to kids, and we were playing."

Karolina ends the story with a quote and explanation: "And then you said, 'Now run home!' because then the old lady would turn us back to trees."

The teacher assists by showing how she said it: "Run, run home!"

When asked directly for a contribution, Amber starts to provide additional details: "Well, Peter and Karolina forgot something. Well, you turned us into trees, first . . ."

The teacher helps the children stay "in character" within their retelling of the story when she asks the clarifying question: "Who turned you into trees first?"

All the children respond in unison, "The old lady!"

The first-grade children in this segment meet the standard for producing and responding to performances by drawing from their repertoire of shared experience to retell a story and reenact it with the help of props. With many children providing bits and pieces from memory, they reconstruct the essentials of the story line. We see evidence that the children have remembered the gist of the story when they dramatize it using movements.

Responding to and Critiquing Their Own Video Performance

Standard 2: Kinds of Talk and Resulting Genres

Producing and Responding to Performances

- Give simple evaluative expressions about a performance and explain their reasoning
- Ask questions about things that they don't understand
- Draw from a rehearsed repertoire to give a brief performance
- Rehearse and memorize short poems or lines of a play
- Critique a performance (especially their own) based on agreed-upon criteria

In kindergarten and first grade, children's responses to performances of all kinds move beyond simple reactions to include more evaluative statements.

This group of first-grade children has choreographed and rehearsed a dance about the seasons, a theme they have been studying in first grade. In this segment, the dance teacher, Ms. Bashaw, asks them to remember the various parts of dance and arrange them in sequence following a story line. The children then view a videotape of their rehearsal of the dance and critique it, noting what they think worked well and what things need work. They decide on a plan for what to do next.

These first graders begin with a talk that goes beyond the "here and now" and recall a sequence of events from an earlier rehearsal. With prompting from Ms. Bashaw, working collaboratively, they recall the sequence of events in their dance performance. To start, the group agrees that the first dance segment represents "birds migrating." We hear Karolina comment that then "the leaves start to fall."

Quickly, Mason corrects her, saying, "No, they start bending and twisting."

"Oh yeah," she agrees.

Staying with the topic, Mason suggests that "someone needs to make pumpkins and apples."

Peter builds on this suggestion by volunteering to make apples, and Lucas chimes in, "I'll make more apple trees."

While watching the dance rehearsal on video, the children listen and watch themselves intently, and they respond with interest and joy at seeing their own work. When Ms. Bashaw asks them, "Are we here yet?" while pointing to the time line they constructed together, Lucas responds, "That's the second time the leaves come out. . . . We are in the middle!" demonstrating that he is following along and noting where they are in the sequence. In the background we hear Peter responding to the music and story line in a playful way, wiggling back and forth and making sound effects, "Bok, bok!"

When Ms. Bashaw asks, ". . . What are the things I need to fix [in my dance]?" Lucas responds, "The end. It's all mixed up."

Ms. Bashaw notes that Mason has made a comment that is more specific and prompts him to repeat his comment. Mason notes, "The pumpkin pickers that are forgetting and apple pickers that are forgetting to go to Disneyland."

Lucas justifies his original comment and says, "But that's all in the end."

Although this segment is included as an example of responding to a performance, we also see evidence of children meeting the standard for language use and conventions when they engage in word play. When we hear Maria giggle after she tries to repeat the words *pumpkin pickers* and says instead "pumpkin pickles," we have an example of children's delight in the sound of the language, specifically of alliteration.

Peter and Mason repeat this and laugh at the mistake, "Pumpkin pickles, apple pickles, ha, ha, ha!"

"What else do we need to work on?" asks Ms. Bashaw.

When Peter says, "We were lining up over there," Lucas raises a question, "Where is [Disneyland]?"

Ms. Bashaw responds to Lucas, "So you aren't sure." Writing on the chart, she says, "I'm going to write a question. Where is it? We could help him find out where it is."

Amber adds, "We could fix up the end when we're making a shape of the end."

Ms. Bashaw then asks the children, "Who can tell me? What are we doing that is working out for us? . . . Give me some evidence."

Maria says, "The birds know when to take off."

Peter jumps in, "When to bend. The leaves know when to start bending."

Then the children start to list all the characters who know when to join the dance: ". . . and the sweepers know when to go; the apple pickers know when to go; the pumpkin pickers know when to go."

Ms. Bashaw asks, "How can I say this so I don't have to name everyone?"

The children offer several suggestions for how this might be said: "And, and, and" or "Everything else worked out" or "Everyone does a good . . . everyone knows what to do in the beginning and the middle."

Lucas sums up his analysis from this lesson when he says, "Ms. Bashaw, you know what I think what we should do . . . is just practice on the end and not the beginning and the middle."

The talk in this video meets the standard for producing and responding to performances because the children critique their own performance based on agreed-upon criteria related to the elements of dance. Using what they know about sequencing of stories, they recall the dance and identify what they did well and what needs work. Lucas gives simple evaluative expressions about the performance and makes suggestions about where to spend time improving the dance.

Standard 3: Language Use and Conventions
Introduction

Standard 3: Language Use and Conventions covers three important aspects of language use: rules of interaction; word play, phonemic (and phonological) awareness and grammatical awareness; and vocabulary and word choice. In kindergarten and first grade, children advance from knowing the most basic rules of interaction to knowing more subtle nuances in speech and social convention, such as apologizing for interruptions, paying attention to the utterances of others and to what type of response is called for, adjusting to different audiences, etc.

Frequent playful interchanges with the sounds and meanings of words help to establish the critical connection between oral language and reading and writing with great efficiency. Children should continue to play with words, through rhyming and using alliteration but also through capitalizing on multiple meanings and repeating tongue twisters. Now children are steeped in deciphering the print-sound code. They should be playing with sentence structure and working orally every day — blending and segmenting word parts and onsets and rimes. They gain awareness at the phonemic level, blending individual phonemes to make words. When it comes to grammar, children are able to form plurals or the past tense of some words they have never encountered before. However, grammatical awareness, knowing the rules of grammar, develops later and only after formal instruction in the higher grades.

Children continue to increase their vocabulary daily, primarily through reading and conversing with adults and peers. Orally defining specific words they already know using simple superordinates, or more general terms, allows children to deepen their knowledge of words they use correctly. (For example, a child might explain, "A buffalo is an animal.") When defining words they already know becomes a well-practiced verbal skill, children can absorb new words through formal definitions, such as vocabulary lists used in the upper grades. The incremental increase in children's linguistic ability during this period is immense.

As a result of reading, being read to and conversing, some children may know as many as 10,000 words (Anglin, 1993). Children who have learned 2,000–3,000 words per year during their preschool years have had many rich language interactions with adults; continuing vocabulary development at this pace during kindergarten and first grade also will depend on exposure to lots of new words in context. Formal vocabulary instruction can offer 10–12 words a week, which is far fewer than could be learned naturally.

Kindergarten & First-Grade Standards

Standard 1: *Habits*

- Talking a Lot — pg. 130
- Talking to One's Self — pg. 138
- Conversing at Length on a Topic — pg. 140
- Discussing Books — pg. 144

Standard 2: *Kinds of Talk and Resulting Genres*

- Narrative — pg. 152
- Explaining and Seeking Information — pg. 158
- Getting Things Done — pg. 168
- Producing and Responding to Performances — pg. 174

Standard 3: *Language Use and Conventions*

- Rules of Interaction — pg. 181
- Word Play, Phonemic Awareness and Grammatical Awareness — pg. 182
- Vocabulary and Word Choice — pg. 190

Rules of Interaction

At this age, children generally have adjusted to the social conventions of the school setting and understand the need for civility and polite interactions. They are more accountable and are ready to expand their awareness of speaking effectively and appropriately in different circumstances. Specifically, by the end of first grade we expect children to:

- know and be able to describe rules for school interactions (for example, using "inside" voices, not pushing in line, taking turns, raising hand to speak);

- learn rules for polite interactions (for example, saying "excuse me" when interrupting or "I'm sorry" when accidentally bumping someone);

- hold self and others accountable to the rules by using verbal reminders to self and others (for example, "Only one person on the slide at a time"); and

- speak one at a time, look at and listen to the speaker, yield and/or signal for a chance to speak, and adjust volume to the setting.

Kindergarten & First-Grade Standards

Standard 1: *Habits*
- Talking a Lot — pg. 130
- Talking to One's Self — pg. 138
- Conversing at Length on a Topic — pg. 140
- Discussing Books — pg. 144

Standard 2: *Kinds of Talk and Resulting Genres*
- Narratives — pg. 152
- Explaining and Seeking Information — pg. 158
- Getting Things Done — pg. 168
- Producing and Responding to Performances — pg. 174

Standard 3: *Language Use and Conventions*
- Rules of Interaction — pg. 181
- Word Play, Phonemic Awareness and Grammatical Awareness — pg. 182
- Vocabulary and Word Choice — pg. 190

Word Play, Phonemic Awareness and Grammatical Awareness

Children in kindergarten and first grade are ready to extend word play, as they have developed an appreciation for rhyme and alliteration and have a general awareness of word meanings. Now they are ready to produce certain types of words and become more conscious of their own grammatical constructions. These two years are critical for the development of phonemic awareness — that is, the notion that words can be broken down into smaller sounds and that those smaller sounds recombine to make all words. Specifically, by the end of first grade we expect children to:

- produce rhyming words and recognize pairs of rhyming words;
- isolate initial consonants in single-syllable words (for example, saying "/t/" when the teacher asks, "What is the first sound in *top*?");
- segment the onset and the rime in single-syllable words (for example, saying the onset "/c/" and then the rime "/at/," if the teacher says, "Cat");
- segment the individual sounds in single-syllable words by saying each sound aloud (for example, saying "/c/-/a/-/t/" if the teacher says, "Cat");
- blend onsets and rimes to form words (for example, saying "cat" when the teacher says, "/c/-/at/");
- blend separately spoken phonemes to make a meaningful word (for example, saying "mom" when the teacher says, "mmm—ahhhh—mmm");
- play with alliteration, tongue twisters and onomatopoeia (for example, "Peter Piper picked a peck of pickled peppers");
- begin to use double meanings or multiple meanings of words for riddles and jokes;
- vary sentence openers and use a wide range of syntactic patterns; and
- examine and discuss the structure of words.

Kindergarten & First-Grade Standards

Standard 1: *Habits*
- Talking a Lot — pg. 130
- Talking to One's Self — pg. 138
- Conversing at Length on a Topic — pg. 140
- Discussing Books — pg. 144

Standard 2: *Kinds of Talk and Resulting Genres*
- Narrative — pg. 152
- Explaining and Seeking Information — pg. 158
- Getting Things Done — pg. 168
- Producing and Responding to Performances — pg. 174

Standard 3: *Language Use and Conventions*
- Rules of Interaction — pg. 181
- Word Play, Phonemic Awareness and Grammatical Awareness — pg. 182
- Vocabulary and Word Choice — pg. 190

Morning Word Work

Standard 3: Language Use and Conventions

Word Play, Phonemic Awareness and Grammatical Awareness

- Blend onsets and rimes to form words

- Segment the onset and the rime in single-syllable words

- Segment the individual sounds in single-syllable words

The images and commentary in this section refer to performances available on the accompanying CD-ROMs.

The children in this combined kindergarten and first-grade class might be considered above standard for phonemic awareness. They clearly are able to segment individual sounds in words, isolate consonants, and blend onsets and rimes, but they do so with words containing digraphs, which is slightly more difficult than single consonants, and they do so in print rather than in a purely oral activity.

In addition, when the teacher asks, "Next line, please. Cynthia, loud voice," Cynthia is required to deduce the meaning of a word that is only partially printed. "You'll have to c-h, choose, which, c-h . . . honey you like best." Here she is blending the onset /ch/ with the rime /ooz/ to make *choose*. Then she isolates the final consonant, in this case the digraph /ch/, and blends it with /wh/-/i/ to make *which*.

These children are reading already, yet they continue to work on phonemic awareness. Reeshie takes care to segment the individual sounds he identifies in the word *sweet*: "Have a /sw/-/e/-/e/. . . sweet day."

The sound of the day is clearly /ch/, and the teacher is aware of other opportunities to focus on it throughout the day.

She also focuses on a particular point of punctuation: "You know what, I'm noticing that there's a mistake in here. I think I forgot to put something in or somebody erased it. Anybody know what it is?"

Though unsure what it is called, Claudia locates the problem, "Um, something like between *you'll*." When asked why the apostrophe is needed, "What two words does that mean? Claudia? What does *you'll* stand for?" she knows that it is two distinct words: "You will."

To conclude, the teacher returns to the /ch/ sound and asks, "Can you think of some words that begin with that /ch/, either have it at the beginning or have it at the end? Annabelle?" To arrive at their answers, the children must segment the beginning sounds mentally to identify the /ch/. Annabelle offers "cheese," and Reeshie offers "chess."

Kindergarten & First-Grade Standards

Standard 1: *Habits*
- ◆ Talking a Lot — pg. 130
- ◆ Talking to One's Self — pg. 138
- ◆ Conversing at Length on a Topic — pg. 140
- ◆ Discussing Books — pg. 144

Standard 2: *Kinds of Talk and Resulting Genres*
- ◆ Narrative — pg. 152
- ◆ Explaining and Seeking Information — pg. 158
- ◆ Getting Things Done — pg. 168
- ◆ Producing and Responding to Performances — pg. 174

Standard 3: *Language Use and Conventions*
- ◆ Rules of Interaction — pg. 181
- ◆ Word Play, Phonemic Awareness and Grammatical Awareness — pg. 182
- ◆ Vocabulary and Word Choice — pg. 190

Phonemic Awareness: Twice Told, with Good Reason

Careful readers will notice that there is a standard for phonemic awareness here and in our companion book, *Reading & Writing grade by grade*. This overlap is intentional.

Clearly, phonemic awareness belongs in this *Speaking & Listening* book; by definition, phonemic awareness is the ability to hear separate sounds, or phonemes, and say, or blend, separate phonemes to make meaningful utterances. These are oral language skills.

The New Standards Primary Literacy Committee decided to include phonemic awareness in the reading and writing standards for a good reason. In their review of research and instructional practices, committee members realized that phonemic awareness is an essential foundation for reading and writing — but many beginning reading programs do not have instructional targets to measure children's progress. By including it as a standard, the committee put phonemic awareness on par with other components of reading and writing — exactly where it belongs.

Kindergarten & First Grade: Standard 3/Commentary on Student Performances

Spontaneous Rhymes

Standard 3: Language Use and Conventions

Word Play, Phonemic Awareness and Grammatical Awareness

◆ Produce rhyming words and recognize pairs of rhyming words

This is an excellent example of the kind of spontaneous word play we hope to see in kindergarten and first grade. In this segment, the teacher says, "And number three is going to be . . ."

Chelsea identifies the rhyme and calls the teacher's attention to it: "Miss Rivera, you rhymed: 'Number three is going to be.'"

The teacher, though ready to begin a lesson, is quick to pause and appreciate this: "You're right."

Another child adds a third rhyming word to the sequence: "A big knee."

Again, the teacher is quick to acknowledge: "Number three is going to be a big knee," and the whole class is delighted.

New Standards

The Importance of Word Play

Word play continues to remain important even as children master phonemic awareness and work on the print-sound code. Kindergarten and first-grade children continue to play with words, not only rhyming and using alliteration, but also capitalizing on the multiple meanings of words to entertain their friends: "Why are fish so smart? Because they go around in schools!" Children at this age especially enjoy the *form* of joke-telling that often produces nonsense riddles.

Kindergarten & First-Grade Standards

Standard 1: *Habits*
- Talking a Lot — pg. 130
- Talking to One's Self — pg. 138
- Conversing at Length on a Topic — pg. 140
- Discussing Books — pg. 144

Standard 2: *Kinds of Talk and Resulting Genres*
- Narrative — pg. 152
- Explaining and Seeking Information — pg. 158
- Getting Things Done — pg. 168
- Producing and Responding to Performances — pg. 174

Standard 3: *Language Use and Conventions*
- Rules of Interaction — pg. 181
- Word Play, Phonemic Awareness and Grammatical Awareness — pg. 182
- Vocabulary and Word Choice — pg. 190

Kindergarten & First Grade: Standard 3/Commentary on Student Performances – 187 –

Miss Mary Mack

Standard 3: Language Use and Conventions

Word Play, Phonemic Awareness and Grammatical Awareness

- Play with alliteration, tongue twisters and onomatopoeia
- Produce rhyming words and recognize pairs of rhyming words

In this simple word-play exercise, children recite a familiar rhyme. The teacher asks the children to clap their hands every time they hear the /ack/ sound. They chant along, clapping on *Mack*, *black* and *back*. The teacher could adjust this type of play easily and ask the children to listen for the long /i/ sound, clapping on *high*, *sky* and *July*. This type of word play, including songs and chants of nursery rhymes, jump-rope tunes and hand-slap games, continues to be important in kindergarten and first grade.

> # Grammatical Awareness in Kindergarten & First Grade
>
> Children at this age have acquired an impressive, if largely unconscious, mastery of many grammatical constructions. By the end of first grade, children are using full, nonreversible passives ("The lunch was eaten by the dog."), relative clauses ("We ate the lunch that my mom made.") and many irregular forms. They usually will not overregularize common words any longer (for example, children will use frequent irregular forms like *fell* and *ate*). More complex derived forms are produced now, both correctly and in ways that are overgeneralized (for example, *happily* from *happy* but also *loveily* from *lovely*), sometimes playfully (for example, "I want something saladic to eat.").

Kindergarten & First-Grade Standards

Standard 1: *Habits*
- Talking a Lot — pg. 130
- Talking to One's Self — pg. 138
- Conversing at Length on a Topic — pg. 140
- Discussing Books — pg. 144

Standard 2: *Kinds of Talk and Resulting Genres*
- Narrative — pg. 152
- Explaining and Seeking Information — pg. 158
- Getting Things Done — pg. 168
- Producing and Responding to Performances — pg. 174

Standard 3: *Language Use and Conventions*
- Rules of Interaction — pg. 181
- Word Play, Phonemic Awareness and Grammatical Awareness — pg. 182
- Vocabulary and Word Choice — pg. 190

Kindergarten & First Grade: Standard 3/Commentary on Student Performances

Compound Words

Standard 3: Language Use and Conventions

Word Play, Phonemic Awareness and Grammatical Awareness

◆ Examine and discuss the structure of words

The students in this class clearly are interested in words and language in general. The teacher has just finished transcribing what some volunteers have shared with the class. She then asks the children to think about the words she circles — *background* and *beehive* — and tell what they notice about them. Sarah suggests that they are "compound words." When asked, she explains that this means "two words put together."

Another child clarifies this definition, adding that a compound word is "two words that you put together to make *one* word."

One child clearly understands the concept of compound words when he explains that *banner* would not be considered a compound word because "*ban* and *ner* aren't words." (Actually, *ban* is a word, but this is not mentioned.)

Next is a wonderful example of just how comfortable these children are in the computer age, as well as how tuned in they are to language. One girl tells that she noticed something amusing: "Um, I just noticed something. Um, *beehive* and *background* . . . I just remembered that *compound* has, is a compound word."

While the teacher is asking, "You think the word *compound* is a compound word?" some children agree. Children say, "/*com*/ and /*pound*/."

The teacher presses them: "What's a *com*?"

One child pipes up immediately, "Short for computer."

"Ah-hah!" the teacher agrees, "but is it a word?"

Another child says, "It's a name."

She explains, "I know you see it . . . dot com, but no . . . but you're thinking and that makes me proud." This is well-deserved praise as the children are alert, interested and already aware of the evolution of language.

New Standards

Vocabulary and Word Choice

Through conversation, daily interaction with adults and peers, and especially reading and being read to, children in kindergarten and first grade continue to increase their vocabulary at an astounding rate. By the end of first grade, their vocabulary likely will double from what it was in preschool. The importance of vocabulary acquisition cannot be overstated. Continually expanding known word domains and understanding the relationships among words allows students to build new concepts. Specifically, by the end of first grade we expect children to:

- build word maps that show the relationship between words, placing newly acquired words in categories that are relevant (for example, when studying special interests like dinosaurs, understanding that a Tyrannosaurus eats meat and a Brontosaurus eats plants, but that both are dinosaurs);
- begin to define words they know using simple superordinates (for example, "A violin is an instrument.");
- show flexibility within the domain, i.e., alter word choice based on audience (for example, when talking to a toddler, "Try the horn," but when talking to an adult, "Want to try my trumpet?");
- learn new words from reading, being read to daily and classroom study experiences;
- study word families;
- know more than one way to describe a particular referent or verb (for example, "Mrs. Benton" is called "teacher" by children in her class and "mom" by her daughter in the third grade);
- recognize multiple meanings of words (for example, go to school, school of fish, my aunt home-schools her kids);
- understand that clusters of words refer to the same events or phenomena but from different perspectives (for example, if someone is buying, another person must be selling; if someone lost the game, another person won); and
- increase vocabulary of verbs, adjectives and adverbs to gain fluency and exercise options in word choice.

Kindergarten & First-Grade Standards

Standard 1: *Habits*
- Talking a Lot — pg. 130
- Talking to One's Self — pg. 138
- Conversing at Length on a Topic — pg. 140
- Discussing Books — pg. 144

Standard 2: *Kinds of Talk and Resulting Genres*
- Narrative — pg. 152
- Explaining and Seeking Information — pg. 158
- Getting Things Done — pg. 168
- Producing and Responding to Performances — pg. 174

Standard 3: *Language Use and Conventions*
- Rules of Interaction — pg. 181
- Word Play, Phonemic Awareness and Grammatical Awareness — pg. 182
- Vocabulary and Word Choice — pg. 190

Defining *Metamorphosis*

Standard 3: Language Use and Conventions

Vocabulary and Word Choice

◆ Learn new words from reading, being read to daily and classroom study experiences

Miss Salafia's first-grade class has been studying metamorphosis, and these studies have been reinforced by watching a classroom caterpillar turning into a butterfly. Mr. Sopyla, a storyteller, plans to build upon this work by telling a story about metamorphosis during his weekly time with the class. While this is not a vocabulary lesson, his introductory inquiry about the meaning of *metamorphosis* clearly indicates that the children have a working knowledge of this word.

Lucas begins the children's efforts to define *metamorphosis* by offering an appropriate synonym, *transform*. This prompts other children to apply this word to examples from their own experiences with toys, superheroes and cartoon characters who are transformed from one form to another. A distinction is then made between transforming and evolving, as the children characterize the processes they know from television examples. Maria remembers another real-life metamorphosis: "When the frog is the egg and it changes to a tadpole and then a frog." This new word is now part of the children's expanding vocabulary.

Research Perspectives

"Through teacher and peer interactions in sociodramatic play, children use new language as they plan, negotiate, compose, and carry our the 'script' of their play."

From Burns, M., Griffin, P. and Snow, C., eds. (1999). *Starting Out Right: A Guide to Promoting Children's Reading Success.* Washington, D.C.: National Academy Press, 49.

Second & Third Grades

Second & Third Grades

Teachers have a tremendous role to play in developing the oral language proficiency of seven- and eight-year-olds. Moreover, this persistent attention can have a direct and positive impact on students' social and academic success.

Using Language for Real-World Purposes

In second and third grades, children increasingly are grounded in reality and less dependent on their imaginations to make sense of the world. Their interest in fantasy play fades as they become interested in "real" activities, such as starting a coin collection, playing on a sports team or joining a scout troop. For seven- and eight-year-olds, the real world holds a fascination all its own: Children become acutely interested in the rules, rituals and routines that govern their lives. This fixation extends to appropriate behavior in the classroom, the fair and correct way to play games and sports on the playground, and a strong awareness of right and wrong.

Second and third graders tend to view life in black-and-white terms — a tendency that manifests itself into passionate objections when they believe they have been wronged. They police one another's behavior and, like alert watchdogs, raise a ruckus when someone falls out of line. Pitched "he-said-she-said" encounters often result.

Despite these flaps, second and third graders generally play well together. Team play is especially popular. Whereas younger students find it difficult to focus on the object of the game or a common goal (beyond their own heroic efforts), seven- and eight-year-olds relish team games and sports that involve whole-class participation, such as kickball. The rules, of course, are a topic of keen interest.

Second and third graders also generally enjoy and value friendships with other children. Beginning in second grade and especially in third grade, children start to socialize in small groups and to have "best" friends. Newcomers sometimes have a hard time fitting in with children who have known one another for a few years. Boys and girls begin to play separately. Indeed, many playground spats center on the age-old complaint: "The girls (or boys) won't leave us alone."

Also at this age, children have a strong sense of their own likes, dislikes, strengths and weaknesses — and those of their classmates. They begin to buddy up with children who have similar interests, so that two boys who like jokes or science fiction books or two girls who like science or art will become friends. Some of these friendships among two or three students develop into tight relationships. There are no hard-and-fast rules, though, about how friendships form. Sometimes two quiet children bond; sometimes a boisterous child finds balance with a quiet friend.

Children also start to define themselves based on their interests and talents, as in "I'm a fast runner" or "I am a good writer." This newfound awareness can be either empowering or devastating. Children who are "good" at something gain an empowering feeling of affirmation and confidence; they enjoy the recognition that their skills bring them. Other children suffer from cruel teasing for their limitations, which amplifies their sense of failure. Children seek approval from their peers at this age — and they are crushed if they don't get it. For this reason, this period is a critical time in school; children who cannot read and write well by this time face not only real academic hardships, but also social consequences.

Speaking and Listening: What to Expect

By second grade, most children are speaking distinctly, with almost perfect pronunciation. By third grade, children who have problems with pronunciation should be referred to a speech and language specialist. Most people, not just family members and familiar adults, can understand children at this age when they talk.

And talk they do. In many ways, second and third graders are more sophisticated in their use of language than younger students are. In preschool or even earlier, children start

Second & Third Grades: Speaking & Listening

to mumble to themselves. As second and third graders, this self-monitoring language takes on a different quality. At this age, children talk themselves through their actions, particularly when they encounter a hard task. Muttering doesn't necessarily mean that they will be more successful with the task, but it is a good indication that they are working hard.

Second and third graders also are learning and using more and more specific words to describe their world and explain their meaning. They stretch their minds to find the right words to express themselves — and this mental exercise is a good sign. Children at this age have a working vocabulary that is big enough to afford them choices when they speak. They enjoy this word choice and should be able to supply specific words to make their meaning clear. They can pick bigger, better, more descriptive words; a "good" snack now seems too ordinary when a "tasty," "delicious," "scrumptious" or "delectable" description is possible.

Children should be using these kinds of challenging words in their everyday speech. Children who routinely do *not* use precise vocabulary may have a language impairment. Likewise, when children regularly use "filler" words to substitute for accurate labels, a language delay or other language impairment may be the reason. For example, a child at this age who overuses words such as *thing*, *that* or *it* or who struggles to make a vague statement such as, "He took the thing," needs attention from a speech and language specialist.

Most second- and third-grade children, though, can use language to tell nicely formed, elaborate stories that make sense. They can comprehend and use more complex sentence structures than do younger children. They give useful explanations and directions. They support their explanations with examples. They give detailed directions that others can follow. They negotiate, persuade, elaborate and embellish skillfully.

Second and third graders usually are more sophisticated in their word play than younger students are. Their rapidly expanding vocabularies permit them to be more precise in describing their meaning, but this precision makes them less likely to come up with dazzling descriptive metaphors. Children at this age can be very reflective about word meanings and ambiguities. With instruction, they will attend closely to word choices in text. For example, children at this age can explain similes and metaphors, discussing at length what "fast as a fox" means and why an author chooses these words — if the teacher prompts this kind of discussion. They also will play with alliteration, tongue twisters, double or multiple word meanings, made-up languages, jokes, and limericks, to name a few.

> Second and third graders also are learning and using more and more specific words to describe their world and explain their meaning.

New Standards

Developing Oral Language

The fact that second and third graders speak more like little adults than like wide-eyed innocents belies their continuing need for the teacher's daily guidance in speaking and listening. Teachers have a tremendous role to play in developing the oral language proficiency of seven- and eight-year-olds. Moreover, this persistent attention can have a direct and positive impact on students' social and academic success.

Now is the time, after all, when children's growing bodies can inflict real harm if disputes turn physical. One of the teacher's most important responsibilities is helping students use language to express emotions, control anger, negotiate and settle differences. "Use your words" is just as apt a reminder for second and third graders as it is for preschoolers. Time-pressed teachers may find it easier to calm a squabble by separating children quickly, diverting their attention or reprimanding them for inappropriate behavior. To develop their speaking and listening skills, though, teachers can try a different approach: Teach children to sort out their differences — with language — on their own.

Children no longer see teachers and other adults as the all-knowing, all-seeing referees and arbiters of all situations. Children themselves can have conversations about how they feel, what they think, what they want, what they will compromise and so on.

This is not to say that these conversations happen easily or spontaneously. Teachers need to model these exchanges daily and arrange opportunities for them to take place.

Common ground rules are important. Teachers need to teach children to be polite and respectful of others' feelings — even if they are communicating about sensitive issues. Children need to learn to express even negative comments in a positive way, without a volatile or accusatory tone that makes matters worse. For example, children can learn to say, "I feel really upset when you tease me," instead of, "You are an idiot, and I hate you!"

Teachers can set aside a quiet corner in the back of their classroom to have these conversations. They can establish a regular time or forum for children to air and resolve their grievances. They can formalize this process by having children write their names on the board if they want to talk about something. Other children can offer advice as well.

Some schools use peer mediation or conflict resolution programs, often with older students as moderators, to allow children to talk through their differences on their own. Older students gain from this experience as well by offering their own observations, experiences and suggestions — another powerful way for them to practice speaking and listening. Usually, a teacher, a principal or another adult is within earshot of these exchanges, just in case, but they do not participate. The idea is for children to do the thinking and the talking.

Teachers who model and use these techniques regularly find that second and third graders can be positive and kind to one another. Their abiding interest in issues of right and wrong primes them for these conversations as well. Second and third graders can be reflective and genuinely sorry about their behavior, particularly when they hear another child's perspective. They can have meaningful, responsible conversations — without whining. In a word, they can handle these situations with maturity.

Children at this age can be equally mature in academic conversations, if teachers provide them with ample opportunities to talk. Book talks are a natural forum for participating in conversations about academic topics. Second and third graders tend to like books with heavy, emotional topics told with humor. Books about heroic, funny children with realistic problems — *The Boxcar Children, A Chair for My Mother, The Great Gilly Hopkins, The Kids of Polk Street School* and *Pippi Longstocking,* for example — elicit lengthy, in-depth book talk conversations. Children respond to good literature with themes aimed right for their hearts and minds. Again, they wrestle out loud with the issues of right and wrong. Teachers can pick good books that will move children. And they can model appropriate ways to explain their interpretations and connect them to their own experiences, using the text to back up their assertions and question those of others.

Likewise, teachers can model effective speaking and listening strategies as children talk about their writing. Daily writing provides opportunities for academic talk to occur. In brainstorming sessions, writing conferences and revising sessions and during the Author's Chair, when children read their writing and then discuss it with others, children need to learn how to make their points kindly and constructively. The author needs to learn how to use the power of the chair to respond to comments considerately and thoughtfully — and to recognize everyone's voice. This takes explicit role-modeling from the teacher.

Second and third graders also should work together frequently in small groups to complete tasks or assignments. Working with others requires students to talk to each other and use language to accomplish a common goal. There are natural tensions and struggles that come with small-group work; only by working through them can children get better at it. Teachers should make sure that the same children don't work together all the time; changing the mix of students changes the dynamic of the conversations.

Throughout these encounters, teachers should constantly and deliberately plant new vocabulary words in the conversations. A rigorous core curriculum has an abundance of challenging concepts and words; teachers should use them and encourage children to use them all the time. They should challenge children to come up with more interesting words to express their meaning. They should make a game of substituting precise or unusual words for drab or common ones.

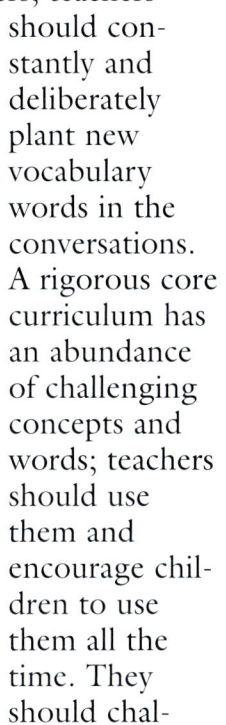

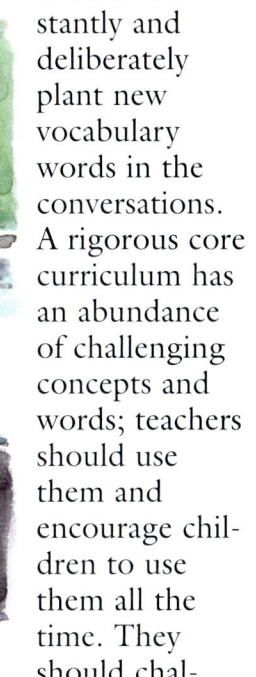

Many of these suggestions for developing speaking and listening skills have an important implication: For children to talk *more*, teachers have to talk *less*. Only with structured opportunities to practice talking can children develop speaking and listening habits. Teachers have to cede the floor, move to the background and simply *listen*.

Standard 1: Habits
Introduction

Lots and lots of purposeful talk remains an important part of children's literacy development. Talking a lot, talking to one's self, conversing at length on a topic and discussing books are four habits that should be a part of children's daily activities in second and third grades. At this age, children become more adept at holding their audience's attention because they understand the various genres of talk and can anticipate questions. They now can predict reliably others' expectations for clarity, brevity, relevance and truth.

Children in second and third grades continue to express their own preferences, negotiate with peers and talk about particular interests. However, now the talk begins to involve collaboration as well as negotiation. When speaking on topics that particularly interest them, their talk is lengthier, and there is more considered conversation. Children should begin to be more skilled at sustaining the conversation by extending others' ideas and soliciting opinions.

In reading, children now should self-monitor almost automatically. When children at this age read, their self-monitoring is primarily silent; however, talking aloud to guide themselves through a difficult task or reasoning aloud to reach a conclusion should be encouraged.

The incremental leap in the quality of book discussions that appears in second and third grades reflects the growth in children's competency as readers and writers. Thus, we expect them to bring their knowledge to bear during discussion, drawing on an understanding of composition and of structuring a text for an audience. Children read longer, more challenging texts now, as well as chapter books, and they can hold the memory of a story over time. Children begin to appreciate books as a way of learning about new topics, unfamiliar people and cultures. More of what they talk about comes from what they have read.

Second- & Third-Grade Standards

Standard 1: *Habits*
- Talking a Lot — pg. 202
- Talking to One's Self — pg. 207
- Conversing at Length on a Topic — pg. 208
- Discussing Books — pg. 218

Standard 2: *Kinds of Talk and Resulting Genres*
- Narrative — pg. 230
- Explaining and Seeking Information — pg. 236
- Getting Things Done — pg. 244
- Producing and Responding to Performances — pg. 251

Standard 3: *Language Use and Conventions*
- Rules of Interaction — pg. 254
- Word Play and Grammatical Awareness — pg. 256
- Vocabulary and Word Choice — pg. 260

Research Perspectives

"Language plays a central role in learning, and the success of children in school depends to a very large degree on their ability to speak and listen."

From Christie, J., Enz, B. and Vukelich, C. (1997). *Teaching Language and Literacy, Preschool Through the Elementary Grades.* Addison-Wesley Educational Publishers Inc., 35.

Talking a Lot

By the second and third grades, students are used to talking and asking questions about their own or others' reading and writing. Their use of language to learn, negotiate, work and play with one another sharpens to the point that they can tackle more complex tasks and communicate more complex concepts.

Specifically, by the end of third grade we expect children to:

- talk about what they think, read or experience;

- explain or speak from another person's perspective (for example, "Claire doesn't think it's fair that she didn't get a speaking part. She's been in the drama group longest.");

- talk about ideas or information gained from sources beyond personal experience (for example, "I read that the moon pulls the ocean tides.");

- talk in small groups to collaborate on a project, ask questions, and make comments or suggestions to facilitate work on a task or project (for example, "We need to assign jobs. Who wants to be the group recorder?"); and

- talk in front of a group on a regular basis (for example, giving book reports, reporting out to the class from a small-group discussion).

Soliciting responses to writing should be a regular part of the writing process. Students should have daily practice giving and receiving oral feedback in response groups or whole-class settings. They should be able to:

- solicit and provide feedback daily about writing, asking questions or commenting in terms of genre features and clarity and making suggestions for where or how to elaborate or edit.

Second- & Third-Grade Standards

Standard 1: *Habits*

- Talking a Lot   pg. 202
- Talking to One's Self   pg. 207
- Conversing at Length on a Topic   pg. 208
- Discussing Books   pg. 218

Standard 2: *Kinds of Talk and Resulting Genres*

- Narrative   pg. 230
- Explaining and Seeking Information   pg. 236
- Getting Things Done   pg. 244
- Producing and Responding to Performances pg. 251

Standard 3: *Language Use and Conventions*

- Rules of Interaction   pg. 254
- Word Play and Grammatical Awareness   pg. 256
- Vocabulary and Word Choice   pg. 260

Second & Third Grades: Standard 1/Commentary on Student Performances

Developing Characters

Standard 1: Habits
Talking a Lot

◆ Talk about what they think, read or experience

◆ Solicit and provide feedback daily about writing

This response group segment is an excellent example of two children working together to improve their writing. Aaron reads his analysis of Allen Say's writing, and then Alexandra offers some specific ideas for revision. Aaron comments on Say's use of language; he quotes directly from the text — "bombs fell and scattered their lives like leaves" — and describes the feelings that it inspired in him: "That makes me feel like I was there and was scared."

He then moves on to character and setting: "Say mostly uses characters from Japan. He also mostly places his stories in Japan, too. He developed his scary characters a lot by talking about them a lot."

Alexandra shows that she has been listening carefully when she asks, "Well, what do you mean by develop? How did he develop the characters?"

Aaron then asks, "Do you mean like putting an example of, like, what, like, how . . . the author talked about them?"

This is a good example of students challenging one another to improve; she asks for justification and evidence for his statement about Say developing his characters.

The images and commentary in this section refer to performances available on the accompanying CD-ROMs.

New Standards

Jared and Sophia Talk about Mexico

Standard 1: Habits
Talking a Lot

- Talk about ideas or information gained from sources beyond personal experience
- Talk in small groups to collaborate on a project

By third grade, children use opportunities to talk with one another in the classroom to enhance their learning about things beyond their personal experience. Not only do they expand their knowledge by getting ideas and information from classmates, but they also clarify their thinking as they put their thoughts into words for others to hear.

Sophia and Jared share such a moment during this social studies lesson. The children have been asked to notice features of nonfiction as they examine resources about Mexico, the country they currently are studying. Organized into small groups at tables, the children are encouraged to talk informally with each other about their work. In this segment, Jared's casual remark about a flooded canal prompts Sophia to pursue information about canals. "You know what, I'm going to write that because that's really interesting," she says. She then finds a postcard in her book that mentions a boat trip down a canal built by the Aztecs more than 500 years ago.

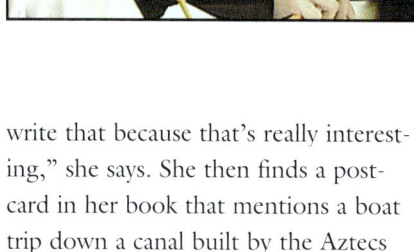

Jared and Sophia use their knowledge of the Aztecs and Mexican history to speculate about how such a canal could have been built. Instead of just wondering about it privately, Jared asks Sophia, "Well, how do you think they built the canal plain? Because they must have had to dig, like, for weeks and weeks."

Sophia emphasizes her understanding of the magnitude of the project by suggesting that it took "years."

In response, Jared modifies his estimate to "two years, maybe," apparently signifying a very long time.

Jared knows that if such a canal were being built presently, "We would use, just like, heavy machinery, like bulldozers."

His comment implies that the Aztecs didn't have the benefit of such machinery, and Sophia agrees with that implication, saying, "Yeah, but they didn't have that. It was the Aztec time."

Jared guesses that the Aztecs must have used "plain shovels," and Sophia acknowledges how hard that would have been: "No wonder it must have taken . . . two years."

In addition to wondering aloud together about what they are learning and making the material come alive as they consider the time and effort put into the canal, the children use each other as resources for making decisions about their work. Sophia asks Jared, "Should I write *postcard*?" for the class list of the features of nonfiction texts.

He responds, "Yeah, you can write *postcard*."

Returning to the content of his investigation, Jared asks Sophia, "Do you think the bullfighters are just a little scared of being with a bull in the ring?"

Sophia instinctively agrees, "Definitely," but then turns to the index — another feature of nonfiction — as a source to look up bullfighters and support their thinking.

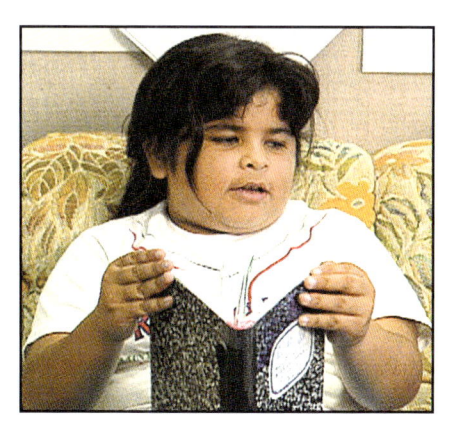

Second & Third Grades: Standard 1/Commentary on Student Performances

Reader Response Pair

Standard 1: Habits
Talking a Lot

◆ Talk about what they think, read or experience

◆ Solicit and provide feedback daily about writing

Discussing Books

◆ Compare one text to another

Listening and speaking to one another about what they are reading and writing continue to be pivotal in children's language development. By second and third grades, children should have daily opportunities to discuss not only books, but also their own writing. In this segment, the two girls are sharing a response to literature.

Gina reads her paper titled "*The Lost Lake* by Allen Say." Her paper includes comments on the feelings of the main character: "This book is about a boy named Luke and his dad. Luke feels bad in this story because his father won't talk to him at all." She also makes a comparison to another text she recently has read: "This book reminds me of *Tree of Cranes* because they both get something they want. For example, in *Tree of Cranes* the, the mother wanted her son to stop going to the pond. And in *The Lost Lake* the boy wanted his dad to talk to him."

Note that Nicole comments on Gina's comparison to another book; Nicole mentions that she liked how Gina "referred back to, um, um, *The Lost Lake*." These response groups normally go on for several minutes, with each child taking a turn to share his or her writing. Children are taught to offer feedback, reinforcing the author's accomplishments, asking questions to clarify meaning, and making suggestions for what they would like to know more about to extend or focus a piece of writing. The idea is to listen attentively, share ideas, and help one another revise and improve their writing.

Revising with a Partner in the Writers Workshop

Standard 1: Habits
Talking a Lot

◆ Talk in small groups to collaborate on a project

◆ Solicit and provide feedback daily about writing

Aaron and Alexandra understand the conventions of working with a partner to revise their written work in a Writers Workshop. They expect to offer and receive constructive suggestions for improving their writing, not just polite feedback about what they liked about each other's work. This daily routine lets Alexandra reflect on her writing as she hears herself reading it aloud and gives Aaron a constructive role as an active listener and editor.

When Alexandra reads her piece about the interesting language of author Allen Say, she seems to hear a problem with the sentence that begins "if authors like Say didn't . . ." She looks over at Aaron and repeats, "like Say, didn't use interesting language . . ."

Aaron makes editorial suggestions about that sentence. He respectfully responds, "Well, there's one thing I would like to ask you, like, to change." They look together at her writing as he describes what to omit and reads the revised version. He justifies his thinking, saying, "See, that makes, like, more sense. . . . It'd be better, 'cause we're talking about, like, the story and it'd be better not to get it, like, off track by saying 'other authors.'"

Alexandra voices her appreciation for Aaron's useful suggestion by saying, "Thanks."

As she tries to make sense of it herself, though, she still isn't quite clear what he has in mind. They work together again, word by word, as she erases the problem phrase and makes the suggested changes on the spot. We expect third graders to engage easily in this kind of focused and functional talk.

Talking to One's Self

By now, most children have internalized the use of language to self-correct and guide their thinking and problem solving. In some areas, such as reading, self-monitoring becomes silent, though children still may work out loud on pronunciations. In other areas — such as remembering complex tasks, mathematics or memorization — students almost always talk aloud. Specifically, by the end of third grade we expect children to:

- make spontaneous corrections (for example, trying out alternate sounds for the letter *c*, "san . . . can . . . canyon");

- talk to themselves out loud to make plans, guide behavior or monitor thinking (for example, while on the computer, "Okay, cut . . . cut . . . right, go to Edit, drag to cut.");

- rehearse steps they will use to solve a problem (silently or by subvocalizing);

- mimic adult language used in problem solving;

- recite facts to confirm what has been memorized (for example, geographical facts, poems, multiplication tables, lines of a play); and

- silently monitor their comprehension of text, including understanding of individual words, using a variety of self-correcting strategies (see *Reading & Writing grade by grade*).

Second- & Third-Grade Standards

Standard 1: *Habits*
- Talking a Lot — pg. 202
- Talking to One's Self — pg. 207
- Conversing at Length on a Topic — pg. 208
- Discussing Books — pg. 218

Standard 2: *Kinds of Talk and Resulting Genres*
- Narrative — pg. 230
- Explaining and Seeking Information — pg. 236
- Getting Things Done — pg. 244
- Producing and Responding to Performances — pg. 251

Standard 3: *Language Use and Conventions*
- Rules of Interaction — pg. 254
- Word Play and Grammatical Awareness — pg. 256
- Vocabulary and Word Choice — pg. 260

Conversing at Length on a Topic

By second grade, children have learned to solicit others' contributions to sustain conversation, and they know to mark new topics explicitly. Their skills in second and third grades grow to incorporate a variety of strategies that enable them to sustain conversations with even lengthier exchanges than in previous years. Specifically, by the end of third grade we expect children to:

◆ initiate and sustain a conversation with eight or more lengthy exchanges;

◆ consistently ask for clarification (for example, "Friday? I don't think that's right. What do you mean?");

◆ consistently recognize and respond to indirect and direct indications that others need clarification (for example, responding to puzzled looks or shrugs with "Right?" or correcting their information by saying, "Wait. No, not Friday. Sign-ups must be Saturday because we'd be in school Friday.");

◆ initiate topics within conversations that are in progress (for example, "It's spring tryouts for Little League? Have you ever tried baseball?");

◆ sustain conversation by extending others' contributions (for example, "Do you really think baseball's harder? I think basketball is harder.");

◆ express and solicit opinions (for example, "The basketball clinic is open all weekend now. Do you like the double practices?");

◆ ask open-ended or long-answer questions (for example, "What did you see at the Sports Fair?");

◆ repair and revert to the topic when necessary (for example, "But wait a minute. Tell me again when baseball sign-ups are?"); and

◆ raise topics likely to be of interest to another person.

Second- & Third-Grade Standards

Standard 1: *Habits*

◆ Talking a Lot pg. 202
◆ Talking to One's Self pg. 207
◆ Conversing at Length on a Topic pg. 208
◆ Discussing Books pg. 218

Standard 2: *Kinds of Talk and Resulting Genres*

◆ Narrative pg. 230
◆ Explaining and Seeking Information pg. 236
◆ Getting Things Done pg. 244
◆ Producing and Responding to Performances pg. 251

Standard 3: *Language Use and Conventions*

◆ Rules of Interaction pg. 254
◆ Word Play and Grammatical Awareness pg. 256
◆ Vocabulary and Word Choice pg. 260

Summary Discussion

Standard 1: Habits
Conversing at Length on a Topic

- Initiate and sustain a conversation with eight or more lengthy exchanges

- Initiate topics within conversations that are in progress

- Sustain conversation by extending others' contributions

- Express and solicit opinions

- Repair and revert to the topic when necessary

These children are in the midst of an author study on Allen Say. Their writing task for the day is to draft a summary. In a group discussion prior to breaking for independent work, the children discuss criteria for a solid summary. Tyler is trying to make the point that a summary must be interesting, not simply a rote accounting of beginning, middle and end: "You just don't say that middle part . . . the beginning is about this, the middle is about this and the end is about this . . . because that would mess up the whole summary and that wouldn't make any sense."

The teacher reminds the class that "when you write a summary, you want it to be brief, but you want it to tell all the information that they need to know."

Tyler then reinforces the importance of sticking to the main idea: "You want to tell them what the story is mainly about, not just go off somewhere else and say, 'Well, I had a puppy once.' You can't do that 'cuz it's mostly about, it's *only* about the story and what happens to the character."

Antonio agrees but reminds them that it's a summary, saying, "Yeah, but you only use two or three lines to tell, tell about the story and don't like put like every detail or they'll know the story."

Gregory agrees that a summary must focus on the main idea.

Finally, Keevy stresses the importance of referring to the text: "The way it is, is you gotta refer to the text."

These children are skilled in group conversation. They have learned to listen to one another and extend contributions of others to further a discussion. They are respectful of each other and work to stay on topic and get ready for their independent writing assignment.

Discussing the Symbolism of a Yoruba Door

Standard 1: Habits
Conversing at Length on a Topic

- Initiate and sustain a conversation with eight or more lengthy exchanges

- Consistently ask for clarification

- Consistently recognize and respond to indirect and direct indications that others need clarification

- Initiate topics within conversations that are in progress

- Sustain conversation by extending others' contributions

- Express and solicit opinions

- Ask open-ended or long-answer questions

- Repair and revert to the topic when necessary

This segment shows a group of third graders talking at length on a topic. The class has been studying the practice of accountable talk (i.e., a way of talking based on accountability to knowledge, reasoning and community) as a vehicle for getting smarter. The behaviors and talk you see are not random events; the strategies employed for exploring a topic have been taught explicitly. The students are attempting to use these strategies deliberately to stay with a topic, explore ideas using evidence, question one another's reasoning in polite ways and share what they know.

This segment is especially interesting because the students are using what they have learned in the context of book talk and extending it to a different form of text, a poster. To prepare for a visit to a museum in which they will see artifacts from the Yoruba culture, these boys and girls discuss the significance of the decorations on the Yoruba door on the poster.

The segment begins with Joanna asking the group, "Who do you think is the person that is in the back on the second row?"

Clorissa responds, "Maybe it's like, to tell the horse which way to go, move the horse or to protect the king from harm."

Ivan responds to this idea: "If someone is going to come and do harm to the king from his back, instead they could do harm to the soldier, not the king."

Paraphrasing what she thinks Ivan said, Joanna says, "So you think that person is in the back so they can protect him?"

Michael says, "I would like to add to what Ivan said. Maybe the person in back of the horse tries to control the horse. Like if the horse tries to goes fast or if it tries to jump up, it holds it down so it doesn't go out of control."

Joanna continues the conversation by agreeing with Michael and asking a question that shows why she agrees: "I agree with you, Michael, because if there was only one in the front, who would protect the horse and the king?"

Ivan makes an analogy by comparing the portrayal on the door with their school: "This is kind of like our school. The principal is kind of like, in the middle, and Miss Mammolito is kind of like the linguist."

Joanna adds, "I think I wanted to add on to what you said. Our guard that we have downstairs? Where do you think you should put that guard?"

Ivan explains his thinking further when he responds to Joanna's question without hesitation, saying, "Where the screen [is]."

Joanna seeks further clarification by asking, "Why do you say that?"

Ivan answers, "Because the people with the screen are like protecting the king. It's like the security guard protects Mr. Spatola [the principal]. The king [the principal] also protects us. I would put us on top."

Continuing this scenario, Michael asks Ivan, "Who would you put on the bottom then?"

"The teachers," replies Ivan.

Joanna and Clorissa press him by asking, "Why?"

" 'Cause without teachers, there really wouldn't be a school," he says. " 'Cause if there were no teachers, then who would teach us?"

Joshua suggests that perhaps some of the other adults in the building, such as the assistant principal or the counselor, could teach the kids.

Ivan sticks to his argument and counters, "There are too many kids. The kids would go wild."

Joanna adds, "And, without kids there would be no school because teachers got to teach the kids."

Ivan asks a follow-up question that extends his analogy: "Where would you put the aides?"

Clorissa responds, "Maybe we could put them where the net is because they also protect, they kind of protect us, and they protect the principal a little."

Ivan doesn't directly confront her but politely offers a different idea: "They don't protect; they mostly help. It's sort of like they help; they mostly help. Sometimes they help us not to be out of control in the lunchroom."

Joanna asks a new question: "Who else do you think is important?"

Michael answers, "The nurse probably will go where the stream is because she helps the kids when they are sick."

"If there was no nurse . . ." Ivan begins to speculate.

Clorissa finishes his sentence, ". . . then everybody would be sick."

Ivan agrees, "Yeah."

"Then they would be spreading diseases," says Joshua.

Clorissa adds, "And then the other children might get sick, and a lot of kids would be absent day after day in school."

Joanna repairs and reverts to the topic when she links what the children have been saying about the nurse to the poster they are analyzing: "So you think the nurse is important, just like a guard would be."

The group agrees.

"Really everybody, mostly everybody has an important job to do on the door," Ivan continues. "We have an important job. We have to learn and remember what they teach us; what the teachers teach us."

Joanna adds, "When you say we have an important job to do. . . . See the woman on the top who is kneeling down with the babies, the womans [sic], they have to teach the kids just like the teachers have to teach us."

Michael asks, "I wonder why they are kneeling and not standing up."

Ivan conjectures, "Maybe they are kneeling for the king. You know, when in the movies, they bow to the king. They kneel."

Clorissa puts forth an interpretation: "They show respect."

Signaling that she is switching topics, Clorissa asks a question of her own and moves the conversation forward: "I have a question, what's a linguist?"

Ivan attempts a definition, "A linguist is a person who talks, speaks for the king, because, um, the king is too busy and too important to speak, so he even has a person who speaks for him."

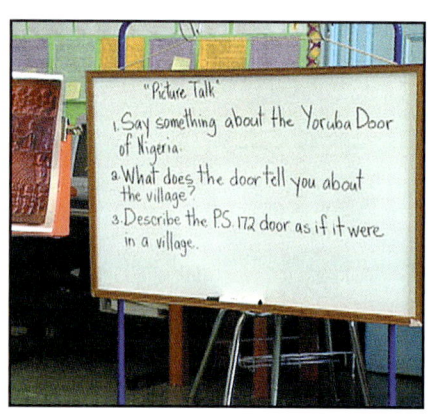

In this portion of the segment, we see six exchanges between Michael and Ivan in which they entertain one another's ideas and seem to finish each other's sentences.

Clorissa asks a follow-up question: "What do you think he is busy with?"

Michael answers, "Helping the villagers survive and support them with food."

Continuing with examples of what might keep the king busy, Ivan says, "Sometimes the king might be in a war with the soldiers."

Michael adds, "He could be like, training them, maybe."

Ivan says, "It could be like, just like a practice war where no one really dies."

Michael continues, "Just in case a war really happens, sometime."

Ivan continues, "They are just getting ready."

"What do you think this door is telling us about this little village?" asks Joanna.

Ivan responds, "Um, without no people protecting the king . . ."

Clorissa finishes the sentence, "There wouldn't be a king."

"Yeah!" agrees Ivan. "And I think the most important person is the women. With no women there would be no king, no people."

Michael adds, "Because they are the only ones . . ."

Ivan finishes, ". . . who can have babies."

Joanna summarizes, "I think the women are important too because they are the ones who have to make a people."

Ivan restates, "They have to make the babies, to make the king and to make the soldiers."

Clorissa continues this line of thinking when she says, "It's like, the king had to have a mother who gave birth to him. And like, he grew up and became king. And the soldiers had to have mothers too. And they grew up to protect the king."

Tiffany, who has been quiet up until now, demonstrates that she has been following the conversation when she poses a question about the design of the door: "Why do you think they put the soldiers on the bottom and not in the middle or in the rest of the parts?"

Ivan again proposes an idea: "The soldiers, without soldiers, people with knives could come in and cut the screen, like when, the people, they are not watching too good, two people could come in the back and attack them and cut through the screen."

Joanna agrees, "I think the soldiers are on the bottom, too, because they are the ones who are protecting the king, the woman, the linguist and all those people who are helping the king. So I think they are very important, so they should go on the bottom."

Michael responds to this question also: "I think the soldiers should be on the bottom. Say if the women were on the bottom, then somebody could come in. Because they are important, so they had to be most protected or if they die there's not going to be a king or anyone else."

Clorissa introduces a new idea when she says, "When I look at this door, it sort of reminds me of a story."

Ivan asks her for more elaboration: "What kind of a story?"

She continues, "Like the women gave birth, they had a child. And like he became a king, and he was protected by soldiers, and like . . ."

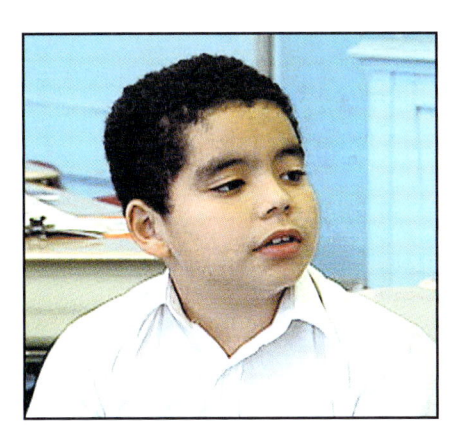

Joanna agrees and explains, "So do I. It's a picture, but it's like a story because it's like it's showing so many pictures and so many details in it; it's like a big story that you can read from pictures and not from words."

Michael builds on this idea and says, "It's like a word book, I mean a picture book not any words."

Ivan says, "It's like the pictures are kinda like the words."

Clorissa responds, "It's like you have to figure out what the words are."

Tiffany adds a new dimension to the conversation and meets the standard for talking a lot when she references ideas beyond her personal experience. She compares reading the symbols on this door to reading Egyptian pictographs: "It's like the Egyptians, like when they used to draw pictures for their writing. It's kind of similar. You have to figure out the writing piece that you can make out of this."

Staying with this idea, Ivan says, "It's like half the story and the other half is the writing and we have to figure out the writing."

Joanna says, "Imagine it's like a story, but it's an interesting story, not just any kind of story."

These students have been taught to use what they know to explore what they don't know. In an attempt to make sense of the symbolism on the Yoruba door, the students explore how this culture is like and unlike things they know. They make four comparisons: to their school, to a story, to a wordless picture book and finally to Egyptian hieroglyphs. When they compare the Yoruba culture to the organization they know best, their school, they create a sequence of analogies between the Yoruba culture and the school. In these analogies, the students consider how the placement of people on the door might make sense given what they know about the organization of their school, its purpose, the role of various personnel, etc.

The third graders in this segment clearly meet the standard for conversing at length on a topic. We see evidence of almost all the bullet points for this strand of the standard, including lengthy turns of conversation initiated by a student and sustained by peers. Without the assistance of an adult, these students explore ideas in smart ways. Different students consistently ask for clarification or recognize and respond to indications that they need to clarify their ideas. New, substantive questions posed by members of the group extend and sustain the conversation. The students stick with the topic and, using what they have learned about accountable talk, develop their ideas, employ reasoning strategies that require them to explain their thinking and back their ideas with evidence or reasons. They know more as a group after this conversation than any one of them did prior to their discussion.

These students also meet the standard for talking a lot to collaborate on a project — preparing for a museum visit — and the standard for rules of interaction by consistently observing politeness conventions, showing mastery of rules for school interaction and talk, and following rules for speaking (looking at the speaker and signaling for a chance to speak).

Cody's Cat, Max

Standard 1: Habits
Conversing at Length on a Topic

- Initiate and sustain a conversation with eight or more lengthy exchanges

- Initiate topics within conversations that are in progress

- Express and solicit opinions

Standard 2: Kinds of Talk and Resulting Genres
Narrative

- Describe information and evaluate or reflect on it

- Orient the listener to the setting with the precise choice of detail

- Develop characters by clearly stating their goals and motivations and by attempting to resolve or satisfy them before the story's end

While sharing his writer's notebook with a visitor, Cody mentioned an entry about his cat, Max. The visitor engages him in conversation about Max by asking, "If you were going to write a story about Max, what would you tell in your story?"

Cody thinks about it, not sure about how he would approach writing about the cat but sharing that he wants to do it.

The visitor probes, "What's special about Max?"

Cody continues the conversation, adding details about Max: "Well, he lived a really long time. He lived um, 100, well, in cat years, he lived like 116. But in our years, he lived like 16 years."

Responding to the visitor asking if Max had a good life, Cody says, "Yeah. He was my favorite cat." He pauses and then shares what he has been holding back: "He got hit by a car." Then he adds, "In the summer."

Cody continues the conversation, acknowledging the visitor's comment about that being a sad part of the summer. He replies, "Yeah. Mm-hmm. That was really at the end of the summer, when we came back from our trip. He died then."

The visitor tries to return to the idea of writing a story about losing his cat, but Cody redirects the visitor, saying, "I'd just, probably, just tell his life."

Knowing his class has been learning about biography as a genre, the visitor suggests he could write "The Biography of Max the Cat."

"Yeah I guess," Cody laughs but continues, "except I wasn't alive the whole time, so . . ."

When the visitor asks how he could find out more about Max, Cody replies, "I could ask my mom and dad."

But rather than focus on gathering information about Max, Cody wants to reminisce as he shares, "We found him in our garage."

Continuing the idea of writing a biography of Max, the visitor asks Cody about other parts of Max's life he would include in the biography. Cody concludes, "I'd do that part as a start, and then I'd do all . . . like when we played . . . when he used to come in my bed every night . . . and — just things like that."

In this conversation Cody demonstrates his ability not only to engage in conversation on a topic at length, but also to gradually tell the story of his cat dying. As his comfort level in sharing this very personal story increases, Cody shares details about Max's life and his relationship with the cat. Cody is able to carry this conversation on two levels: as a recounting of the story of Max's life and as a subject he might write about. The conversation is typical of a writing conference. The visitor engages Cody in talk to help him develop a plan for writing about Max. Cody's performance demonstrates the power of daily classroom talk to help students develop confidence and grow as writers.

The World Is Shrinking

Standard 1: Habits
Conversing at Length on a Topic

◆ Initiate and sustain a conversation with eight or more lengthy exchanges

◆ Initiate topics within conversations that are in progress

◆ Sustain conversation by extending others' contributions

◆ Express and solicit opinions

Tyler and Kirbe are discussing a rather mature idea — that "it's a small world after all." They have been reading several books by different authors whose fictional stories are set in foreign countries. This conversation illustrates the standard for conversing at length. Though brief, it consists of at least eight exchanges, with the children signaling comprehension and extending each other's contributions.

Tyler suggests that other cultures have a lot of things in common with their own so that "it's just like one continent."

Kirbe agrees, "And like a lot of stuff happens and like there's all this stuff that goes on around the world."

The children even refer to the school's Intercultural Fair to help prove their point: "And in Intercultural Fair we started noticing and we, and we bring in all the different cultures so it's all in our playground."

This example highlights the importance of book discussions. Engaging in author studies has prompted these children to look closely at the world they live in, adjusting their viewpoint to recognize similarities.

Research Perspectives

> "One of the most important influences on all talk (some say the most important influence) is the participants themselves — their expectations about interactions and their perceptions of each other. . . . Ways of talking that seem so natural to one group are experienced as culturally strange to another."
>
> From Cazden, C. (1988). *Classroom Discourse, The Language of Teaching and Learning.* Heinemann, 67.

Discussing Books

Year-end second graders recognize and compare works by different authors in the same genre and discuss recurring themes across works. They paraphrase, summarize, ask speakers to give evidence, and politely correct someone who paraphrases or interprets them incorrectly. They may challenge speakers on the accuracy of their facts, logic or inferences.

Second- & Third-Grade Standards

Standard 1: *Habits*
- Talking a Lot — pg. 202
- Talking to One's Self — pg. 207
- Conversing at Length on a Topic — pg. 208
- Discussing Books — pg. 218

Standard 2: *Kinds of Talk and Resulting Genres*
- Narrative — pg. 230
- Explaining and Seeking Information — pg. 236
- Getting Things Done — pg. 244
- Producing and Responding to Performances — pg. 251

Standard 3: *Language Use and Conventions*
- Rules of Interaction — pg. 254
- Word Play and Grammatical Awareness — pg. 256
- Vocabulary and Word Choice — pg. 260

Book talk that occurs in one-on-one or small-group sessions allows children to show deeper comprehension. In these situations, by the end of second grade, children begin to talk about organizing structures; combine information from two different parts of the text; infer cause-and-effect relationships; and discuss how, why and what-if questions about nonfiction texts. They can discuss or write about themes, trace characters and plots across multiple episodes, and relate different parts of the text.

By the end of third grade, we also expect children to:

- note and talk about author's craft: word choice, beginnings and endings, plot, and character development (for example, "The ending comes right back to the beginning. It's like a circle.");
- use comparisons and analogies to explain ideas;
- refer to knowledge gained during discussion (for example, "No that can't be right, because it said the dragon is 'too old to swim across the channel.'");
- use information that is accurate, accessible and relevant;
- restate their own ideas with greater clarity when a listener indicates noncomprehension (for example, "He's too old to get across the channel, so he can't be the dragon that swam across and stole Sarah away.");
- ask other students questions that require them to support their claims or arguments (for example, "Why not? Maybe he took a boat.");
- indicate when their own or others' ideas need further support or explanation (for example, "But there's nothing in the book about a boat. But there are clues that it might be the wizard.");
- cite important details from the text (for example, "She's sad because she's the new girl and hasn't met anybody yet. Plus, it says, 'a lonely flower in a crowded vase.'");
- compare one text to another text they have read or heard (for example, "This is the second book about being new in class too, but I like it better. The words are pretty."); and

Second & Third Grades: Standard 1

- capture meaning from figurative language and explain the meaning (for example, "He said 'she's frilly as a petunia' because her dress and hair are so ruffly and bright.").

With narratives in particular, we expect children to:

- relate a story to real-life experiences (for example, "I was new in second grade; I hated it.");
- explain the motives of characters (for example, "When you're new, sometimes you're afraid to talk to anyone."); and
- discuss plot and setting (for example, "She has to have a partner for the field trip, but you don't know who. I hope she doesn't get the mean girl.").

With informational texts in particular, we expect children to:

- use the structure of information texts to retrieve information (for example, "Chapter 5 is called 'Desert Plants,' so cactus must be there.");
- analyze the causes, motivations, sequences and results of events;
- understand the concepts and relationships described;
- use reasoning and information from within and outside the text to examine arguments (for example, "It says this cactus only blooms every 10 years, but it looks like the one we have, and it's always blooming!"); and
- describe in their own words what new information they gained from a nonfiction text and how that information relates to their prior knowledge (for example, "There's a kind of cactus . . . it looks just like one at my house, but it's a different species. It only blooms every 10 years!").

With functional texts in particular, we expect children to:

- follow instructions or directions they read in more complicated texts (for example, while working on a group craft, "No, look, it says, 'Fold it diagonally,' you're folding it sideways.").

Discussing Books: A Multifaceted Literacy Skill

Careful readers will notice that there is a standard for discussing books in this book about speaking and listening and in our companion book, *Reading & Writing grade by grade*. This overlap is intentional.

Discussing books is a multifaceted literacy skill. Clearly, talking about books, listening to others speak about points of view, taking turns in a group discussion, disagreeing politely and so on are oral language skills.

Just as clearly, discussing books is a vital component of reading and writing. In book talks, students can demonstrate comprehension, compare and contrast authors and books, find justification for their remarks in the text, and explain their interpretations. These literacy skills are distinct from oral language skills. The reading and writing standards approach discussing books from a different perspective than the speaking and listening standards do.

The Singing Man Discussion

Standard 1: Habits
Discussing Books

- Note and talk about author's craft: word choice, beginnings and endings, plot, and character development
- Cite important details from the text
- Refer to knowledge gained during discussion
- Use information that is accurate, accessible and relevant
- Restate their own ideas with greater clarity when a listener indicates noncomprehension
- Ask other students questions that require them to support their claims or arguments
- Indicate when their own and others' ideas need further support or explanation
- Use comparisons and analogies to explain ideas
- Capture meaning from figurative language and explain the meaning
- Relate a story to real-life experiences

While discussing *The Singing Man* by Angela Medearis, this small group of third graders gives attention to the development of the character Banzar, who becomes the king's personal praise singer. We pick up the discussion as the children are looking at two of the illustrations of Banzar.

Joanna describes Banzar's appearance, saying, "He's like wearing clothes that is like, not like, you know, like regular people would wear. He's wearing something real rich."

"Like silk," adds Joshua.

Ivan comments that "you can see the big difference. Here he, he looks poor and then you see here he, he looks so different."

In response to the teacher's question, "Why?" Michael makes a relevant comment about the reason for the difference in Banzar's appearance, saying, "Because, um, he was at the festival singing, and the chief, um, the king, um made him his personal praise singer. And, so, he was important to the king now."

Clorissa offers an addition: "He was like, I would like to add, he was like, umm, like the, he was like the best of the praise singers."

"Could you speak louder?" Michael asks.

Clorissa restates her idea more clearly using an analogy: "He was like the best one of the praise singers. He's like, almost like the king of the praise singers, their leader."

"Like Sholo used to be," concludes Tiffany.

Ivan says, "Sholo passed away, and Banzar took his place."

This comment serves as a turning point in the conversation. Others build on Ivan's statement, expanding the conversation by explaining what it means to take someone's place across generations.

Joanna adds, "It's like, um, it's like, it's like, like when Sholo died, Banzar took his place. It's like, it's like a repetition, like somebody's dying and then somebody else takes their place. It's never gonna happen that someone never is gonna be in first place, somebody has to . . ."

Clorissa adds greater detail: "Like if Banzar, you know, meets somebody else and, um, teaches the same thing and then when, um, when Banzar died, then he takes the place. It's like that."

Michael adds, "The person that he taught would become like the number one praise singer."

"I think that it was meant for Sholo and Banzar to meet," announces Tiffany.

Several children, recognizing that an explanation is needed, ask in unison, "Why do you say that?"

She explains, "Because Banzar always wanted to become a musician, and Sholo was a praise singer and they . . ."

Ivan supports her, saying, "So they kind of made the dream come true."

"Yeah," she responds.

The conversation shifts back to specifics of the text when Joanna says, "It surprised me too. At the end, I didn't think it was going to end like this way, like, him meeting his, like seeing his parents again. Because since he had to sing for the king and all that kind of stuff, I thought he wasn't really going to come, at the end he wasn't gonna to come back to his family, and you know, see them again."

Ivan asks her to support her statement: "Well, why, why do you think he wouldn't come back to his family?"

Joanna explains, "I mean, I would think that he would come. But I didn't, like, it didn't get up to my head that it would be at the end. Because he would have to like sing for the king and maybe he would be busy a lot. Because he would maybe have to think of songs to sing to the king, so maybe he wouldn't have time to go to the village where his family was at."

Clorissa offers her support: "I, I kind of agree with Joanna because I didn't think that, like, Banzar would go back to the village or anything, to his boyhood. Because, it's like, because he'd be like very . . . I wouldn't think that the king, would like let him go like anywhere. I think he would just like let him stay there and like figure out songs and sing them to him, new songs. I wouldn't think that the king would like let him go anywhere else, only stay in where he is."

Joanna builds on Clorissa's statement: "I would like to add a little bit to what you said, Clorissa. What I want to say is that maybe too he wanted to go over there because he wanted to show everybody that, um. . . . He wanted to show everybody that, um, a musician isn't bad because you can,

um, be able to not be just a musician. You can be even more than that."

Michael expands on the comments, saying, "Like he wanted to teach and after that he probably wanted to teach others that it's good to be a musician sometimes."

Ivan directs the group back to the text, using a quote from the book: "Yeah, 'cause, um, if you turn to the last page, it says that 'now there is a new saying. Yams fill the belly, money fills the pockets, but music fills the heart.' "

The teacher's questions, "What do you think about that? Why do you think they end with that?" launch the group into a discussion of the value of music in people's lives.

Clorissa answers, "I kind of like it because it's like, 'cause in the first part the elders didn't really know that music was like to impress you and like to fill your heart. You need happiness too, not only like, um, money and stuff, and money and, um, you need food but you don't always only need that. You need happiness in your heart too."

Michael expands the point: "And they only thought that like music was for entertaining, um, like the . . ."

▶▶

"It won't help people," Ivan interjects.

"Yeah," Michael agrees, "it won't help people at all."

Ivan continues expanding the point: "If you really look at it, um, music does help people. It fills the heart with joy."

"And caring," adds Clorissa.

"Yeah," says Ivan, "and they, they remember what happened in the past because Sholo said a person, a person with no past has no future."

"Yeah," Clorissa agrees.

Joanna refers back to the text, saying, "I think that, um, on the last page when it says, 'but music fills your heart,' I think that it's trying to tell, that little sentence right there, I think it's trying to tell us that music, when you like sing it or you, um . . ."

"Play it," says Ivan.

"Play it, um," continues Joanna, "you could, it could make you happy if you're sad. It could make you happy. I think it's trying to say it fills your heart with happiness."

Joshua relates the discussion to his real-life experience, saying, "It kind of reminds me because of, of my own life. 'Cause, um, one time I, I, I was like . . . I was sad because my great-grandmother died. And, I was like walking around, um, Manhattan and I saw this guy who, who, um, was with, um, like, um, a few other guys. And they were like playing drums and they were like, um, they were singing. And, and I stood there for like a, five minutes. And, it made me feel a little bit happier because my gramma, my great-grandmother, she used to like music. And, and I gave them like at least a dollar."

"I know," Joanna says, referring back to the text. "It happened too to Banzar. Because over here, um, when Sholo died, he, um, you could see him, um, sitting there somewhere around here, when Sholo died, he was sad, right? But then . . ."

Ivan begins to read from the text: " 'started playing his flute. He sat by the river for hours gently tapping Sholo's omele drum and thinking about his friend. He remembered Sholo's words.' "

Joanna completes the character development discussion by connecting real life back to the text. She says, "So that like tells us that it happened, the same thing like Joshua and you. You thought about the music. So, when you heard it, um, it made you feel better. And, when Banzar, he played his flute and it made him feel better. So, he said, 'Why am I sitting here? Why shouldn't I play my flute and not get sad. Because why shouldn't I do what, um, Sholo told me to do?' "

Throughout the discussion, the children refer to specific, relevant parts of the text, often with direct quotes. The children demonstrate that they are listening carefully to each other by asking for clarification and building on and supporting each other's comments. They demonstrate an understanding of figurative language, using comparisons and analogies to explain their thoughts. One child validates the story by making a relevant connection to his own real-life experience. Note that the teacher asks only a few open-ended questions, "Why?" "What did you think of that?" and "Why do you think they end with that?" This end-of-the-year student performance meets the standard and demonstrates the group's ability to independently sustain an in-depth book discussion.

Interesting Language

Standard 1: Habits
Discussing Books

◆ Note and talk about author's craft: word choice, beginnings and endings, plot, and character development

◆ Compare one text to another text they have read or heard

These students exhibit the kind of talk about books that shows discussing books has become a habit they enjoy. Tyler explains, "I really like this book because of all the interesting language it had." Then he shares a specific example, which is one of his favorite passages: "Let me see if I can find it, like, where is it? 'The older, the older children waved flags and headbands and shouted at the top of their lungs until the mountain echoed the noise like rumbling thunder.' "

Alexandra agrees, remembering that another author she is familiar with also uses rich language, "Well, I agree with you. I mean, and I think that some of these interesting words are kind of interesting like Byrd Baylor's words."

The group agrees, saying, "Yeah, I agree with you because it's like . . ." and "Yeah, they're like connected in some way."

Did He Die?

Standard 1: Habits
Discussing Books

- Note and talk about author's craft: word choice, beginnings and endings, plot, and character development
- Cite important details from the text
- Compare one text to another text they have read or heard
- Refer to knowledge gained during discussion
- Use information that is accurate, accessible and relevant
- Restate their own ideas with greater clarity when a listener indicates noncomprehension
- Ask other students questions that require them to support their claims or arguments
- Indicate when their own or others' ideas need further support or explanation
- Use comparisons and analogies to explain ideas
- Capture meaning from figurative language and explain the meaning

This performance includes just the type of spirited conversation we hope to see. All of the students obviously have thought about this text, and they are all quick to voice their opinion when there is a disagreement about the author's intent.

The teacher simply asks, "Did [Allen Say's grandfather] ever go back to Japan?"

This question sparks quite a debate — some people think he returned, others think he passed away and never did. Tyler says, "[He went to] California, but he never went [to Japan]," while another student says, "And he died." Alexandra adds, "Because it said he never did," as Kirbe claims, "It gives us a *thought* that he did die."

Then the children begin interpreting the text to justify their claim. Kirbe begins to interpret some of the figurative language used, saying, "The only way you could be really sure he died was because, like, in the end of the book it said something about that being like the last memory, like that being the last time Allen Say saw his grandfather."

Alexandra agrees, citing the text and making inferences, "Yeah, he said, 'The last time I saw my grandfather, he was longing for California, he never did [go back to Japan].' You would like think that he was dead. I mean, 'cuz, like, if you never did, you died or something like that."

Next there is a disagreement as Raymond attempts to transfer the discussion to another book by the same author. Raymond says, "I don't think he died because in *Tea with Milk*, it, um, it shows him with Miscoko [sic] so that kind of proves that he didn't die and . . ."

Quickly and politely, Alexandra corrects him, explaining that the two cannot be compared on this particular point: "No, this was like before Allen Say was born, this was like, this was like whenever, like, his grandfather was young and he was married and he just had his child."

The children continue responding to the issue of how this series of books by Allen Say informs the question of the grandfather's death. Victor states, "*Tea with Milk* could've happened, could've happened after that story."

Tyler references several texts, saying, "Yeah, 'cuz *Grandfather's Journey* for instance, it's like its own story of its own, then it goes into *Tree*, then it goes into *Tea with Milk*, and then it goes into *Tree of Cranes*. Then it's a whole 'nother story."

Tyler goes on to bring the conversation back around to the question of the one character in the particular book. He says, "So I agree with Victor because he probably *did* die because some stories give you a hint that they die, a lot of stories do that." He goes on to offer some evidence for his idea: "And I agree with you because it's like *Grandfather's Journey*, the very last part, the last fourth of it, it goes into way after *Tea with Milk*, so I agree with you, Victor."

The children clearly are discussing author's craft, referring to an author's strategy of purposely leaving things vague or for the reader to infer. Jordan says, "I agree with you too, Tyler, because it's kind of obvious that he died and that . . . in other stories, they say things like that, too. And you're sure, for sure that they died in other stories, but we're not sure in this . . . and it's real obvious that he did."

This is an excellent discussion of author's craft, including word choice and endings. The students cite details from the text and compare different works by the same author. They are careful to restate their own ideas with greater clarity and to offer evidence when others question them.

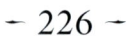

Word Choice

Standard 1: Habits
Discussing Books

- Note and talk about author's craft: word choice, beginnings and endings, plot, and character development

- Capture meaning from figurative language and explain the meaning

These children obviously are enjoying the word choice — an element of author's craft — in this story. Aaron explains that the descriptive language makes him feel like he is part of the story: "When you're reading it, you could really, like, almost feel like you're in the story, like by hearing that language."

Tyler agrees, citing a page of the text as an example, "Yeah, it's like I'm one of the kids, and I'm enjoying him riding the bicycle because it's like, it tells so much language to describe what he's actually doing. And like this, 'He seemed to be flying free, crushing *[sic]* like an enormous dragonfly, oh, oh, he exclaimed and gasped and turned.'"

Book discussion with this level of detail will help children become better readers and accomplished writers.

Research Perspectives

> "... the basic purpose of school is achieved through communication."
>
> From Cazden, C. (1988). *Classroom Discourse, The Language of Teaching and Learning.* Heinemann, 2.

Standard 2:
Kinds of Talk and Resulting Genres
Introduction

In second and third grades, children should continue to have opportunities for speaking and listening in the four genres identified in Standard 2: narrative, explaining and seeking information, getting things done, and producing and responding to performances. While they already have made a full transition from speech to print by writing for specific purposes and consciously appropriating author's craft, this oral work continues to be very valuable.

When it comes to narratives, children are still better at factual accounts than at fictional ones, as fictional narratives are the most difficult to master. Children's fictional stories may have climaxes; however, their autobiographical narratives do not have a traditional climax. These narratives often, though, have some sort of evaluative, reflective comment.

Second- & Third-Grade Standards

Standard 1: *Habits*

- Talking a Lot — pg. 202
- Talking to One's Self — pg. 207
- Conversing at Length on a Topic — pg. 208
- Discussing Books — pg. 218

Standard 2: *Kinds of Talk and Resulting Genres*

- Narrative — pg. 230
- Explaining and Seeking Information — pg. 236
- Getting Things Done — pg. 244
- Producing and Responding to Performances — pg. 251

Standard 3: *Language Use and Conventions*

- Rules of Interaction — pg. 254
- Word Play and Grammatical Awareness — pg. 256
- Vocabulary and Word Choice — pg. 260

> By now, children can tackle complex social and cognitive problems; they are intrigued by rules and interested in the process of argument. Their ability to consider point of view and alternative solutions takes a leap.

As in earlier years, teachers are advised to be aware of cultural differences that will affect children's narratives. (For more details and examples, see sidebar on page 231.)

By the second and third grades, children are much more capable of differentiating between narratives and explanations used in their reports. For instance, sharing time for personal narratives is now very different from a report on the life cycle of a butterfly.

The world broadens for most children in second and third grades. They take a huge leap developmentally in the complexity of their responsibilities. Their chores and their extracurricular activities broaden, expanding their knowledge of the world. Their physical boundaries widen, improving their sense of geography. Their vocabulary grows and so does their pragmatic language competence, including the ability to argue. By now, children can tackle complex social and cognitive problems; they are intrigued by rules and interested in the process of argument. Their ability to consider point of view and alternative solutions takes a leap.

Children should be engaged in regular writers response groups or taking the Author's Chair at the close of a Writers Workshop period. In this setting, they have daily opportunities either to perform by reading their own material or to respond to others' with questions or suggestions.

In addition, other types of performances might include presenting a full-length play to an unfamiliar audience or giving an oral report to the class. Students also should attend or watch more complex performances and have opportunities to respond orally and in writing.

Narrative

At this age children's oral narratives increase in length and complexity and are likely to move beyond personally experienced events. The sequence of events lengthens, and character development moves beyond simply stating motivations. The use of detail begins to be sharpened by precise word choice, and resolutions do more than simply comment on final events.

With factual narratives, by the end of third grade we expect children to:

Second- & Third-Grade Standards

Standard 1: *Habits*
- Talking a Lot — pg. 202
- Talking to One's Self — pg. 207
- Conversing at Length on a Topic — pg. 208
- Discussing Books — pg. 218

Standard 2: *Kinds of Talk and Resulting Genres*
- Narrative — pg. 230
- Explaining and Seeking Information — pg. 236
- Getting Things Done — pg. 244
- Producing and Responding to Performances — pg. 251

Standard 3: *Language Use and Conventions*
- Rules of Interaction — pg. 254
- Word Play and Grammatical Awareness — pg. 256
- Vocabulary and Word Choice — pg. 260

- independently give a lengthy and richly detailed account in which the actual sequence of events is clear even though events may be told out of order deliberately to build anticipation or through use of flashbacks; and
- pass along a story they have heard, giving enough detail or nuance to do justice to the original version.

Second- and third-grade children should learn to include these elements for telling more interesting and varied narratives:

- solicit and/or engage the listener's attention (beginning with the time, location or main character of the story) before going into the full account (for example, "One night my friend and I went out to play. It was pitch black and kind of scary.");
- orient the listener to the setting with the precise choice of detail (for example, "We met at the creek. We had a canoe and fishing poles. I had a tub of worms for night fishing.");
- cluster useful descriptive information in the beginning (for example, "We caught some fish right away, but just tiny ones. They were easy.");
- describe information and evaluate or reflect on it (for example, "There was no way, no way I was going to let that fish go! I was fighting so hard my arm ached!");
- describe internal events or reactions as well as external events (for example, "At first I wasn't scared of playing the piano on stage, but when I saw the audience I wanted to run and hide.");
- develop characters by clearly stating their goals and motivations and attempting to resolve or satisfy them before the story's end (for example, "I was so happy to get that fish; I couldn't wait to tell my dad.");
- include quotations (for example, "Dad said, 'Hey, we're going to the rodeo.' ");
- comment and reflect on how things were resolved (for example, "Mom cooked the fish for dinner. It tasted so good."); and
- mark the end of the story directly or with a coda to bring the impact of the past experience up to the present time (for example, "I didn't even get in trouble for going out at night.").

New Standards

Cultural Differences in Narrative Form

North American cultural traditions dominate life in the United States. Thus, the standards for narratives conform to North American narrative tradition.

However, narratives from other cultures are distinctly different; for example, some stories typically combine several experiences linked in the narrator's mind. These narratives, called "topic-associating narratives," are not about a single important event. For instance, African American narrative style (often mislabeled as "rambling") is a thematic linkage of events that occurred at different places and times and often involves different participants.

Hispanic children's stories place family connections and relationships in the foreground; these children worry less about the exact sequence of events. In one study, almost 50 percent of the narratives produced by these children contained no sequencing. Japanese children often conform to their cultural norms by keeping narratives succinct, while Hungarian children use extensive embellishments in their retellings. Hawaiian children, on the other hand, tell "talk-stories" that weave teasing and fantasy into repetitive routines for a number of participants.

Children's native cultures influence how they recount their experiences and tell stories. Teachers must help children develop expertise in North American narrative forms while respecting their students' native ones.

What follows are examples of typical narrative performances by seven- or eight-year-old children from different cultures. When teachers understand and respect students' native narrative style, they can better help them acquire both the oral and written North American narrative forms. Not teaching the North American narrative form disadvantages children from other cultures who are living in the United States.

African American Narrative Form

Consider the way that an eight-year-old African American girl pulls together a variety of teeth-pulling stories to establish herself as a "pullin'-teeth expert." She builds up to a powerful unifying aphorism that encourages self-reliance yet expresses support. (Note that children do not always make their themes as explicit as this girl does.)

Eight-year-old Vivian, African American:
We went to the dentist before and I was gettin' my tooth pulled and the doc, the dentist said, "Oh, it's not gonna hurt."

And he was lying to me. It hurt. It hurted so bad I coulda' gone on screamin' even though I think some. (I don't know what it wasn't like.) I was, in my mouth like, I was like, "Oh that hurt!"

He said no, it wouldn't hurt. 'Cause last time I went to the doctor, I had got this spray. This doctor, he sprayed some spray in my mouth and my tooth appeared in his hand. He put me to sleep, and then, and then I woke up. He used some pliers to take it out, and I didn't know.

So I had told my, I asked my sister how did, how did the man take it out. And so she said, "He used some pliers."

▶▶

I said, "Nah, he used that spray."

She said, "Nope, he used that spray to put you to sleep, and he used the pliers to take it out."

I was, like, "Huh, that's amazin'." I swear to God I was so amazed that, hum. It was so amazing, right, that I had to look for myself, and then I asked him too.

And he said, "Yes, we, I used some pliers to take out your tooth, and I put you to sleep, an, so you wouldn't know, and that's how I did it."

And I was like, "Oouu," and then I seen my sister get her tooth pulled.

I was like, "Oouu" 'cause he had to put her to sleep to, hmm, to take out her tooth. It was the same day she got her tooth pulled, and I was scared.

I was like, "EEEhhhmmm."

I had a whole bunch cotton in my mouth, chompin' on it 'cause I had to hold it to, hmm, stop my bleeding.

I, one day I was in school. I took out my own tooth. I put some hot water in it the night, the, the night before I went to school. And I was taking a test. And then it came out right when I was takin', when I finished the test. And my teacher asked me, was it bleeding.

I said, "No, it's not bleeding 'cause I put some hot water on it."

And so my cousin, he wanted to take out his tooth, and he didn't know what to do, so I told him, "I'm a pullin'-teeth expert. Pull out your own tooth, but if you need somebody to do it, call me and I'll be over."

Hispanic Narrative Form

Hispanic children tend to include many family members and friends as characters in their stories, no matter how slight the role assigned to a character. Teachers often see this flood of names and characters as distracting from the main story line. However, this emphasis on family is typical in narratives told by Hispanic children. The following is an excerpt from a narrative told by a seven-year-old girl from El Salvador:

Seven-year-old Carmen, El Salvadoran:
My Uncle Roberto . . . he has two children who are not twins . . . because first Robertico was born, who is named after his dad, and then Christopher was born. . . .

But my Uncle Roberto has a dog who is one of those German ones, who is already two months old. My uncle whose name is Juan . . . gave him that dog. But that dog bites. He bites Alex . . . he runs and bites. . . . HERE he bit him and he bit him even in the face and here in the arms.

Japanese Narrative Form

In some cultures, a premium is placed on being succinct rather than verbose. In a style reminiscent of haiku, Japanese children produce succinct collections of experiences, often presented in sets of three lines. Sun, an eight-year-old Japanese child, was asked if he ever had an experience involving an injury or requiring a doctor. The structure of the narrative he told is quite different from those told by North American children in response to the same prompt.

Eight-year-old Sun, Japanese:
As for the first . . .
got [it] at Ehime, you know,
hurt a lot.

As for the second, you know,
hurt, you know.
Well, you know, didn't hurt so much. . . .

The next didn't hurt so much, either.
As for the last, you know, didn't hurt at all.

— adapted from McCabe, 1996, *Chameleon Readers*

Second & Third Grades: Standard 2/Commentary on Student Performances — 233 —

Trevor Tells about Rosa Parks

Standard 2: Kinds of Talk and Resulting Genres

Narrative

◆ Pass along a story they have heard, giving enough detail or nuance to do justice to the original version

◆ Solicit and/or engage the listener's attention (beginning with the time, location or main character of the story) before going into the full account

◆ Orient the listener to the setting with the precise choice of detail

◆ Cluster useful descriptive information in the beginning

◆ Describe information and evaluate or reflect on it

Trevor recounts for a classroom visitor the story of Rosa Parks, one of the people about whom his class has read during their genre study of biography.

Trevor establishes a context for his story by describing the racial climate in which Rosa Parks lived: "Well, um, back in the '50s, I think, um, this thing, I don't know, like a civil rights thing, and there was all these white people who wouldn't let black people do the same things as them, like they'd have the blacks drink out of different water fountains and go to different schools for the kids." He gives a specific example of the way people acted out their racial hatred and connects it to an incident in Rosa Parks' early life, saying, "And there was this, um, organization called the, the KKK, which stands for the, um, the Ku Klux Klan, and they would, and they would hate, and they hate blacks, and they would, um, and I think it's still around, I think it still exists. Um, they take black people, like they break into their houses. And when Rosa was a kid, um, she would stay up all night with her grandfather with his shotgun next to him in case they came. And they never came, but she still stayed up."

Trevor knows many details about the singular incident for which Rosa Parks is known: "Um, there was this famous thing that happened. Um, she got on a bus, 'cause I don't think she had a car, I think that's the reason she rode the bus all the time, and um, she rode the bus, and one day she got on the bus and she sat in front." He understands why this act of Rosa's was significant and explains, "And, in those days the blacks weren't allowed to sit in front, and they'd have to sit in back."

Trevor sequences many details of the incident on the bus: "And so she sat there, and a white guy wanted to sit there, so, um, a white man wanted to sit there, so she refused to get up, so he got the, um, he got the, um, bus driver, and the bus driver told her to get up, and she still refused, so the bus driver called the police, and the police arrested her."

Trevor reflects on the importance of biography as a genre that can inform future generations about past events, saying, "So, um, you could, so other people know what people have done."

Equally important, he is able to evaluate the lesson that others can take from these historical examples: "Well, because, um, well 'cause, you, so I and some other kids, um, know what happened and try not that, let that happen again."

Even when a class has had in-depth discussions of the books, it is important to give individual students an opportunity to tell what they have learned from their reading. Teachers can check for understanding of the material, and students can consolidate their thinking by putting it into words.

The images and commentary in this section refer to performances available on accompanying CD-ROM.

New Standards

Timmy's Waterfall Adventure

Standard 2: Kinds of Talk and Resulting Genres
Narrative

- Orient the listener
- Describe information and evaluate or reflect on it
- Describe internal events or reactions

When a listener invites him to tell a story about an interesting experience, Timmy offers a detailed and evocative account of his encounter with a waterfall. Right away, Timmy orients the listener by describing the setting of his story and introducing the main characters: "When, probably, I was in a jungle . . . a forest, I think. And then there was this, there was a bridge, like . . . and there was a waterfall. And then, I just, um — my dad was in the waterfall."

Notice that in this last sentence, Timmy is tempted to dive right into an account of his own experience. He stops himself mid-sentence, however, and adds the important fact that his "dad was in the waterfall." This information helps to reveal Timmy's internal state and his motivation for the journey: He was going not only to the waterfall but also to join his dad.

Once he has established the setting and point of view for his story, Timmy begins to move the narrative forward, describing his approach to the waterfall and taking care to include information about his own reaction: "And then I just walked across the bridge. It was very scary, though, because it was all creaky."

At this point in his story, Timmy backtracks for just a moment to reiterate that he was moving toward his dad, "who was in the waterfall." Timmy clearly has the listener in mind here as he checks for comprehension and restates important facts before continuing his story.

Timmy continues, "My dad was like, he said it was like a massage when he . . . um, stand *[sic]* in the waterfall, and it fell on his back." By including this extra layer of detail, Timmy helps the listener understand why he was so eager to approach the waterfall himself.

Having successfully brought the listener to this point in his journey to the waterfall, Timmy is ready to describe the surprise that awaited him when he finally arrived. He says, "And so I went there. As soon as I got [to the waterfall], it just pushed me down, and it was really freaky." Notice that Timmy concludes his story with an evaluative comment that conveys not only the suddenness of the external event, but also his feelings of shock and dismay at the power of the water.

Piper Goes to the Rodeo

Standard 2: Kinds of Talk and Resulting Genres
Narrative

◆ Solicit and/or engage the listener's attention

◆ Cluster useful descriptive information in the beginning

◆ Develop characters

◆ Include quotations

In second and third grades, children increasingly are adept at using a variety of narrative techniques to develop character and build a story from a sequence of events. Here, Piper demonstrates skill with both spoken and written narrative, moving easily from one to the other.

When asked to summarize a story she has been working on, Piper begins by offering useful background information: "It's about me, my dad and my two sisters.... We went to a rodeo."

Piper then engages the listener's attention by describing a rodeo accident, the memory of which was the original inspiration for her story: "I remembered that we were watching the bucking broncos and a guy fell off and the bronco ran right over his head and hurt the guy."

Piper then reads aloud the story that grew out of this memory:
We woke up and had pancakes. Then my dad came up and said, "Hey, guys! We're going to the rodeo."
"Yes!" I said.
"Yee-ha!" my little sister said.
"Cotton candy," my older sister said.
We went to the rodeo. We sat down. The calf roping was first.
I said, "Get it!"
My little sister said, "No! It's a baby calf."
My older sister said, "Cotton candy."
My dad said, "Fine. I'll get you some cotton candy."
"Yes!" my older sister said.
"Oh," my little sister said.
"Okay," I said.

Notice that Piper uses direct quotations to quickly and efficiently reveal the distinct personalities of the three sisters as they react to the events of the story. The parallel construction in these quotations helps to emphasize the personality differences among the sisters and to develop each girl as a character who can be recognized by her responses.

Piper's use of this quotation structure throughout her story demonstrates that she is aware of parallel construction and repetition as narrative devices and that she is able to effectively integrate these into her storytelling and writing. In this story, repetition adds a layer of humor and also invokes the familiar and powerful structure of myth and fairy tale (" 'Not I,' said the dog. 'Not I,' said the cat").

Piper continues reading:
Then the bucking broncos.
I said, "Yes."
My little sister said, "Aaah!"
My older sister said, "Oh."
Number three was up. He got knocked out and the bronco stepped on his eye and he had to go out. Then the rodeo queens came.
I said they were pretty.
My little sister said, "I want to be one."
My older sister said, "Cool."
On the way back, we ran all the way to the car and went home.
The end.

Talking about their writing process and reading their work aloud helps students become aware of the narrative devices at their disposal and use these devices consciously as they create their own spoken and written narratives.

Explaining and Seeking Information

In second and third grades, children's ability to seek information from adults, the library and the Internet expands. They are able to research and gather more information. Their descriptions, while still evaluative and reasoned, become even more elaborate. Their presentations improve, and their ability to relate complex information to others increases. Specifically, by the end of third grade we expect children to:

◆ seek out multiple resources for information such as libraries, governmental and professional agencies, the Internet, and identified experts;

◆ conduct firsthand interviews (for example, interviewing a peer to write a character sketch, interviewing a parent for a report on a historical event);

◆ give increasingly elaborate and extended descriptions of objects, events and concepts;

◆ support opinions or provide specific examples to support generalizations;

◆ give a short prepared speech or report informing others about some object, event or person (for example, plan and present a brief oral report on a project or a book, with a poster or diorama used in the presentation); and

◆ tutor others in new and somewhat complicated tasks (for example, showing a child how to make origami).

Second- & Third-Grade Standards

Standard 1: *Habits*

- ◆ Talking a Lot — pg. 202
- ◆ Talking to One's Self — pg. 207
- ◆ Conversing at Length on a Topic — pg. 208
- ◆ Discussing Books — pg. 218

Standard 2: *Kinds of Talk and Resulting Genres*

- ◆ Narrative — pg. 230
- ◆ Explaining and Seeking Information — pg. 236
- ◆ Getting Things Done — pg. 244
- ◆ Producing and Responding to Performances — pg. 251

Standard 3: *Language Use and Conventions*

- ◆ Rules of Interaction — pg. 254
- ◆ Word Play and Grammatical Awareness — pg. 256
- ◆ Vocabulary and Word Choice — pg. 260

Second & Third Grades: Standard 2/Commentary on Student Performances — 237 —

Ethan and Graham Elaborate the Categories

Standard 2: Kinds of Talk and Resulting Genres

Explaining and Seeking Information

◆ Give increasingly elaborate and extended descriptions of objects, events and concepts

This third-grade class has reconvened as a large group after the children worked together in small groups to generate ideas about the elements of biographies. They have written their ideas on sentence strips and inserted them into pocket charts. Their task now is to develop some categories to organize all of these ideas.

In this segment, Ethan is testing the usefulness of the categories that already have been suggested by the group. He considers the sentence strip "Important Things" and suggests that "important things come like when you're a like a teenager or something, so we could put, like, um the time of, like the timeline of like what happens . . ." The teacher is responsive to his suggestion for a more specific heading of "Teenager" between the existing categories of "Birth" and "Growing Up."

They continue working together on the charts to refine the categories until Ethan concludes their work with a summary: "First it's like birth, then it's like teenage years, then it's, then they're like grown up, but in the middle there like are things like, like maybe there's like things like, well under teenager there's like things you need to know about and under childhood there's like things you want to do, and under adult is like jobs and stuff." Even while summarizing, Ethan is thinking about other ways the information could be organized under his broad headings: "Things You Need to Know About," "Things You Want to Do," and "Jobs and Stuff."

Graham sees the big picture and demonstrates his experience with polite classroom discourse when he comments about the overarching idea "About a Person's Life." He thinks that it's too broad an idea: "It's growing up and birth. It's a pretty good idea, except it's kinda like the whole thing. That's the meaning of a biography."

This opportunity to suggest categories, evaluate their usefulness, explain their thinking to each other and refine their ideas helped these students develop their capacity to reason logically and express themselves clearly.

New Standards

Second- & Third-Grade Standards

Standard 1: *Habits*
- Talking a Lot pg. 202
- Talking to One's Self pg. 207
- Conversing at Length on a Topic pg. 208
- Discussing Books pg. 218

Standard 2: *Kinds of Talk and Resulting Genres*
- Narrative pg. 230
- Explaining and Seeking Information pg. 236
- Getting Things Done pg. 244
- Producing and Responding to Performances pg. 251

Standard 3: *Language Use and Conventions*
- Rules of Interaction pg. 254
- Word Play and Grammatical Awareness pg. 256
- Vocabulary and Word Choice pg. 260

Explaining, Describing and Seeking Increasingly Elaborate Information

When seeking information or understanding, children now are more apt to speculate about cause and effect, talking in terms of "what if . . ." or "now that . . ." and using complex grammatical structures as they embed multiple possibilities, such as "if/then." In general, compared to younger peers, children at this age are able to speak more extensively and in much more clear terms about almost all events, ideas and people with which they are familiar. In speaking, they begin with topic sentences and give causal explanations, addressing cause and effect in a number of ways:

physical causality:	"He didn't wash the scrape, and so it got infected."
moral or logical connections:	"Tame rabbits don't run away. This rabbit doesn't run away, so it must be tame."

— McCabe & Peterson, 1985

In addition, children give increasingly elaborate and extended descriptions of objects, events and concepts, as in the following example:

Brother (age seven): Mom, what does *guest* mean?

Mother: What does what mean?

Brother: *Guest*. You know how in "Beauty and the Beast," when they said, "Be our guest!"

Sister (age eight): That means that someone is at your house and you have to be nice to your guest. She is your guest if she is over to your house.

— Beals & Snow, 1994

Second & Third Grades: Standard 2/Commentary on Student Performances — 239 —

Timmy Describes Pangaea

Standard 2: Kinds of Talk and Resulting Genres

Explaining and Seeking Information

◆ Seek out multiple resources for information

◆ Give increasingly elaborate and extended descriptions

Timmy clearly is enjoying the learning process and is able to reflect on how his growing knowledge changes his understanding of the world. When asked about what he has been studying, Timmy offers an extended description of Pangaea, as well as an explanation of how he and his classmates have gathered their information.

The visitor begins by asking, "Can you tell me what you've learned about Pangaea?"

In response, Timmy attempts to offer an account of what he's learned, "Um, well, I've learned that um, there was, there, first, like . . ."

At this point, Timmy stops himself and begins again, stumbling a bit but finally hitting upon a way to frame his explanation and engage the listener's attention: "When I was a kid, I always thought that the world was just, like, the way it was." This sentence serves as a compelling introduction not only to the subject of Pangaea, but also to Timmy's story about his own learning process.

Once this introductory information has been conveyed, Timmy feels free to begin his description of Pangaea: "And then, now Pangaea, it probably took like billions of years to make it spread apart . . . and . . ."

The listener asks, "What spread apart?"

Timmy responds, "Pangaea. It's um, like . . . it was all in a cluster, except Antarctica, I think. And then, um, they all moved away, and now, um, now they're like, they moved away, now they're going back in again. And then America, every year, I think, moves one inch towards Europe."

Although Timmy never quite manages to define Pangaea or explain that the things breaking up and moving around are continents, he nevertheless responds to the listener's request for more information by offering detailed descriptions of the breakup of Pangaea, as well as a specific example to illustrate that the continents are moving back together today.

When the listener asks what he has been doing to learn about Pangaea, Timmy explains where he and his classmates sought information: "Well, I'm doing it at home, too. But over here, we learned at a, we looked at a Web site. And then we go like, we turn on something and then it like, moves. All the clusters go together and then they split up again into tiny pieces everywhere."

Later in the conversation, the listener asks Timmy why he thinks it is important to study Pangaea. Timmy's reply shows that he is reflecting on his own motivation for learning. He says, "Well, I don't know about *important*, but . . . well, I would want to know what our land was like before I was here."

Finally, when the listener asks for more detail about what caused the giant land mass to break apart, Timmy is ready with a very detailed description: "Probably lots of earthquakes . . . volcanoes erupted everywhere, and then, um, they like split lines everywhere and then it, like, broke up."

New Standards

Graham's Writer's Notebook

Standard 2: Kinds of Talk and Resulting Genres

Explaining and Seeking Information

- Give increasingly elaborate and extended descriptions
- Support opinions or provide specific examples

Graham is an accomplished writer who, along with his classmates, has been studying and practicing author's craft. Here, Graham shares his writer's notebook with a visitor. Graham offers confident and detailed descriptions of the writing process, complete with visual aids and specific examples of various techniques.

The visitor begins by asking Graham what he has learned about how writers get their ideas. Graham responds by explaining exactly how he and his classmates gather raw material and story ideas in their notebooks: "A lot of our ideas, is what we would do, we would go out around the school and try to hear what people were saying. It's called, we would dialogue, and we would hear gossip of people talking. And we would take that and write it down in our notebook, and maybe sometime later that would become a story idea. Or, we would brainstorm and do lists."

Notice how Graham introduces the word *dialogue* (a word he knows is specific to author's craft) and then follows up with the example of "hear gossip of people talking" as a way to illustrate the meaning of the new term.

Next, the listener asks Graham to describe how he uses his writer's notebook. By way of introduction, Graham explains the general purpose of the writer's notebook, saying, "This isn't for, like, first drafts, even. It's just to write down ideas."

He then pages through his own notebook, showing examples of his work and describing various techniques. Notice that throughout his explanation, Graham uses vocabulary that is specific to the writing process and clarifies his meaning by using the notebook as a visual aid, "Like, I put dialogue pages . . . [points to a page] . . . and these are some memories . . . [turns to another page] . . . and a poem I was writing. [Points to a new page.] This is one of my brainstorming pages. [Turns the page.] That's just a little, um, story."

Here, Graham is teaching and explaining, checking for comprehension as he goes along and giving specific examples that will help the listener make sense of the new information.

When the listener asks Graham if his notebook reminds him of experiences he's had, Graham once again points to a specific page in his notebook and says, "Well, some. Like this poem I was writing about a bat. There was a bat living behind the house we rented."

The listener asks, "Can you tell me about that experience? What happened with that bat?"

Graham replies, "Well, I was just playing, um, hide and seek with my friends, and so, I hid behind the house, and we saw the bat hanging there. We actually saw him like three times after we went inside."

The listener asks, "Did anything happen with the bat?"

Graham takes this question as a cue to provide more information and offers a detailed description of his encounter with the bat and his feelings at the time: "Well, yeah. Well, not . . . kind of. 'Cause I went to check on him because he was going and coming back and going. And once I went to check on him and he wasn't there so I was about to leave, and he flew out right in front of my face and then flew back."

The listener asks, "Ooh. Did that scare you?"

Graham responds, "Yeah. It frightened me."

When the listener asks Graham if there are other experiences he is considering writing about, Graham once again flips through his notebook. Finding a general trend in his writing, he explains, "Kind of about, um, about in Mexico. I usually write about trips."

Graham then follows up with a specific example of the kind of descriptive writing that might be inspired by a trip: "Like in Mexico, there would be hermit crabs crawling under your feet or things like that."

Graham's Story

Standard 2: Kinds of Talk and Resulting Genres

Explaining and Seeking Information

- Give increasingly elaborate and extended descriptions
- Support opinions or provide specific examples
- Tutor others in new and somewhat complicated tasks

In this discussion, Graham gives a thoughtful, articulate description of the writing process. Using his own story as an example, Graham explains to the listener how he goes about turning an original idea into a finished piece of writing. He also describes a number of literary techniques, offering specific examples of how he uses these to make his story more effective.

Graham begins by introducing his story: "It's a story about a kid who has a grandpa that has Alzheimer's. My grandpa *does* have Alzheimer's, except, it's not what, it's not really what happened to me or, and the kid's not me."

He then reads his story aloud:

I opened the door. It was a long way to the bottom. I saw a rocking chair and an old violin, but what interested me most was the box.

Oh, I forgot to tell you who I was. I'm Henry. I'd like to tell you a story about my grandpa. You see, he has Alzheimer's, a disease where you forget everything: to eat, drink and even walk.

One time, I was at the hospital, and I found a basement in his room, and that's where the story begins.

So I found this box. I wiped off the dust and saw a tiny keyhole. I thought, "Where's that key?"

I looked everywhere: no sign of it. Soon, I gave up. I was going to leave when I saw something in my grandpa's hand: "The key!"

I ran to him and took the key. I looked up at his face. He had a slight smile.

I put the key in the keyhole. It opened with a creak. Inside were books; three of them. I wondered why they were there and what did they mean?

That night, I couldn't get it out of my head. It was like a spider web and I was the fly. I finally got to sleep.

I had a dream that night that I saw myself as a baby. I was sitting on my grandpa's lap. He was reading to me. Suddenly, my mom walked by. She said, "You know, he doesn't understand."

"I know," he said.

Suddenly, my alarm clock went off.

The next day, I went to my grandpa's place. I went and got the books. I came and sat down next to him. He still had the smile. I started reading. Suddenly, the nurse came by and interrupted.

"He can't understand, you know," she said.

"I know," I replied.

When Graham finishes reading, the listener asks him to describe his writing process. Graham begins with a description of his original idea and then follows up with a specific example of how he worked to create a compelling first line: "Well, how I got the story was, well because of my grandpa, actually, more . . . and, and also I made the beginning because last year Miss D. would always talk about pulling the person in, so I made up that it just says, the beginning, instead of saying that 'I'm Henry,' it says, 'I opened the door. It was a long way to the bottom,' to make it more . . . like . . ."

"Engaging?" the listener prompts.

"Yeah. To like pull, to make the person who's reading it, like, get into the story already, in the beginning," Graham replies.

The listener then asks Graham what other techniques he used to make his story better. Once again, Graham uses an example from the text to explain his process: "Well, to use, like how it said 'I know' two times, it's kind of like the grandpa has become the child and he has become the, more of like a grandpa, but a kid, though."

Later, Graham describes how he made a conscious effort to include rich detail in his story. Once again, he offers a clear example: "Trying to um, kind of, but it's, to make it not just 'I opened, I opened the . . .' to kind of make more details, like making the grandpa have the key in his hand. Things like that."

Finally, the listener asks Graham if there are any other things he's thinking of doing to make his story even better. Graham replies, "I don't know. There are some, like, sentences that I wrote that, like, don't make sense. . . . I just fixed them up while I was reading it. Or some there's like too much double spacing, or things like that. That would be more of the punctuation."

"But overall, you're happy with the story?" the listener asks.

"Yeah," Graham says.

"Well, I think you should be," the listener responds.

Throughout this extended conversation, Graham offers explanations that are clear, detailed and specific to the topic at hand. As he talks about his writing, Graham not only shares his creative vision, but also is able to explain the process by which he takes that vision and transforms it into a finished story.

Getting Things Done

By now children have increased the specificity and complexity of directions they are able to give or receive. They begin to entertain alternate viewpoints and do more than just *listen* to opposing arguments. They have understood the value of fair negotiation and/or trading since preschool, but now they advance to generating alternative solutions and collaborating. Specifically, by the end of third grade we expect children to:

◆ listen to, comprehend and carry out directions with eight or more steps (for example, be able to follow: "Read page 54 and 55 in your social studies book and take notes. When you finish, get your writing folder and review your report draft. Think about where you need to include more information and use your notes to decide where to try to find it. Then get started.");

◆ ask (or answer) specific questions to clarify a novel task, persisting if necessary to get the information;

◆ give directions for technically complex tasks (for example, math problems, science procedures, computer games);

◆ ask clarifying questions to learn what a person knows (for example, "Do you know how plants turn sunlight into food?");

◆ describe alternate ways to complete a task or reach a destination (for example, "Look, now you can subtract to see if you added right" or "You can find a trail behind school, instead of going around the block.");

Second- & Third-Grade Standards

Standard 1: *Habits*
- ◆ Talking a Lot — pg. 202
- ◆ Talking to One's Self — pg. 207
- ◆ Conversing at Length on a Topic — pg. 208
- ◆ Discussing Books — pg. 218

Standard 2: *Kinds of Talk and Resulting Genres*
- ◆ Narrative — pg. 230
- ◆ Explaining and Seeking Information — pg. 236
- ◆ Getting Things Done — pg. 244
- ◆ Producing and Responding to Performances — pg. 251

Standard 3: *Language Use and Conventions*
- ◆ Rules of Interaction — pg. 254
- ◆ Word Play and Grammatical Awareness — pg. 256
- ◆ Vocabulary and Word Choice — pg. 260

- use visual aids, such as charts, diagrams or maps, to augment language;
- engage in extended conversations (seven or more exchanges) about a problem, with both sides presenting and listening to arguments and solutions;
- disagree with another person's argument and then generate and promote alternative solutions to reach agreement (for example, "Everybody's been to the aquarium. Why don't we go to the museum? They've got rock collections like we've been doing in science."); and
- collaborate by seeking out peers to solve problems, disagreeing diplomatically, and assigning or delegating tasks to organize a group.

Arguing and Collaborating

In second and third grades, children spend quite a bit of time in self-directed activity. They work in small groups on social studies projects, on science experiments and in games on the playground. Speaking and listening in all of these activities are very important to the success of the group.

Children's ability to argue now is based on reasoned justification, evidence and logic rather than mere force of will. They are becoming more skilled at elaborating on their arguments and may refer often to social norms or rules to help convince others. They attempt to weave together related arguments, deliberately connecting their own suggestions or arguments to the other person's.

Children also are learning to be diplomatic in the way that they challenge and disagree with others. Most importantly, they know how to bring a group together with complementary skills to solve a problem, plan an event or construct something. They understand the importance of delegating and scheduling.

Ethan Perfects His Poem

Standard 2: Kinds of Talk and Resulting Genres
Getting Things Done

◆ Ask (or answer) specific questions to clarify a novel task

◆ Use visual aids

Ethan is able to give very specific information about the writing process his third-grade class has learned. Even more important, he demonstrates that this is not just an abstract concept for him to talk about but a series of useful steps that help him achieve the effect he intends for his writing.

He begins by talking in general terms about how he and his classmates brainstorm their writing ideas: "Well, we usually just put like, um, we get a piece of paper and we, um, put ideas in the middle and then we write, and then we write all the ideas we could think of, then we choose one that we like the most, and, um, that's the one we would do."

He specifically got inspiration for his poem "Silence" from his brother's writing: "Well, my brother, he, um writes a lot of stuff about like silence and noise and stuff like that, so I just decided to write this story about silence."

With a shy smile, Ethan willingly reads his poem aloud. This kind of informal performance should be a regular event for third graders in addition to more formal, rehearsed performances of their work in front of larger audiences.

Silence is gold.
If we didn't have silence
Nothing would be right.
We couldn't sleep all day and night.
People would keep on going.
The word "talk" would be
  overflowing.
You couldn't go anywhere without
  hearing noise.
People would be fighting like boys
  with toys.
Silence is gold,
That's what I'm saying.
Now you could go now,
And keep on playing.

Ethan gives an elaborate description of the steps he has taken so far and his thinking at each step in the development of this poem. "First I wrote it down in my book, but there was some things that I wanted to do, but I was just doing it really quick, so I decided to add on more," he says.

He gets even more specific about his writing decisions, saying, "Well, I just went through it and read the first one. Then I decided, you know what, I'm going to copy some of it . . . the parts I don't like, I'm going to take out and add new things in there, that would sort of rhyme or something."

Ethan clearly believes that this is an authentic writing task because satisfying his audience and publishing a final product influence his editing. He wants his poem to be "something that people would really like. Instead of just saying, 'Silence is gold, that's great, the end,' I wanted to make it better, like more complex."

He knows what he means by "complex": "I think the rhyming and stuff make it more complex 'cause it's kind of harder to do, to make every word rhyme and stuff."

That hard work is worth the effort to make his poem something his readers will enjoy. "Well, I think I may add on more, and then I would edit it and finish it and make it into a book, maybe, a book of poems," he says.

Ethan also has drawn a cautionary cartoon to further make his point about the value of silence. It depicts "all these kids trying to get silence in a golden box. And, they're all like jumping and everything bad is happening like, and it kind of annoys you because there's like no silence or anything in it." The dialogue of the characters in Ethan's drawing reinforces his message about the chaos and aggravation of continuous noise.

Ethan understands the way his illustration supports his poem. He says, " 'Cause some people get annoyed if they don't have any silence, and if you keep on like repeating this and stuff, you'll get someone annoyed eventually, and, well, the main part of it is they're all trying to get silence in a golden box. Like it says, 'Silence is gold.' "

In this segment, Ethan uses language effectively for various purposes. He clarifies his thinking during the writing process, explains the origin and meaning of his poem in elaborate detail, and articulately reads his work. His performance demonstrates the convergence of the many speaking skills delineated in these standards.

Hannah's Writing Ideas

Standard 2: Kinds of Talk and Resulting Genres
Getting Things Done

◆ Answer specific questions to clarify a novel task

The students in this third-grade class write regularly about topics they have generated in their writer's notebooks. In this short segment, Hannah clearly describes her plans for enhancing the next draft of her story about her family's vacation trip: "Well, I'm just, well, to finish it and make it better, I have some pictures at home of my, of my trip, and I think I'm going to bring them in so I could look at them and get some ideas so I don't forget."

She is able to be more specific about how her vacation photos will help her remember the incident about which she is writing. She says, "Because you'll see, like my dad took a picture of when the eagle went down and catched the fish, and I could remember that, how it swept down and got the fish." She even hints at some of the language she may use in her story when she says that the eagle "swept down." This strategy of using artifacts from their personal experiences helps children recall important details to make their writing more vivid.

Aaron and Alexandra Clarify the Assignment

Standard 2: Kinds of Talk and Resulting Genres

Getting Things Done

- Listen to, comprehend and carry out directions with eight or more steps
- Ask specific questions to clarify a novel task, persisting if necessary to get the information

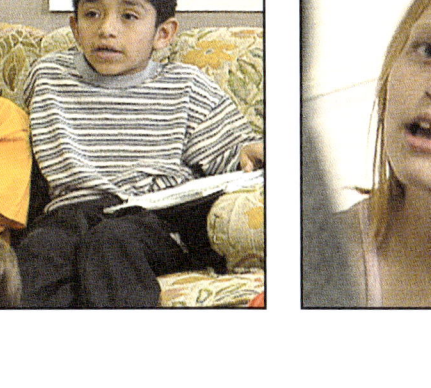

In second and third grades, children spend considerable amounts of time in self-directed activity. They must be able to listen to, comprehend and carry out a set of instructions for independent tasks. In this class meeting, the children are listening to instructions about their writing response for the day. Instead of asking the children to make the usual "connections between the text and yourself or the world," the teacher asks them to make a connection to another book by Allen Say, an author whose writing the class has been studying.

Part of knowing that you understand the teacher's instructions correctly is asking questions to clarify the task. In this segment, Aaron first makes certain that he may expand on a previous book talk by asking if they have to do "a different one, instead of, like, the one we shared."

The teacher affirms that this is a "good idea" and reminds the class that talking about a book before writing a response to it "helps us get our ideas clear in our head."

Aaron persists in clarifying the assignment, wanting to know "if we need, like, a theme or a connection, can we get it off that . . . ?"

The teacher helps him remember that the tool to which he is referring is an "attribute chart," a "tool to help you remember the thoughts you had about the book." Aaron's question about the attribute chart prompts the teacher to elaborate on her original instructions and to encourage the class to use the attribute chart, other charts they have made together and anything else they have in their source books that will give them ideas.

In addition to asking direct questions to clarify an assignment, children sometimes make comments that indirectly imply a question or concern that needs to be resolved. When Alexandra states, "But I can't connect it, like, up to any other Allen Say books," she really is asking the teacher for help in how to proceed on this task.

The teacher understands her implication and offers a helpful suggestion: "Can you tell how it's not like them?"

Alexandra confirms with a nod and says that she can use this suggestion.

Cody Asks for Clarification

Standard 2: Kinds of Talk and Resulting Genres
Getting Things Done

- Ask (or answer) specific questions to clarify a novel task

This third-grade class has been reading a series of biographies, and now the teacher wants the children to consider the common elements of biography as a genre. As the class prepares to begin small-group work to develop lists of the elements of biography, the teacher checks their understanding of the task, asking, "What's the first step for what we're going to do?"

Owen confirms the format for the work: "Get in your group."

Kevin adds, "Start brainstorming," indicating that these students are very familiar with this strategy for generating a set of ideas.

Cody then asks, "Are we doing it on the book we just read or on a different book?" His question reveals more than just a confusion about which book to consider. He has misunderstood the basic nature of the task — to consider the elements of biography in general, not just the elements of a specific biography.

The teacher acknowledges the importance of this question without calling attention to Cody's misunderstanding, thus encouraging the students to ask for clarification. When she solicits an answer from another student instead of giving the answer herself, she creates an opportunity to see if other students have a similar misconception. She restates Cody's question and frames the central issue of the task: "Are we doing this on the book we just read or can we think about other things?"

Graham's response indicates that he has understood the purpose of the task, asking, "Well, we're not really doing it on a book, it's just what we would want to include on a biography."

This kind of restating the purpose of a task before the children set to work both teaches students the value of asking specific questions to get information they need and provides teachers with an opportunity to be certain the students will be doing the intended lesson.

Producing and Responding to Performances

As in earlier grades, children should have frequent opportunities to give author performances of their own material and to respond to the author performances of their peers. In responding to more challenging performances, children continue to offer reactions and learn to support their opinions.

At this age, students speak before the class to read their work, present a report or propose an idea. These activities, as well as other, lengthier group activities, are considered performances. In other areas, children's performances move beyond the classroom setting and grow in length. Specifically, by the end of third grade we expect children to:

- describe their reaction to a performance, giving details to support opinions;

- attend to more challenging performances that go beyond entertainment or present unfamiliar material (for example, a museum slide show on native plants, a video on Martin Luther King Jr.);

- draw from a rehearsed repertoire to give a brief performance (for example, reciting a poem or famous speech, leading a class or club in a pledge, presiding over a class meeting);

- conduct and/or make lengthier presentations to the class or take part in full-length performances in front of larger groups or unfamiliar audiences (for example, taking the floor in a formally defined setting; presenting a report with visual aids, costumes, props or sound effects); and

- give an author performance, reading from their own material out loud (for example, in daily reader response groups during the Writers Workshop).

Second- & Third-Grade Standards

Standard 1: *Habits*
- Talking a Lot — pg. 202
- Talking to One's Self — pg. 207
- Conversing at Length on a Topic — pg. 208
- Discussing Books — pg. 218

Standard 2: *Kinds of Talk and Resulting Genres*
- Narrative — pg. 230
- Explaining and Seeking Information — pg. 236
- Getting Things Done — pg. 244
- Producing and Responding to Performances — pg. 251

Standard 3: *Language Use and Conventions*
- Rules of Interaction — pg. 254
- Word Play and Grammatical Awareness — pg. 256
- Vocabulary and Word Choice — pg. 260

Standard 3: Language Use and Conventions
Introduction

Standard 3: Language Use and Conventions covers three important aspects of speaking and listening: rules of interaction, word play and grammatical awareness, and vocabulary and word choice. By second and third grades, students are expected to master the rules of interaction. They should be communicating competently in academic and social situations. They have acquired different and deeper domains of expertise and have developed the associated vocabulary and word knowledge. Therefore, they can be expected to hold forth at some length on familiar topics while speaking in a group setting.

By second grade, children should have mastered phonemic awareness and the ability to orally blend and segment sounds in words. Much of their focus is on developing accuracy and fluency with the print-sound code. However, children continue to display increased levels of experimentation with sounds, meaning and grammar. And their awareness of ambiguities in language expands.

In second and third grades, building concepts behind words in an ever-increasing number of domains is very important. By now, students have acquired different domains of expertise. While students at this age are capable of learning new words through

Second- & Third-Grade Standards

Standard 1: *Habits*
- Talking a Lot — pg. 202
- Talking to One's Self — pg. 207
- Conversing at Length on a Topic — pg. 208
- Discussing Books — pg. 218

Standard 2: *Kinds of Talk and Resulting Genres*
- Narrative — pg. 230
- Explaining and Seeking Information — pg. 236
- Getting Things Done — pg. 244
- Producing and Responding to Performances — pg. 251

Standard 3: *Language Use and Conventions*
- Rules of Interaction — pg. 254
- Word Play and Grammatical Awareness — pg. 256
- Vocabulary and Word Choice — pg. 260

> Children continue to display increased levels of experimentation with sounds, meaning and grammar. And their awareness of ambiguities in language expands.

vocabulary lists and definitions, this approach is not as effective as using advanced words that are relevant to whatever the class is studying. Children acquire words at a phenomenal rate now. They learn new words naturally — by talking, asking, listening and *primarily* by reading. Researchers estimate that children at this age are capable of acquiring a 15,000- to 20,000-word vocabulary (Anglin, 1993). A student's vocabulary should grow across many domains. Yet the specific words in that vocabulary are less important than its steadily growing size.

An important aspect of children's growing vocabularies is that they now should be developing elaborated networks of semantic, phonological, orthographic and grammatical relationships among words. Semantic relationships include knowing about superordinates and subordinates, antonyms and synonyms, and words with similar but only partially overlapping meanings (for example, *pretty, beautiful, gorgeous, attractive* and *pleasing*). In addition, semantic knowledge includes knowledge of polysemous meanings (for example, *rich* people, *rich* food and *rich* fabric) and homonyms.

Phonological relationships include a conscious understanding of alliterations, onomatopoeias, syllable structure, stress and rhyme, building on the word play that children have been engaged in for years. Orthographic relationships help children understand word origins (for example, words in which *ph* spells /f/ are likely to be Greek in origin) as well as appropriate various forms of word play (for example, "I'm a gnu, a gnother gnu"). Knowing a word means understanding what morphological processes it can undergo (for example, verbs ending in *-ate* usually can become nouns ending in *-ation*) as well as how the word can be used in grammatical constructions (for example, the Lakers *beat* the Jazz and *won* the championship). Thus, *beat* is like *play, challenge, threaten, engage* and other verbs that take animate direct objects, whereas *win* is like *paint, break, eat, sell* and other verbs for which the direct object is inanimate and affected by verb action.

Rules of Interaction

In second and third grades, children work on the mastery of important conventions in the school and social settings by speaking in a group. More and more, their class work should require them to speak, listen and collaborate in small or large groups. Specifically, by the end of third grade we expect children to:

◆ consistently observe politeness conventions (for example, use "please," "thank you" and "excuse me" consistently; apologize spontaneously when appropriate; occasionally compliment others);

◆ hold themselves and others accountable to the rules by using verbal reminders (for example, anticipate being treated politely by others, *Child 1:* "Give me that pencil." *Child 2:* "But you didn't say please."); and

◆ speak one at a time, look at and listen to the speaker, signal for a chance to speak, adjust volume to the setting, and hold the floor and yield when appropriate.

Second- & Third-Grade Standards

Standard 1: *Habits*
- Talking a Lot — pg. 202
- Talking to One's Self — pg. 207
- Conversing at Length on a Topic — pg. 208
- Discussing Books — pg. 218

Standard 2: *Kinds of Talk and Resulting Genres*
- Narrative — pg. 230
- Explaining and Seeking Information — pg. 236
- Getting Things Done — pg. 244
- Producing and Responding to Performances — pg. 251

Standard 3: *Language Use and Conventions*
- Rules of Interaction — pg. 254
- Word Play and Grammatical Awareness — pg. 256
- Vocabulary and Word Choice — pg. 260

Research Perspectives

"The child's wish to communicate about something which interests him at one particular moment should draw the attention of an adult who will talk with him, in simple, varied and grammatical language. We should arrange for language-producing activities — activities where adult and child must communicate in order to co-operate."

From Clay, M. (1991). *Becoming Literate.* Heinemann, 72.

Word Play and Grammatical Awareness

At this point, children have mastered the ability to blend and segment onsets and rimes and have mastered phonemes. Children should exhibit a continuing interest in words and experimentation with language, though in a more sophisticated fashion than in earlier years. Specifically, by the end of third grade we expect children to:

- identify the number of syllables in a word;
- play with alliteration, tongue twisters and onomatopoeia (for example, generally playing with forms like limericks and parodies of familiar tunes);
- use double meanings or multiple meanings of words for riddles and jokes (for example, using puns like, "Why is bread lazy? Because it loafs around.");
- detect a variety of speech ambiguities and understand the intended meaning;
- start to play with made-up languages (for example, pig Latin or other secret codes); and
- identify subjects and verbs in simple sentences.

Second- & Third-Grade Standards

Standard 1: *Habits*
- Talking a Lot — pg. 202
- Talking to One's Self — pg. 207
- Conversing at Length on a Topic — pg. 208
- Discussing Books — pg. 218

Standard 2: *Kinds of Talk and Resulting Genres*
- Narrative — pg. 230
- Explaining and Seeking Information — pg. 236
- Getting Things Done — pg. 244
- Producing and Responding to Performances — pg. 251

Standard 3: *Language Use and Conventions*
- Rules of Interaction — pg. 254
- Word Play and Grammatical Awareness — pg. 256
- Vocabulary and Word Choice — pg. 260

Second & Third Grades: Standard 3/Commentary on Student Performances

Adam Tells Jokes

Standard 3: Language Use and Conventions

Word Play and Grammatical Awareness

◆ Use double meanings or multiple meanings of words for riddles and jokes

Children and adults of all ages love to play with words. By third grade, children's developing awareness of the ambiguities of language and the resulting multiple meanings of words permits them to experiment with more sophisticated language manipulation.

Adam, who aspires to be either a comedian or a professional wrestler, demonstrates in this segment his own comprehension of the comedic twists language can take. His droll delivery belies his obvious pleasure in surprising his audience with the double meanings of his punch lines. Each joke works in a different way.

The first joke: "One day a girl was talking to her teacher. She told her teacher, would he be mad for something she didn't do. And he said, 'No.' And she said, 'Good,' because she didn't do her homework." This joke gets its punch by surprising the listener, who is set up to expect "something I didn't do" to refer to a naughty behavior rather than a homework assignment.

The second joke: "The boy in the band said, 'We had to play Beethoven last night.' And guess what the gym student said, 'Who won?' " In this joke, the listener understands the correct meaning of "had to play Beethoven last night," and it's a character in the joke, the gym student, whose misunderstanding of the word *play* makes it funny.

The images and commentary in this section refer to performances available on the accompanying CD-ROMs.

New Standards

Acute Awareness of Language and Ambiguities

Children at this age bring an impressive array of linguistic resources to the classroom. By now they have a strong, unconscious understanding of grammar. They comprehend anaphoric use of pronouns (for example, "John told Mike that he hurt himself.") They can use full reversible passives (for example, "The criminal was shot by the policeman"). And research shows that second and third graders speak in whole clauses most of the time, except when doing so is not practical.

Their tendency to follow rules comes with an unfortunate side effect, however. Unless encouraged to do otherwise, children may stop forming metaphors because it's "using the wrong words." Teachers can point out metaphors in the context of stories and encourage the use of them in children's writing.

Children continue to display increased levels of experimentation with the sounds, meaning and grammar of language; however, their play with all these dimensions is more sophisticated than in earlier years. They may begin to reproduce strong poetic forms such as limericks and can even be invited to parody familiar discourse or songs. In general, children are becoming more and more aware of language and are able to detect ambiguities, especially where they affect comprehension.

Struggles with and manipulation of ambiguities are sophisticated forms of language experimentation that clarify multiple meanings. This type of awareness supports comprehension in speaking, listening, reading and writing. For instance, deep structure ambiguities may affect comprehension of text, while ambiguities in morpheme boundaries more often affect listening.

Exploitation of language ambiguities can make for playful fun. Following are some different types of ambiguities that can be detected by most second and third graders.

Phonological: joking vs. choking
A: "Bob coughed until his face turned blue."
B: "Was he choking?"
A: "No, he was serious."

Lexical: dog's bark vs. bark of a tree
A: "How can hunters in the woods best find their lost dogs?"
B: "By putting their ears to a tree and listening to the bark."

Surface Structure: man-eating fish vs. man eating fish
A: "Where would you go to see a man-eating fish?"
B: "A seafood restaurant!"

Deep Structure: having grandmother for Thanksgiving (as a companion versus a cannibalistic course)
A: "We're going to have grandmother for Thanksgiving."
B: "You are? Well, we're going to have a turkey!"

Morpheme Boundary: engineer vs. engine ear
A. "How do trains hear?"
B: "Through their engine ears!"

— Hirsh-Pasek, Gleitman & Gleitman, 1975

Research Perspectives

"Talking to adults is children's best source of exposure to new vocabulary and ideas."

From Burns, M., Griffin, P. and Snow, C., eds. (1999). *Starting Out Right: A Guide to Promoting Children's Reading Success.* Washington, D.C.: National Academy Press, 19.

Vocabulary and Word Choice

Children continue to acquire new vocabulary at a phenomenal rate, and their increased vocabulary will have a direct correlation to their academic success — their ability to read more and more difficult texts, write in the different genres, and learn new concepts. Using new, advanced words that are relevant to what the class is studying is more important than teaching children specific words on a vocabulary list.

Second- & Third-Grade Standards

Standard 1: *Habits*
- Talking a Lot — pg. 202
- Talking to One's Self — pg. 207
- Conversing at Length on a Topic — pg. 208
- Discussing Books — pg. 218

Standard 2: *Kinds of Talk and Resulting Genres*
- Narrative — pg. 230
- Explaining and Seeking Information — pg. 236
- Getting Things Done — pg. 244
- Producing and Responding to Performances — pg. 251

Standard 3: *Language Use and Conventions*
- Rules of Interaction — pg. 254
- Word Play and Grammatical Awareness — pg. 256
- Vocabulary and Word Choice — pg. 260

Specifically, by the end of third grade we expect children to:

- build word maps that show the relationship between words, placing newly acquired words in categories that are relevant (for example, knowing a chandelier is a source of light and a piece of furnishing; knowing all dogs are mammals but not all mammals are dogs);

- use specialized vocabulary related to school subjects (for example, Ancient Egypt: hieroglyphs; space travel: gravitational pull);

- provide definitions of words they know and learn new words from definitions using simple superordinates (for example, going beyond "A buffalo is an animal" to "A buffalo is an animal with a humped back that lives in the western United States.");

- learn new words from reading or being read to daily;

- demonstrate flexibility by choosing from word options to show precision or effect (for example, going beyond "She had a fancy hat" to "She had long peacock feathers in her hat.");

- study word families;

- develop a basic awareness of meaningful word parts and identify how they relate to certain words (for example, prefixes such as *un-*, *pre-* and *tri-* and suffixes such as *-able* and *-er*);

- increase vocabulary of verbs, adjectives and adverbs to speak fluently and exercise options in word choice;

- use and explain metaphoric language (for example, "He's called cold-hearted because he doesn't have any warm feelings for anyone.");

- understand and produce antonyms and synonyms; and

- understand and produce homonyms, homographs and homophones.

Whole or *Hole?*

Standard 3: Language Use and Conventions

Vocabulary and Word Choice

◆ Understand and produce homonyms, homographs and homophones

Piper, Charlie, Cynthia and Graham are brainstorming a list of elements that characterize the genre of biography. Graham watches as Piper records their ideas and notices that she needs help spelling the word *whole*. He provides her with the final three letters: "I think you need to spell it *o-l-e*."

Charlie chimes in, "No, it's *w*," to make sure Piper is spelling the entire word correctly.

Graham clarifies Charlie's suggestion: "That's *whole* with a *w*. It depends what *whole* you're trying to spell."

Piper explains, "*Hole* is like a hole, like you dig a hole, like I think it's *h*."

Charlie is really enjoying this *whole* and *hole* conversation: "*Hole* starts with an *h*, but *whole* starts with a *w*."

Cynthia understands the distinction he's making but comments on the confusion that can be caused by homophones when she says, "That doesn't make sense."

Graham laughs in agreement, "I know."

Cynthia playfully repeats, "*Hole* starts with an *h*, and *whole* starts with a *w*."

Piper has gotten a bit confused by now and just needs to confirm with her teacher that indeed the word she is writing starts with a *w*. "Yeah, yeah, it's *w*," Piper says.

This kind of talk in the immediate context of children's real work helps them make sense of these confusing elements of the English language and helps them understand the importance of accurate spelling to convey the meaning they intend.

Defining *Biography*

Standard 3: Language Use and Conventions

Vocabulary and Word Choice

◆ Provide definitions of words they know

Timmy, Camille, Nora and Brailon are exchanging ideas about what constitutes a biography. By combining the elements they have discussed in the many individual biographies they have read as a class, this group of children is creating a definition of this genre as a whole.

Timmy correctly describes their task: "We put down like the things that most biographies have."

The children then begin to tell their teacher some of the ideas they have been talking about together. Timmy starts off with his idea that a biography is about "a person that did something to help the world or something." He also adds "athletic ability."

Camille offers that writers of biography write about "people that like are famous, like had a good life, that they helped someone, they got lots of medals or they won, people that are very famous."

Brailon expands the definition to include "people that believe in theirselves."

Children are better able to grasp the nuances of their expanding vocabularies when they have such opportunities to talk together about the new words they are encountering in their school work.

Second & Third Grades: Standard 3/Commentary on Student Performances

What's the Word for "Old"?

Standard 3: Language Use and Conventions

Vocabulary and Word Choice

◆ Demonstrate flexibility by choosing from word options to show precision or effect

This third-grade class is developing life-span categories to organize the ideas they have generated in small groups about the elements of biographies. This segment begins in the middle of Timmy's attempt to name the category he is proposing. He can't think of the word, but he remembers the context in which it is used: "Like movies and stuff, or when you go see something, there's like, you say you're like, I don't know, you're like older, and there's a word for it and then you don't need to pay as much money."

The teacher recognizes this description and asks if he means "senior, senior citizens." Timmy acknowledges that that's what he had in mind.

The conversation continues, and Ethan tries to delineate the stages of life beyond senior citizen. "Isn't there like a name for the, um, like after senior citizen?" he says.

This sparks great enthusiasm among the children, and they begin to call out some possibilities: "old grandpa," "old," "elder," "elders," "elderly." Timmy suggests that an "elder is a senior," and Graham (off camera) agrees that "senior is like all the way up." Timmy defines that further as "over 50."

Ethan thinks they need to have still another category after senior citizen and completes their life cycle list, saying, "Then we have to have a whole new one, and it should be death."

This kind of practice refining their use of words to capture the exact meaning prepares children not only to speak precisely but also to be able to choose just the right word for the effect they want to create as writers.

Appendix

Glossary

Accountable talk. A way of talking based on accountability to knowledge, reasoning and community. Accountable talk promotes learning by regularly engaging students in respectful discussion of academic content that requires them to explain, connect, compare and contrast, provide evidence from text, and use other principles of rigorous thinking in their talking together.

Coda. The part of a story that indicates the story is over. A coda can be more formal, such as "And they all lived happily ever after," or more informal, such as "And I'll never, ever do that again!"

Code switching. Switching back and forth between language patterns based on the social and cultural contexts.

Discourse. Purposeful talk that consists of a few utterances from one speaker or includes a few turns between speakers.

Genre. A form or style of speaking or writing, such as narrative (a story), informative (a report) or functional (instructions).

Grammatical awareness. A sense of appropriate word choice and sentence structure.

Grapheme. A written symbol of language (i.e., a letter of the alphabet). Graphemes can represent one or more sounds in alphabetic languages. For example, the letter *s* can symbolize different sounds, depending on the word in which it appears (e.g., *s* can represent the /sh/ sound in *sure*, or the /s/ sound in *snake*).

Homographs. Words that are spelled the same but sound different and have different meanings, such as *minute* (a minute of time) and *minute* (very small).

Homonyms. Words that sound the same and have the same spelling but have different meanings, such as *table* (a piece of furniture) and *table* (a list of information).

Homophones. Words that sound the same but are spelled differently and have different meanings, such as *hear* and *here*.

Knowledge domain. A broad sphere of knowledge, such as *animals, transportation* or *sports*.

Metalinguistic awareness. The ability to think about and discuss language as a symbolic system.

Morpheme. The smallest units of a word that convey meaning or serve a grammatical function. A morpheme can be a word, such as *plant* or *walk*. A morpheme can also be part of a word, such as the plural marker *s* in *plants* or the past tense marker *ed* in *walked*. Both *plants* (*plant + s*) and *walked* (*walk + ed*) contain two morphemes. (Adapted from Berko Gleason, 1997.)

Morphological markers. Prefixes or suffixes that change the meaning of a word. For example, the addition of the suffix *ed* often changes the meaning of a verb to past tense, thereby functioning as a morphological marker. (See *morpheme*.)

Morphology. The study of the way morphemes are combined into words and how word meanings are changed through these combinations.

Narrative. A story, usually about the past. Narratives contain at least two chronologically ordered phrases about a single event. (Adapted from Berko Gleason, 1997.)

Phonemes. The smallest units of sound in a given language. The phonemes in a word are not always the same as the letters in a word. In the word *dog*, there are three phonemes (d-o-g) and three letters. In the word *snow*, there are three phonemes (s-n-o) but four letters.

Phonemic awareness. The ability to hear sounds in words and to identify particular sounds.

Phonological representation. A representation in memory of the sound and meaning of a word, but not the written representation.

Phonology. The study of the sound system of language, including both the individual phonemes and the rules for their combination and pronunciation. (Adapted from Berko Gleason, 1997.)

Pragmatic knowledge. The ability to use language appropriately and effectively for varying contexts, depending on the audience, situation and intent.

Pragmatics. The understanding of the way language is used in varying social contexts (e.g., word choice, tone, formality).

Semantics. The study of the ways language conveys meaning.

Story grammar. Predictable organizational elements that follow a distinct pattern in a story.

Subordinate. A word whose meaning is more specific and restricted than its superordinate term. For example, *Lazy Boy* is a subordinate of the superordinate *chair*. *Chair* is a subordinate of the superordinate *furniture*.

Superordinate. A word whose meaning is general or broad enough to encompass multiple subordinate terms. (See *subordinate*.)

Syntax. The rules by which words are combined to form grammatically correct sentences (e.g., plurals, future tense, etc.).

Topic. The shared focus of a conversation.

Committee's Selected Bibliography

Members of the New Standards Speaking and Listening Committee were asked to recommend publications for readers interested in further research. Here is a selection of their choices.

Accountable Talk

Resnick, L. and Hall, M. (2001). *The principles of learning: Study tools for educators.* CD-ROM version 2.0; also available at www.institute-forlearning.org.

Dialect

Labov, W. (1972). *Language in the inner city: Studies in the Black English vernacular.* Philadelphia, Pennsylvania: University of Pennsylvania Press.

Perry, T. and Delpit, L., eds. (1998). *The real ebonics debate: Power, language, and the education of African-American children.* Boston, Massachusetts: Beacon Press.

Smitherman, G. (1977). *Talkin and testifyin: The language of Black America.* Boston, Massachusetts: Houghton Mifflin.

Explanations

Barbieri, M. (1991). The origin of explanations. *Contributi di Psicologia,* 4, 153–76.

Barbieri, M., Colavita, F. and Schener, N. (1990). The beginning of the explaining capacity. *Children's language series,* 7, 245–71.

Beals, D. (1993). Explanatory talk in low-income families' mealtime conversations. *Applied Psycholinguistics,* 14(4), 489–513.

Beals, D. (1997). Sources of support for learning new words in conversation: Evidence from mealtimes. *Journal of Child Language* 24(3), 673–94.

Beals, D. and Snow, C. (1994). 'Thunder is when the angels are upstairs bowling:' Narratives and explanations at the dinner table. *Journal of Narrative and Life History,* 4(4), 331–52.

Beals, D. and Tabors, P. (1995). Arboretum, bureaucratic, and carbohydrates: Preschoolers' exposure to rare vocabulary at home. *First Language,* 15(43), 57–76.

Bloom, L. and Captides, J. (1987). Sources of meaning in the acquisition of complex syntax: The sample case of causality. *Journal of Experimental Child Psychology,* 43(1), 112–28.

Bloom, L., et al. (1980). Complex sentences: Acquisition of syntactic connectives and the semantic relations they encode. *Journal of Child Language,* 7(2), 235–61.

Donaldson, M. (1986). *Children's explanations: a psycholinguistic study.* Cambridge, England: Cambridge University Press.

Hood, L., et al. (1979). What, when, and how about why: A longitudinal study of early expressions of causality. *Monographs of the Society for Research in Child Development,* 44(6), 1–47.

Getting Things Done

Fulkerson, R. (1996). *Teaching the argument in writing.* Urbana, Illinois: National Council of Teachers of English.

Kirsh, B. (1983). The use of directives as indication of status among preschool children. *The Developmental Issues in Discourse.* Eds. Jonathan Fine and Roy O. Freedle. Norwood, New Jersey: Ablex Publishing Corp., 269–90.

Knudson, R. (1992). Analysis of argumentative writing at two grade levels. *Journal of Educational Research,* 85(3), 169–79.

Knudson, R. (1992). The development of written argumentation: An analysis and comparison of argumentative writing at four grade levels. *Child Study Journal,* 22(3), 167–84.

Piccolo, J. (1987). Expository text structure: Teaching and learning strategies. *The Reading Teacher,* 40(9), 838–47.

White, J. (1989). Children's argumentative writing: A reappraisal of difficulties. *Writing in schools: Reader.* Edt. 418. Ed. F. Christie. Geelong,

Victoria, Australia: Deakin University Press, 9–23.

Metalinguistics

Anglin, J. (1993). Vocabulary development: A morphological analysis. *Monographs of the Society for Research in Child Development,* 58(10), 1–166.

Beals, D., deTemple, J. and Dickinson, D. (1994). Talking and listening that support early literacy development of children from low-income families. *Bridges to literacy: Children, families, and schools.* Ed. David K. Dickinson. Cambridge: Blackwell, 19–40.

Cazden, C. (1992). Play with language and metalinguistic awareness: One dimension of language experience. *Whole language plus: Essays on literacy in the United States and New Zealand.* New York, New York: Teachers College Press, 59–75.

Clark, E. (1993). *The lexicon in acquisition.* Cambridge, England: Cambridge University Press.

Dickinson, D., Cote, L. and Smith, M. (1993). Learning vocabulary in preschool: Social and discourse contexts affecting vocabulary growth. *The development of literacy through social interaction.* Ed. Colette Daiute. *New Directions in Child Development,* 61. San Francisco, California: Jossey-Bass, 67–78.

Dickinson, D. and Smith, M. (1994). Long-term effects of preschool teachers' book readings on low-income children's vocabulary and story comprehension. *Reading Research Quarterly,* 29(2), 104–22.

Fenson, L., et al. (1993). *The MacArthur Communicative Development Inventories: User's guide and technical manual.* San Diego, California: Singular Publishing Group.

Fenson, L., et al. (1994). Variability in early communicative development. *Monographs of the Society for Research in Child Development* 59(5), 1–173.

Gombert, J. (1992). *Metalinguistic development.* Trans. Tim Pownall. New York, New York: Harvester Wheatsheaf.

Hirsh-Pasek, K., Gleitman, L. and Gleitman, H. (1978). What did the brain say to the mind? A study of the detection and report of ambiguity by young children. *The child's conception of language.* Eds. A. Sinclair, R.J. Jarvella and W.J.M. Levelt. Berlin, Germany: Springer-Verlag, 97–132.

Nelson, K. (1973). Structure and strategy in learning to talk. *Monographs of the Society for Research in Child Development,* 38(1–2), 1–135.

Pan, B. and Berko Gleason, J. (2001). Semantic development: Learning the meanings of words. *The development of language.* 5th ed. Ed. J. Berko Gleason. Boston, Massachusetts: Allyn and Bacon.

Preece, A. (1992). Collaborators and critics: The nature and effects of peer interaction on children's conversational narratives. *Journal of Narrative & Life History,* 2(3), 277–92.

Metaphor

Gardner, H., et al. (1975). Children's metaphoric productions and preferences. *Journal of Child Language,* 2(1), 125–41.

Winner, E. (1998). *The point of words: Children's understanding of metaphor and irony.* Cambridge, Massachusetts: Harvard University Press.

Morphology and Grammar

Berko Gleason, J. (1958). The child's learning of English morphology. *Word,* 14, 150–77.

Tager-Flusberg, H. (2001). Putting words together: Morphology and syntax in the preschool years. *The development of language.* 5th ed. Ed. J. Berko Gleason. Boston, Massachusetts: Allyn and Bacon.

Narrative

Bamberg, M., ed. (1997). *Narrative development: Six approaches.* Mahwah, New Jersey: Lawrence Erlbaum Associates.

Berman, R. and Slobin, D., eds. (1994). *Relating events in narrative: A crosslinguistic developmental study.* Hillsdale, New Jersey: Lawrence Erlbaum Associates.

Bliss, L., Covington, Z. and McCabe, A. (1999). Assessing the narratives of African American children. *Contemporary Issues in Communication Science and Disorders,* 26, 160–7.

Botvin, G. and Sutton-Smith, B. (1977). The development of structural complexity in children's fantasy narratives. *Developmental Psychology,* 13(4), 377–88.

Invernizzi, M. and Abouzeid, M. (1995). One story map does not fit all: A cross-cultural analysis of children's written story retellings. *Journal of Narrative and Life History,* 5(1), 1–19.

McCabe, A. (1992). *Language games to play with your child: Enhancing communication from infancy through late childhood.* Revised, New York, New York: Insight Books.

McCabe, A., ed. (1996). *Chameleon readers: Teaching children to appreciate all kinds of good stories.* New York, New York: McGraw-Hill.

McCabe, A. and Peterson, C. (1985). A naturalistic study of the production of causal connectives by children. *Journal of Child Language,* 12(1), 145–59.

Michaels, S. and Foster, M. (1985). Peer-peer learning: Evidence from a kid-run sharing time. *Kid watching: Observing the language learner.* Eds. Angela Jaggar and M. Trika Smith-Burke. Newark, Delaware: International Reading Association; Urbana, Illinois: National Council of Teachers of English, 143–58.

Michaels, S. (1991). The dismantling of narrative. *Developing narrative structure.* Eds. Allyssa McCabe and Carole Peterson. Hillsdale, New Jersey: Lawrence Erlbaum Associates, 303–51.

Minami, M. and McCabe, A. (1991). Haiku as a discourse regulation device: A stanza analysis of Japanese children's personal narratives. *Language in Society,* 20(4), 57–99.

Ninio, A. and Snow, C. (1996). *Pragmatic Development.* Boulder, Colorado: Westview.

Peterson, C. and McCabe, A. (1983). *Developmental psycholinguistics: Three ways of looking at a child's narrative.* New York, New York: Plenum Press.

Snow, C. (1983). Literacy and language: Relationships during the preschool years. *Harvard Educational Review,* 53(2), 165–89.

Private Speech

Berk, L. (1992). Children's private speech: An overview of theory and the status of research. *Private Speech: from social interaction to self-regulation.* Eds. Rafael M. Diaz and Laura E. Berk. Hillsdale, New Jersey: Lawrence Erlbaum Associates, 17–53.

Berk, L. (1994). Why children talk to themselves. *Scientific American,* 271(5), 78–83.

General

Barrett, M., ed. (1999). *The development of language.* London, England: UCL Press.

Bear, D., et al. (1996). *Words their way: Word study for phonics, vocabulary, and spelling instruction.* Upper Saddle River, New Jersey: Merrill.

Berko Gleason, J., ed. (1997). *The development of language.* Boston, Massachusetts: Allyn and Bacon.

Berko Gleason, J., ed. (2001). *The development of language.* 5th ed. Boston, Massachusetts: Allyn and Bacon.

Blum-Kulka, S. (1997). *Dinner talk: Cultural patterns of sociability and socialization in family discourse.* Mahwah, New Jersey: Lawrence Erlbaum Associates.

Burns, M., Griffin, P. and Snow, C. (1999). *Starting Out Right: A Guide to Promoting Children's Reading Success.* Washington, D.C.: National Academy Press.

Ervin-Tripp, S., Guo, J. and Lampert, M. (1990). Politeness and persuasion in children's control acts. *Journal of Pragmatics,* 14(2), 307–31.

Finnegan, E. (1994). *Language: Its Structure and Use.* New York: Harcourt Brace.

Fletcher, P. (1985). *A child's learning of English.* London, England: Blackwell.

Fletcher, P. and MacWhinney, B., eds. (1995). *Handbook of child language.* London, England: Blackwell.

Hampson, J. and Nelson, K. (1993). The relation of maternal language to variation in rate and style of language acquisition. *Journal of Child Language,* 20(2), 313–42.

Hart, B. and Risley, T. (1995). *Meaningful Differences in the Everyday Experience of American Children.* Baltimore, Maryland: Paul H. Brookes.

Jordan, G., Porche, M. and Snow, C. (in press). Project EASE: Easing children's transition to kindergarten literacy through planned parent involvement. *Reading Research Quarterly.*

Appendix: Committee's Selected Bibliography

Language development in early childhood: The role of social interaction in different care environments. *Infants and toddlers in out-of-home care.* Ed. D. Bailey. Baltimore, Maryland: Paul H. Brookes.

Lawrence, V. and Shipley, E. (1996). Parental speech to middle- and working-class children from two racial groups in three settings. *Applied Psycholinguistics,* 17(2), 233–55.

MacWhinney, B., ed. (1999). *The emergence of language.* Mahwah, New Jersey: Lawrence Erlbaum Associates.

MacWhinney, B., ed. (1987). *Mechanisms of language acquisition.* Hillsdale, New Jersey: Lawrence Erlbaum Associates.

Menn, L. and Ratner, N., eds. (2000). *Methods for studying language production.* Mahwah, New Jersey: Lawrence Erlbaum Associates.

Nelson, K. (1986). *Event knowledge: Structure and function in development.* Hillsdale, New Jersey: Lawrence Erlbaum Associates, 137–60.

Ninio, A. and Bruner, J. (1978). The achievements and antecedents of labelling. *Journal of Child Language,* 5, 1–15.

Oller, D., et al. (1997). Development of precursors to speech in infants exposed to two languages. *Journal of Child Language,* 24(2), 407–25.

Pinnell, G. and Fountas, I. (1998). *Word Matters.* Portsmouth, N.H.: Heinemann.

Schieffelin, B. and Ochs, E., eds. (1986). *Language socialization across cultures.* Cambridge, England: Cambridge University Press.

Smit, A., et al. (1990). The Iowa articulation norms project and its Nebraska replication. *Journal of Speech and Hearing Disorders,* 55(4), 779–98.

Snow, C., Burns, M. and Griffin, P. (1998). *Preventing Reading Difficulties in Young Children.* Washington, D.C.: National Academy Press.

Snow, C. and Dickinson, D. (1990). Social sources of narrative skills at home and at school. *First Language,* 10(2), 87–103.

Snow, C., et al. (1991). *Unfulfilled Expectations: Home and school influences on literacy.* Cambridge, Massachusetts: Harvard University Press.

Snow, C., Scarbrough, H. and Burns, M. (1999). What speech-language pathologists need to know about early reading. *Topics in Language Disorders,* 20(1), 48–58.

Strucker, J., Snow, C. and Pan, B. (2000). Family literacy for ESL families: Challenges and design principles. *Family literacy, an annotated bibliography.* Ed. Barbara Hanna Wasik. Washington, D.C.: U.S. Department of Education, Office of Educational Research and Improvement, National Institute on Early Childhood Development and Education.

Tabors, P. (1997). *One child, two languages: A guide for preschool educators of children learning English as a second language.* Baltimore, Maryland: Paul H. Brookes.

Teale, W. and Sulzby, E. (1986). *Emergent literacy: Writing and reading.* Norwood, New Jersey: Ablex Publishing Corp.

Tomasello, M., ed. (1998). *The new psychology of language: Cognitive and functional approaches to language structure.* Mahwah, New Jersey: Lawrence Erlbaum Associates.

Uccelli, P., et al. (1999). Telling two kinds of stories: Sources of narrative skill. *Child psychology: A handbook of contemporary issues.* Eds. Lawrence Balter and Catherine S. Tamis-LeMonda. Philadelphia, Pennsylvania: Psychology Press.

Acknowledgments

As principal investigators of the New Standards early literacy project, we wish to acknowledge the many people whose contributions to the work of the committee and the preparation of this publication and companion CD-ROMs have been invaluable. Their specific contributions are noted.

Phil Daro

Sally Hampton

Lauren B. Resnick

Martha Vockley, for writing, editing and project management; **Judith Lang,** for art direction and graphic design; **Kathy Ames,** for copyediting and production management; **Beth McConnell,** for proofreading and indexing; and their colleagues at KSA-Plus Communications, Arlington, VA, all of whom transformed the manuscript and student work into this engaging publication.

Donna DiPrima Bickel, University of Pittsburgh, Institute for Learning, Learning Research and Development Center, for significant contributions to the development of the standards, video production, and the selection and writing of the commentary on student performances.

Kathy Darling, Learning in Motion, Inc., Santa Cruz, CA, for organizing and editing the committee's drafts of the standards, video production, and the selection and writing of the commentary on student performances.

Nancy Artz, University of Pittsburgh, Learning Research and Development Center, for coordinating the work of the staff team for video production and video editing of student performances and for writing commentary on student performances.

Marie-Luise Caster, media producer/video editor, University of Pittsburgh, Institute for Learning, Learning Research and Development Center.

Amy Crosson, research specialist, and **Pauline Kraly,** administrative assistant, University of Pittsburgh, Learning Research and Development Center.

Judy Codding, vice president; **Dottie Fowler,** senior associate, primary language arts specialist; **Mary Anne Mays,** director of National College and chief of staff; **Suzie Sullivan,** special assistant to the president; and **Pat Whiteaker,** director for contracting,

Acknowledgments

National Center on Education and the Economy, for professional and administrative support to the project.

Marge Cappo, Mike Fish, Yael Lachman, Lisa Paul, Devin Wilson, Learning in Motion, Inc., Santa Cruz, CA, for design and development of the companion CD-ROMs.

Ron Bricker and **Emil Gallina,** Gallina-Bricker, Washington, DC, for video production and editing.

Student performances in speaking and listening were collected from urban schools around the country with strong literacy programs that prepare students to meet high standards of performance. For their assistance in producing videos of students demonstrating performances related to the standards, we thank the following teachers, administrators and staff:

Barry Edwards, principal; **Gloria Arias,** literacy leader; and **Daisy White,** teacher, Horizon Heights, Socorro Independent School District, El Paso, TX.

Celia Salazar, principal, and **Melissa Ramirez,** teacher, Ysleta Pre-K Center, Ysleta Independent School District, El Paso, TX.

Dona Descamps, principal; **Tina Madrid,** literacy coordinator; and **Imelda Heredia** and **Karla Bazan,** teachers, Pebble Hills Elementary, Ysleta Independent School District, El Paso, TX.

Michele Wells, program director, El Paso Collaborative for Academic Excellence, for coordinating the selection of classrooms for video production in El Paso, TX.

Maria Lamb, principal, and **Joey Mantecon, Nikki Prindle, Grace Escovedo** and **Nancy Box,** teachers, Fort Worth Independent School District, Alice Carlson Applied Learning Center, Fort Worth, TX.

Margaret Heritage, principal; **Hasmik Avetisian, Susan DiBlazio, Julie Kern, Alejandra Rivera, Lisa Rosenthal** and **Sarah Wischnia,** teachers; and **Rick Lee, Doris Levy** and **Jessica Fairbanks,** assistant teachers, Corinne A. Seeds University Elementary School, UCLA, Los Angeles, CA.

Lorraine Boyhan, principal; **Arthur Mattia,** assistant principal; and **Beth Huff, Kathy Mullen, Kathy Palestino, Holly Bowers, Bernadette Fitzgerald, Debra Mastrianno, Irene Gonzalez** and **Gina Garofalo,** teachers, Public School 372, New York, NY.

Tina Volpe, principal; **Nora Polansky,** acting assistant principal; **Claire Dougherty, Yvonne Derrick-Girela, Siham Tadros, Barbara Bashaw, Deanna Salafia** and **Linda Mazza,** teachers; and **Ronald Sopyla,** storyteller from ArtsConnection, Public School 295, New York, NY.

Jack Spatola, principal; **Jacqueline Mammolito,** assistant principal; **Marie Papaleo** and **Lucille Santoro,** teachers; and **Antoinette Coppa** and **Antoinette Michocki,** school staff developers, Public School 172, New York, NY.

Frank DeStefano, superintendent, and **JoAnna Maccarrio,** deputy superintendent, Community School District 15, Brooklyn, NY.

Ann Loney, director; **Kathy Keller** and **Shari Gewanter,** teachers; **Sandra Nystrom,** assistant teacher; **Betty Moore, Mary Ramm, James Belchick** and **Jerelene Taylor,** aides; and **Karen Howard,** storyteller, Shady Lane School, Pittsburgh, PA.

Denise Yates, principal, and **Michele Gnora, Dr. Robin Ittigson** and **Jack Zewe,** teachers, John Minadeo Elementary School, Pittsburgh, PA.

Andrea Robinson, principal; **Dr. Gerri Harper-Carter,** literacy coach; and **Arona McNeill-Vann, Diane Tunis, Latonya Porter** and **Natalie Berry,** teachers, Community Academy Public Charter School, Washington, DC.

About New Standards

New Standards is a joint project of the Learning Research and Development Center (LRDC) at the University of Pittsburgh and the National Center on Education and the Economy (NCEE). Since it began in 1991, New Standards has led the nation in standards-based reform efforts. New Standards, heading a consortium of 26 states and six school districts, developed the New Standards® performance standards, a set of internationally competitive performance standards in English language arts, mathematics, science and applied learning in fourth, eighth and 10th grades.

New Standards also pioneered standards-based performance assessment, developing the New Standards® reference examinations and a portfolio assessment system to measure student achievement against the performance standards. With support from the U.S. Department of Education's Office of Educational Research and Improvement, New Standards has produced a collection of publications addressing early literacy. These include the award-winning 1999 book *Reading & Writing grade by grade* — primary literacy standards for kindergarten through third grade, a parent handbook, a book on helping English language learners meet the standards and videos on literacy program practices for preschool and kindergarten.

Index

How to Use This Index

This is not a traditional index. To help readers easily find the information they seek, the index is divided into several sections of increasingly specific information. A brief description at the beginning of each section lets you know the kind of information you will find there.

About the Standards: Use this section to find in-depth explanations of the standards, which are listed by age span and subtopic.

Standards: Use this section to find the standards, which are listed by age span and subtopic. This section also includes a list of the student performances that show students meeting the standards.

Student Performances: Use this section to find student performances, which are listed alphabetically.

Focus Topics: Use this section to find topics that elaborate on points made in the standards.

Other Works and Authors: Use this section to find student performances, referenced by the title or author of the literary work that is being read.

About the Standards

Use this section to find in-depth explanations of the standards, which are listed by age span and subtopic.

Habits
age spans
> preschool, 46
> K–1, 128
> 2–3, 200

introduction to, 11
standard subtopic
> conversing at length on a topic, 19
> discussing books, 21
> talking a lot, 16
> talking to one's self, 18

Kinds of Talk and Resulting Genres
age spans
> preschool, 72
> K–1, 151
> 2–3, 228

introduction to, 23
standard subtopic
> explaining and seeking information, 26
> getting things done, 27
> narrative, 25
> producing and responding to performances, 28

Language Use and Conventions
age spans
> preschool, 98
> K–1, 180
> 2–3, 252

introduction to, 29
standard subtopic
> rules of interaction, 30
> vocabulary and word choice, 34
> word play and language awareness, 31

Standards

Use this section to find the standards, which are listed by age span and subtopic. This section also includes a list of the student performances that show students meeting the standards.

Standard 1: Habits

Conversing at Length on a Topic
age spans
> preschool, 60
> K–1, 140
> 2–3, 208

student performances
> Cody's Cat, Max, 214
> Discussing the Symbolism of a Yoruba Door, 210
> Evie Lifts Dirt Clods, 61
> Fredric's Cat, 62
> Kevin on Bees, 141
> Summary Discussion, 209
> Talking Buddies Discuss What They Want to Learn, 142
> The World Is Shrinking, 216

Discussing Books
age spans
> preschool, 64
> K–1, 144
> 2–3, 218

student performances
> Adam's Favorite Part of the Book, 71
> Did He Die?, 224
> Discussing Eric Carle Favorites, 70
> Emma on Title, 146
> "He Was Still Hungry," 67
> Interesting Language, 223
> *Jeremiah Learns to Read*, 145
> Nirjhar Retells the Story, 150
> Reader Response Pair, 205
> *The Singing Man* Discussion, 220

Summarizing *The Little Red Hen*, 65
Telling the Story, 68
Tess, Talia and Carina Analyze a Poem, 148
Wish Books, 147
Word Choice, 226

Talking a Lot
age spans
  preschool, 48
  K–1, 130
  2–3, 202
student performances
  Alex Expresses a Need, 49
  April's Story, 51
  Austin's Planets, 135
  Cane's Beehive, 133
  Developing Characters, 203
  Friends Play with Words, 56
  Informal Snack Table Conversation, 52
  Jared and Sophia Talk about Mexico, 204
  Mariah's Writing, 134
  Reader Response Pair, 205
  Revising with a Partner in the Writers Workshop, 206
  Sherry Analyzes Her Poem, 136
  Talk about /ch/ Sounds, 137
  Tessa on Being Jealous, 131
  Water Talk, 54

Talking to One's Self
age spans
  preschool, 58
  K–1, 138
  2–3, 207
student performances
  Stephen Spells *Volcanoes*, 59

Standard 2: Kinds of Talk and Resulting Genres

Explaining and Seeking Information
age spans
  preschool, 82
  K–1, 158
  2–3, 236

student performances
  Anna Explains the Body Alphabet, 86
  Carlos and Research, 160
  Crickets, 87
  Ethan and Graham Elaborate the Categories, 237
  Graham's Story, 242
  Graham's Writer's Notebook, 240
  Handling Nervousness before a Class Play, 163
  Is It a Ladybug?, 166
  Jacelyn Finds Some Bugs, 83
  Lucas's Scenery, 164
  Music for the Play, 161
  The Neighborhood Jewish Community Center, 162
  Philip Talks about the Orchestra, 84
  Reporting Research on Bees, 159
  Stephanie Lifting a Rock, 167
  Thorny, 88
  Timmy Describes Pangaea, 239

Getting Things Done
age spans
  preschool, 90
  K–1, 168
  2–3, 244
student performances
  Aaron and Alexandra Clarify the Assignment, 249
  Block Play, 93
  Cody Asks for Clarification, 250
  Conflict Resolution, 172
  Ethan Perfects His Poem, 246
  Evie Knows How to Feed Her Dog, 92
  Hannah's Writing Ideas, 248
  How to Wear the Flower Costume, 170
  How to Write a Play, 171
  Negotiate Recess Game, 169
  Philip Knows How to Solve a Conflict, 91

Narrative
age spans
  preschool, 74
  K–1, 152
  2–3, 230
student performances
  Angel's Computer Game, 81
  Anna Is Jealous, 75
  Charles's Trains, 77
  Cody's Cat, Max, 214
  Emma's Fight with Her Brother, 154
  Evie's Lost Ball, 79
  Informal Snack Table Conversation, 52
  Piper Goes to the Rodeo, 235
  Stephanie's Spider Story, 155
  Story of a Play, 153
  Timmy's Waterfall Adventure, 234
  Trevor Tells about Rosa Parks, 233
  When Chris Was Five, 156

Producing and Responding to Performances
age spans
  preschool, 94
  K–1, 174
  2–3, 251
student performances
  Chavez "Reads" a Familiar Poem, 96
  Five Fishies, 97
  Meagan's Portfolio, 175
  Philip Wonders about Sheet Music, 95
  Responding to and Critiquing Their Own Video Performance, 178
  Retelling and Reenacting the Frog Fairy Dance, 176

Standard 3: Language Use and Conventions

Rules of Interaction
age spans
  preschool, 100
  K–1, 181
  2–3, 254

Index

student performances
    Alex's Spill, 102
    Are Dinosaurs Extinct?, 101

Vocabulary and Word Choice

age spans
    preschool, 112
    K–1, 190
    2–3, 260

student performances
    Anna's Feelings Vocabulary, 116
    Benjy's Science Journal, 118
    "Buckle My Shoe," 105
    Charles's Train Vocabulary, 113
    Defining *Biography*, 262
    Defining *Busy*, 120
    Defining *Metamorphosis*, 191
    Informal Snack Table Conversation, 52
    Insects and Spiders, 117
    Philip's Orchestra Vocabulary, 115
    What's the Word for "Old"?, 263
    Whole or *Hole*?, 261

Word Play and Language Awareness

age spans
    preschool, 104
    K–1, 182
    2–3, 256

student performances
    Adam Tells Jokes, 257
    "Buckle My Shoe," 105
    Compound Words, 189
    It's So Chocolate, 107
    Miss Mary Mack, 187
    Morning Word Work, 183
    The Restaurant Sign, 111
    Spontaneous Rhymes, 185
    The Water "Bingo" Song, 109
    What I Wrote, 110

Student Performances

Use this section to find student performances, which are listed alphabetically.

Aaron and Alexandra Clarify the Assignment, 249
Adam's Favorite Part of the Book, 71
Adam Tells Jokes, 257
Alex Expresses a Need, 49
Alex's Spill, 102
Angel's Computer Game, 81
Anna Explains the Body Alphabet, 86
Anna Is Jealous, 75
Anna's Feelings Vocabulary, 116
April's Story, 51
Are Dinosaurs Extinct?, 101
Austin's Planets, 135
Benjy's Science Journal, 118
Block Play, 93
"Buckle My Shoe," 105
Cane's Beehive, 133
Carlos and Research, 160
Charles's Train Vocabulary, 113
Charles's Trains, 77
Chavez "Reads" a Familiar Poem, 96
Cody Asks for Clarification, 250
Cody's Cat, Max, 214
Compound Words, 189
Conflict Resolution, 172
Crickets, 87
Defining *Biography*, 262
Defining *Busy*, 120
Defining *Metamorphosis*, 191
Developing Characters, 203
Did He Die?, 224
Discussing Eric Carle Favorites, 70
Discussing the Symbolism of a Yoruba Door, 210
Emma's Fight with Her Brother, 154
Emma on Title, 146
Ethan and Graham Elaborate the Categories, 237
Ethan Perfects His Poem, 246
Evie Knows How to Feed Her Dog, 92
Evie Lifts Dirt Clods, 61
Evie's Lost Ball, 79
Five Fishies, 97
Fredric's Cat, 62
Friends Play with Words, 56
Graham's Story, 242
Graham's Writer's Notebook, 240
Handling Nervousness before a Class Play, 163
Hannah's Writing Ideas, 248
"He Was Still Hungry," 67
How to Wear the Flower Costume, 170
How to Write a Play, 171
Informal Snack Table Conversation, 52
Insects and Spiders, 117
Interesting Language, 223
Is It a Ladybug?, 166
It's So Chocolate, 107
Jacelyn Finds Some Bugs, 83
Jared and Sophia Talk about Mexico, 204
Jeremiah Learns to Read, 145
Kevin on Bees, 141
Lucas's Scenery, 164
Mariah's Writing, 134
Meagan's Portfolio, 175
Miss Mary Mack, 187
Morning Word Work, 183
Music for the Play, 161
Negotiate Recess Game, 169
The Neighborhood Jewish Community Center, 162
Nirjhar Retells the Story, 150
Philip Knows How to Solve a Conflict, 91
Philip's Orchestra Vocabulary, 115
Philip Talks about the Orchestra, 84
Philip Wonders about Sheet Music, 95
Piper Goes to the Rodeo, 235
Reader Response Pair, 205
Reporting Research on Bees, 159
Responding to and Critiquing Their Own Video Performance, 178
The Restaurant Sign, 111
Retelling and Reenacting the Frog Fairy Dance, 176
Revising with a Partner in the Writers Workshop, 206

New Standards

Sherry Analyzes Her Poem, 136
The Singing Man Discussion, 220
Spontaneous Rhymes, 185
Stephanie Lifting a Rock, 167
Stephanie's Spider Story, 155
Stephen Spells *Volcanoes*, 59
Story of a Play, 153
Summarizing *The Little Red Hen*, 65
Summary Discussion, 209
Talk about /ch/ Sounds, 137
Talking Buddies Discuss What They Want to Learn, 142
Telling the Story, 68
Tess, Talia and Carina Analyze a Poem, 148
Tessa on Being Jealous, 131
Thorny, 88
Timmy Describes Pangaea, 239
Timmy's Waterfall Adventure, 234
Trevor Tells about Rosa Parks, 233
The Water "Bingo" Song, 109
Water Talk, 54
What I Wrote, 110
What's the Word for "Old"?, 263
When Chris Was Five, 156
Whole or *Hole*?, 261
Wish Books, 147
Word Choice, 226
The World Is Shrinking, 216

Focus Topics

Use this section to find topics that elaborate on points made in the standards.

Acute Awareness of Language and Ambiguities, 258
Arguing and Collaborating, 245
Basic Linguistics: What Should Children Learn?, 32
Building Knowledge Domains, 114
Collecting Touchstone Books, 64
Coming Soon: *From Spanish to English*, iii
Cultural Differences in Narrative Form, 231
Developmental Sequence of Early Narratives, 76
Different Cultures, Different Rules, 24
Discussing Books: A Multifaceted Literacy Skill, 219
Encouraging Narratives, 78
Encouraging Talk, 132
Explaining, Describing and Seeking Increasingly Elaborate Information, 238
For Talk at Its Best, Try Familiar, Informal and Comfortable Settings, 18
Full-Day Kindergarten? Yes!, 127
Grammatical Awareness in Kindergarten & First Grade, 188
Grammatical Awareness in Preschool, 106
How Children Exhibit Talking to One's Self, 58
The Importance of a Literacy-Rich Environment, 66
The Importance of Word Play (K–1), 186
The Importance of Word Play (preschool), 108
The Joy of Collecting Words, 19
Meaningful Differences and Implications for Schools and Teachers, 20
More Complete Narratives, 80
Ordering the World with Superordinates and Subordinates, 27
Personal and Cultural Differences, 48
Phonemic Awareness: Twice Told, with Good Reason, 184
Playful Manipulation of Language, 50
Research Note, 104
Responding to Performances, 94
Settings That Get Children Talking, 17
Smart Mistakes, 106
Take Time to Listen and Model Good Habits, 29
Talk: A Very Important Topic, 13
Talk, Talk and Talk Still More, 15
Topic-Relevant Responses in Conversation, 140
What Should Children Talk About?, 10
What's the Point? Talking for a Purpose, 23

Other Authors and Works

Use this section to find student performances, referenced by the title or author of the literary work that is being read.

Amazing Grace, 147
Baylor, Byrd, 223
Best Wishes for Eddie, 150
The Boxcar Children, 198
Carle, Eric, 67, 70, 117, 120
Cinderella, 147
A Chair for My Mother, 198
Clever Sticks, 147
Dahl, Roald, 71
Fanny's Dream, 147
Grandfather's Journey, 225
The Great Gilly Hopkins, 198
I Wish I Were a Butterfly, 147
James and the Giant Peach, 71
Jeremiah Learns to Read, 145
The Kids of Polk Street School, 198
"A Lazy Thought," 148
The Little Red Hen, 65
The Lost Lake, 205
Medearis, Angela, 220
Merriam, Eve, 148
Minnie and Moo Go Dancing, 146
Nayer, Judy, 150
Pippi Longstocking, 198
The Quiet Cricket, 70
The Rainbow Fish, 147
Rush Hour, 149
Rylant, Cynthia, 64
Say, Allen, 203, 205, 206, 209, 224, 249
The Singing Man, 220
Tea with Milk, 224, 225
Three Wishes, 147
Tree of Cranes, 205, 225
The Very Busy Spider, 70, 120
The Very Hungry Caterpillar, 67, 70
Winter, Becky, 142
The Wish, 142
Yolen, Jane, 64